"Entrepreneurship is a journey that's full of stories, best learned from doing rather than from classroom training or a theoretical framework. Andrew has structured *The Entrepreneur's Odyssey* in such a way as to capture this fluid nature of startups, writing it as a work of fiction and not as a how-to manual. Having been an entrepreneur now for over 40 years and having helped countless founders in their journeys, I believe that every startup is a new work of fiction, working to turn their dream into something real. I hope that you enjoy the book."

David Brown, *co-founder and former CEO, Techstars*

"*The Entrepreneur's Odyssey* is a startup guide like no other. Packed with real-world experience and practical advice, this humorous novel-style guide is the perfect companion for anyone navigating the complex startup world. A fresh, insightful and enjoyable read for aspiring entrepreneurs."

Dr. Noam Wasserman, *Dean, Sy Syms School of Business at Yeshiva University and bestselling author of* The Founder's Dilemmas *and* Life Is a Startup

"Most students come into my course with only vague ideas of what building a startup is really like. *The Entrepreneur's Odyssey* is real, practical, and memorable. It makes learning entrepreneurship much more fun."

Ira Weiss, *Clinical Professor of Entrepreneurship and Accounting, Chicago Booth and General Partner, Hyde Park Venture Partners*

"*The Entrepreneur's Odyssey* is a must-read for anyone stepping into the world of startups. Having worked with Andrew at Dreamit, I know firsthand the depth of his expertise. This book distills years of experience into a gripping narrative that is both practical and engaging. Whether you're a founder navigating your first venture, a student of entrepreneurship, or simply curious about the startup grind, *The Entrepreneur's Odyssey* will give you the real, unfiltered insights you need. It's not just another guide—it's a story that stays with you, helping you avoid pitfalls and guiding you to success."

Steve Welch, *Founder, Dreamit Ventures and CEO/Co-founder Restore Hyper Wellness*

"Andrew Ackerman has masterfully captured the entrepreneurial journey in *The Entrepreneur's Odyssey*, offering invaluable insights into the many challenges founders will face when launching a startup. By embedding these lessons into a compelling story, Andrew provides practical advice that shares both the entrepreneur's and advisor's perspectives. Whether you're building a business or mentoring those who are, this book offers a clear, engaging roadmap for navigating the startup landscape."

Mike Levinson, *Founder, Dreamit Ventures*

"Andrew Ackerman's *The Entrepreneur's Odyssey* offers a refreshing and highly practical approach to startup success. Unlike conventional business books, this novel-style guide blends storytelling with valuable insights on the startup journey, covering everything from crafting the perfect elevator pitch to securing investors. Entrepreneurs will find it an engaging, memorable resource that breaks down complex concepts into actionable steps, making it easier to understand critical strategies for building a successful startup. This book is ideal for both aspiring and seasoned entrepreneurs looking for a comprehensive yet relatable guide. Ackerman's hands-on experience as a founder and investor shines through, offering real-world advice that goes beyond theory. Entrepreneurs will appreciate the blend of humor, candidness, and hard-won lessons shared in an approachable format that keeps them engaged while imparting invaluable wisdom on the realities of startup life. It's an essential read for anyone serious about turning an idea into a thriving business."

Jeffrey Berman, *General Partner, Camber Creek*

"*The Entrepreneur's Odyssey* is an absolute must-read for anyone looking to take an idea from concept to reality. Andrew Ackerman has taken years of hard-earned wisdom from his time guiding startups through accelerators and mentorship and distilled it into a narrative that's both engaging and deeply practical. Whether you're a seasoned entrepreneur or just starting out, this book will guide you through the critical steps needed to build a successful startup, all while keeping you entertained."

Avi Savar, *Former CEO, Dreamit Ventures*

"A captivating and pragmatic read on what it takes to launch a startup and embrace the entrepreneurial adventure! Andrew's relatable and witty storytelling on how to navigate the turbulent waters of building a business inspires resilience and creativity at every turn. An authentic glimpse for anyone eager to dive in on their entrepreneurial journey!"

Anvesh Rai, *Venture Capitalist*

"*The Entrepreneur's Odyssey* brilliantly blends the excitement of a novel with the depth of a startup manual. Andrew Ackerman takes readers on a lively journey, covering everything from developing an idea to securing funding. His knack for explaining complex concepts in an engaging, accessible way sets this book apart. This is your guide if you're a founder looking for clear, actionable advice wrapped in an entertaining narrative."

Steve Barsh, *former Managing Partner, Dreamit Ventures*

The Entrepreneur's Odyssey

The Entrepreneur's Odyssey is an authentic window into what it really takes to turn an idea into a viable startup. It is both an essential how-to guide for would-be startup founders as well as an entertaining novel for the startup curious.

This textbook-as-novel has fictional first-time entrepreneur Marcus Williams recount his journey from would-be founder with a half-formed idea to a funded startup. His mentor, Jason Murath, a seasoned angel investor, guides Marcus step by step through customer discovery, validating and refining the product, market sizing, and more, all the way through closing his first round of financing.

There has never been a more fun – and effective! – way to learn how to build a startup.

Andrew Ackerman is a serial entrepreneur, startup mentor and early-stage investor. He has invested in over 70 startups and mentored hundreds more over the past 15 years. Previously, Andrew founded two companies and has a keen appreciation for how hard it is to build a successful startup, even under the best of circumstances. In addition to investing, Andrew consults for startups, venture and corporate venture funds, accelerators and venture studios.

The Entrepreneur's Odyssey

A Novel Approach to Startup Success

Andrew Ackerman

Routledge
Taylor & Francis Group

LONDON AND NEW YORK

Designed cover image: Cover art by Good Knife Studio (GoodKnifeStudio.com)
Illustrator: Juan Pablo Dellacha
Artistic direction: Noam Steinerman

First published 2025
by Routledge
4 Park Square, Milton Park, Abingdon, Oxon OX14 4RN

and by Routledge
605 Third Avenue, New York, NY 10158

Routledge is an imprint of the Taylor & Francis Group, an informa business

British Library Cataloguing-in-Publication Data
A catalogue record for this book is available from the British Library

ISBN: 978-1-032-89404-1 (hbk)
ISBN: 978-1-032-88354-0 (pbk)
ISBN: 978-1-003-54261-2 (ebk)

DOI: 10.4324/9781003542612

Typeset in Adobe Garamond Pro
by Newgen Publishing UK

Contents

About the Author

Andrew Ackerman is a recovering consultant turned serial entrepreneur, startup mentor and early-stage investor. He has invested in over 70 startups and mentored hundreds more over the past 15 years. Previously, Andrew founded two companies and has a keen appreciation for how hard it is to build a successful startup, even under the best of circumstances. In addition to investing, Andrew consults for startups, venture and corporate venture funds, accelerators and venture studios.

Andrew began his career at Booz & Co consulting on strategy and operations for Fortune 100 clients. After a brief stint at Kaplan Test Prep helping transition their traditional classroom into online products, he then joined Bunk1.com as founding COO where he spent eight years building it into the leading provider of web services to the summer camp industry. After being bought out, Andrew managed over $50M of alternative assets and incubated new ventures for a family office. Andrew then founded Layercake, a digital memory startup. Later, Andrew joined Dreamit and helped build its new, later stage accelerator platform and launched its Edtech and then its Urbantech (Proptech and Construction tech) verticals. Andrew is currently the Strategic Advisor/Head of REACH Labs for Second Century Ventures.

Andrew has written over 60 published articles for Fortune, Forbes, Propmodo, CREtech, Builders Online, Architect Magazine, Multifamily Executive, AlleyWatch, Edsurge, The 74 Million et al. He is a frequent speaker at conferences and consults for startups, venture and corporate venture funds, accelerators and venture studios.

Andrew received his MBA in Operations & Marketing from Chicago Booth and a BA in Economics & Political Science from Johns Hopkins University.
For more information, go to http://andrewbackerman.com/

P.S. CallJar is real!
CallJar is based on a startup currently in development (at the time of writing this book) called CallVault. To learn more, go to http://callvault.app/

Dear Potential Buyer of this Book

Should *you* buy this book?

Maybe.

(Not what you were expecting the author to say? Read on.)

Here is who should buy this book:

1. Entrepreneurs thinking about founding, or anyone who has already founded, a startup. You need to read this book *yesterday*. From starting with a vague idea all the way through closing your first round of funding, this book has everything you need to know about building a startup.
2. Students taking a course on entrepreneurship. Same reason, just with slightly less urgency. Plus, odds are your professor assigned it and you risk failing the course if you do not buy the book. Why chance it?
3. Anyone who has ever wondered, "What the heck do startup founders actually do?" Startup life is not like the most recent Steve Jobs biopic. It is much more boring (there is a lot of staring at computer screens) and also much more exciting at the same time. If you really want to know what goes into making a successful startup, this is the book for you.

   Hey entrepreneurs from Part 1 above! You might even want to get this book for your parents or partner so they finally stop asking you, "But what do you actually do all day?" I can't help you with the, "When are you going to get a real job?" question, though.

Why should you buy *this* book?

There is no shortage of advice out there for startups. Why take mine?

Most of the advice sucks. I have built two startups, invested in over 70, and coached or mentored hundreds. Let's just say, I know a thing or two about what it takes to build successful businesses.

Most of the advice out there exists as random, scattered, bite-sized blog and social media posts. Even if you could easily separate the wheat from the chaff, it would be a full-time job to piece together anything even remotely comprehensive.

Most of the longer form content (a.k.a. books) about startups are biographies of famous founders and focus more on the human side and on the dramatic moments. None of them offer practical, critical guidance about what it takes to really nail your Total Addressable Market slide or how to work your network to find potential investors. Which brings me to my last point …

Most of the advice is, to be brutally honest, mind-numbingly boring. Textbooks, while they at least cover what you really need to know, are bone dry and best for curing insomnia and crushing very large bugs. At least blog posts are short but do you know how hard it is to explain what full ratchet anti-dilution protection can do to your cap table if you have a down-round without making a reader's eyes glaze over? (hey, wake up!)

And then there is this book. This *novel*. Stories – novels, myths, fables, legends, etc. – are *memorable*. They make it easier for us to absorb and retain important information. This book is an all-you-need-to-know textbook disguised as a novel with (I hope) interesting characters in engaging situations as they navigate the startup journey.

What would you rather read?

(More or less) sincerely,
Andrew Ackerman

Acknowledgements

Long ago, when the earth was young and I was in business school, I took a course on business operations and strategy. In addition to a typically boring textbook, we were also assigned *The Goal* by Eliyahu Goldratt. This textbook-disguised-as-a-novel had colorful characters navigating a fictional plot that contained, along the way, real lessons on how to run a business in general and specifically how to apply the author's "Theory of Constraints." The format was so memorable that *The Goal* stuck with me for decades, after the main textbook was long forgotten, and was the inspiration for this book. *The Entrepreneur's Odyssey* is essentially *The Goal* for startups.

Most of the example slides used in this book come from real startups that I have had the privilege of investing in. I would like to thank Reuben Levine (Stringbean), Tarun Nimmagadda (Ruckit, acquired by Command Alkon), Daniel Farb (Flower Turbines), Stephen Carter & Daniel Turner (TRAXyL), Albert Bou Fadel (SmartBarrel), Franco Giaquinto (Outbuild, fka IPSUM), LD Salmanson (Cherre), Resha Shroff (Lynx Automation), Joe Troyen (Go Pangea, fka PenPal Schools), Ravi Sahu (Strayos), and Matias Klein (Kognition) for giving me permission to use their slides here and I wish them all continued success and good exits.

Next in chronological order, I am sincerely grateful to Dr. Noam Wasserman, Dean of Yeshiva University's Sy Syms School of Business and author of the award-winning "The Founder's Dilemmas", who suggested that I test out early drafts of the book by actually teaching Entrepreneurship at Sy Syms ... and who somehow also managed to sucker me into teaching two other courses.

Thanks to Oliver Mitchell for the introduction that led me to my publisher for this book, Routledge Press. Ironically, Routledge publishes *The Goal* outside the US so I could not have asked for a better publisher.

Special thanks also to Peter Akman and Joe Covey for proofreading the book cover to cover and all their invaluable suggestions as well as to everyone else who contributed in smaller but no less appreciated ways.

Cover art by Good Knife Studio (GoodKnifeStudio.com)
Illustrator: Juan Pablo Dellacha
Artistic direction: Noam Steinerman

Preface

"What a long, strange trip it's been."

And it has only just begun. Pretty much nothing went the way I thought it would but the money is in the bank so that is definitely a win.

So many of you, my friends, have been asking me what it was like to plunge into the startup world. Most of you seem to think it is all glamor and excitement. It's actually been the most confusing (and sometimes outright terrifying) period of my life. And when I tell you this, you seem to think I am being modest. So, I pulled together my journal entries (yes, I keep a journal. You want to make something of it?), the notes I took on my meetings with Jason, thousands of emails and calendar entries, and put it all together here for you to read in all its messy glory.

Here is how it went down.

– Marcus

Part I

Laying the Foundations for a Great Startup

Before you can raise money for your startup, you need to make sure that startup is ready for funding. That means making sure that you are solving a painful, prevalent, and persistent problem and boiling your solution down to a minimum valuable product. Then you need to clearly define your ideal customer profile and get actionable feedback from them. Once you are fairly certain you have something the market wants, you need to identify the critical assumptions that can make or break your startup ... ideally all *before* even starting product development.

DOI: 10.4324/9781003542612-1

Chapter 1

Open Mic Night, Startup Style

The room was bland-upscale-inoffensive as only a midtown Manhattan law firm's conference room could be.

At this point, I'd been to a few dozen events hosted by law firms and they all kinda look the same. The food table in the back of the room was slightly better than average. The typical fruit and cheese platters were there along with some deli meat. There was wine in addition to beer and – wait. Are those macadamia nuts? Classy. But I am not here for the food.

A couple of the scruffier looking entrepreneurs in the room might have been. I have seen them around at several events. They are "killing it" as always but never seem to raise a round, add people to their team, push new features ... basically no visible progress that I can see. Unless you count moving towards the deli meat as progress.

On the other hand, they might be thinking the same thing about me. Except that tonight is different. Tonight, I am pitching.

A few people are wearing suits and ties. Lawyers, accountants, and other service providers. Useless to me. I am hunting investors.

Jeans, button down and blazer is the unofficial venture capital dress uniform. It is too warm out for the sleeveless Patagonia vest jacket and some of the angel investors are dressed even more casually but it is definitely a 'look' that you learn to recognize. The tricky part was that some software development shops and marketing consultants dress this way too – like nonpoisonous snakes that mimic the colors of poisonous ones to get all the benefits without the hassle. By now I know many of those guys by sight and have mastered the smile-nod-avoid maneuver. They know I have no money so they are not particularly interested in wasting their time on me either.

DOI: 10.4324/9781003542612-2

Mostly, I am focused on finding the judges. I did my homework and I know what they look like.

The first one I spot is an Associate at A Prime Capital Partners, Kani Green. According to LinkedIn, Kani joined the firm about six months ago, just after graduating business school. He looks to be about 27 or 28. But he was easy to spot; he is basically the only other Black man in the room. While he is too new to VC to rely on his advice, if he likes what I am pitching, it could be a foot in the door.

The second, Angela Weiss, is a Principal from Brand New Ventures. Solid firm. I have seen her at pitch events before. She typically gives good advice. It is a shame that they only invest in direct-to-consumer brands and I am doing nothing of the sort.

The third judge, Jason Murath, is a bit of a wild card. Not much information about him on LinkedIn. He has a reputation for investing actively in early-stage startups but, to be honest, looks like a crotchety old man. I have not seen him at any other pitch events so I will reserve judgment.

I have another half hour to kill before the pitch. Might as well chat with some of the 'wantrapreneurs.' Maybe someone will know good sales or marketing people for me to hire once I have raised my seed round.

*   *   *

Finally! They are telling people to take their seats so the pitches can begin. I have already chatted up the Associate a bit but the other two judges sneak in at the last minute and go straight to the table at the front of the room. Smooth.

The first pitch is meh at best. Two kids, real estate agents, working on the leasing side, put together an app that lets them take photos and videos of the apartment they are trying to lease. The photos go on their app for renters to view. Right now, they are just using it for their own listings but have hopes – fantasies? – of selling the software to other agents. Or maybe they think renters will download their app to search. That part is a little vague.

The Associate gives them the standard encouragement about solving problems that they know firsthand followed by the equally standard caveat that they are too early for that fund to invest in them but to please keep them posted as to their progress. For a guy who has only been in the industry six months, Kani's got the 'soft no' down pat.

The Principal leads off with how this is not within her investment thesis – nice of Angela to nip any hope they had in the bud before they got too excited – but then starts asking about customer acquisition. Apparently, these guys have not thought much about it. Their plan to sell to other brokerages seems to be limited to picking up the phone and calling people. They have not even thought about how the direct-to-renter side customer acquisition will work yet.

"I may have a couple of suggestions on how to get your app into renters' hands," she says. "Many apps like yours, as well as most e-commerce sites, rely on a mix of Search Engine Optimization and paid search. If you push each listing to your website and you are careful using the right keywords, you might get some traffic that way. Unfortunately, any broker with any listing is doing the same so I am not sure how much mileage you will get from SEO. That leaves paid search. Depending on the demographic you are targeting, you should be looking at Google, Facebook, Instagram, maybe even TikTok. Have you experimented with any of those?"

The founders look a bit uncomfortable. "Not yet. We were planning to do that once we raise our seed round."

"Why wait? For a couple of hundred dollars per platform you can test out whether these channels will work for you. You can figure out what your Cost Per Click is, what percent of those clicks download the app, how many of those book an apartment tour through the app, all the way down to how many of them end up leasing an apartment. If your CPC is low enough relative to the money you make on the renters who close, you put that into your pitch. Startups are inherently risky. Anytime you can prove an assumption and replace it with supporting data, you reduce the risk involved. And as the risk goes down, it gets easier for you to actually raise your seed round."

Good, actionable feedback. Experience matters.

There is a longish pause and finally the angel investor, Jason Murath, weighs in.

"Don't do this. Shut this down and move on to something else." In the stunned silence that follows, Jason continues. "There is nothing new here. I have seen dozens of startups like this over the past ten years. You are going to die on customer acquisition cost. Everyone and their mother is bidding on those keywords.

"More importantly, you have no 'Why Now?' Listen up. Any time an idea becomes feasible – technologically, legally, whatever change makes it suddenly possible to do something that was previously impossible – thousands of hungry entrepreneurs rush in and try to exploit the new opportunity. If an idea could have been done for several years, I guarantee you many people have tried it. Either there are competitors who are very far ahead of you or all of the other upstarts have failed. If you have a competitor way ahead of you, I would not bet on a horse leaving the gate far behind the pack. And if everyone else who has tried it has failed, it is probably a flawed idea. To get me to write a check, you would have to prove to me that you know exactly why *every one* of those dozens or hundreds of other startups failed and that you were going to do something amazingly and dramatically different than all of them in order for you to have a chance, in my not so humble opinion, of succeeding. Life is too short to waste time on dead ends. Dump this and come up with something else."

Well, that was different. No sugar coating, no encouragement. Not mean, but yet … firm. Maybe even a touch of genuine sorrow in the old guy's tone.

And not at all what the founders wanted to hear. There was some mumbling about millennials and how the rental search process is changing but the angel cut them off.

"That has all been playing out for over a decade. Ten years ago that might have cut it, but that train has left the station. Listen, it is your time, it is your money, it is your call. But you are very late to this party. I would not do this if I were you and I would not put money in at this point. Nothing would make me happier than to see you come back in a year and prove me wrong … but you are going to have to be able to do it while bootstrapping because any angel worth his salt is going to feel the same way."

As much as I agree with Jason, I am pretty relieved that I do not have to follow that pitch.

As I listen to the next pitch, I waver between thinking it is the dumbest idea I have ever heard and that it might possibly be brilliant. I am at about an 80/20 split right now. The guy is pitching his startup as "Untuck'd for ties," ties that only sit loosely around your neck, that you never untie, just pull over your head.

That is right in Angela's strike zone so she goes first and she goes deep. Apparently, this guy comes from the industry and has all the logistics nailed down pretty well.

She ends with, "Until you actually put out a line and are seeing sales, you are early for us. But I would like to make some introductions to a couple of other investors who get involved a little earlier than we do." For a pitch event like this, that is a pretty big win.

Kani, who was looking lost during most of the prior exchange, finally settles on this response: "This is not a fit for us but it sounds like the kind of thing that would definitely interest a more fashion-focused investor. You should talk to as many investors as you can because this is not a tech startup per se so a lot of investors are going to pass before you find the right ones for you." Supportive and vaguely helpful. This kid will go far.

Jason? "I am one of those guys who doesn't invest in your kind of startup so I am not going to be one of those angels who gives you random advice of questionable value. Good luck."

Gramps is definitely growing on me. But now I am up. Fingers crossed!

"My name is Marcus Williams and my startup CallJar is bringing the phone call back. How many times do you get off the phone call, only to forget critical details that you just discussed? Maybe you took notes around the call but as you look at your notebook, you can't make out what you wrote down. CallJar can help.

"CallJar uses speech diarization to split the audio streams of your call, records them separately, and automatically transcribes them. It then escrows the transcripts and requests retroactive opt-ins from the various call participants, only releasing the call parts that it is authorized to release."

(Definitely started off a little shaky but I am hitting my stride. All that rehearsing helped. The more I get into the pitch the more I feel like I am in the zone. Time to close strong.)

"I am not only the CEO but also the CTO. I have been working in speech recognition for over a decade creating ASR models for AVR applications. My alpha is mostly done and I am looking for $500,000 to launch the service and hire a salesperson to sell the solution to the sales departments of large corporations."

I think I pretty much killed it, if I do say so myself.

So then why is Jason frowning?

"You are way too early for him," pointing to Kani, "and totally out of her strike zone," pointing to Angela, "so I guess I will go first.

"Your pitch sucks. It's full of jargon and I am not entirely sure how the product works and yet I strongly suspect you got the product wrong. But if you can do what I think you can do, I think there is something interesting here at its core. I have been watching speech recognition for a while and I think it is finally at the tipping point so I am interested.

"Are you a solo founder?"

"Yes"

"I hate solo founders. There is too damn much for any one person to do. Plus, everything sounds great inside your own head. There's no substitute for having to say your plans out loud to somebody on the other side of the table and have him poke holes in it. But that is fixable."

Jason continues, "What about the legality of recording phone calls without a person's consent?"

"Federal Law requires one party consent in order to record a phone call. On top of that, 11 states have two party consent."

"That is enough. I wanted to make sure you were on top of it and had thought that part through. I have got enough. Come talk to me afterwards."

Honestly, I am not sure I want to. But if there is one thing going to all these pitch events has taught me, it is that when an investor shows interest, you talk to that investor. Worst case scenario, it will be good practice for someone who is not a complete asshole.

*   *   *

"Hi, I am Marcus. You told me to come to you after the pitch."

"I am Jason. And no, I am not a complete asshole."

What the hell. "What percent asshole are you?"

That got me a smile.

"Ask my wife. But seriously. I used to go to a lot of these things but there is so much crap out there. I got tired of throwing up in my mouth most of the evening. So I stopped going. But Jim McCaffee is my lawyer and he had a last-minute cancellation so I came as a favor. How many times have you pitched CellJar?"

"CallJar. Including this event?"

"Yup."

"Once."

"This was your first time? Huh. Maybe I should have been a little more … gracious. Look, I meant what I said. There is a lot wrong about your startup but there may be one or two really good things at its core. If you can stomach 30 minutes alone in a room with me, let's find a time to meet in person. Here's my card."

Key Takeaways

- Startup pitch events can be good opportunities for entrepreneurs to practice their pitches, meet potential investors and mentors, and network with other entrepreneurs.
- An overarching question investors want startups to be able to answer is "Why now?" If a concept could have been done five years ago, odds are there are startups far ahead of you or there is a graveyard full of failed prior startups proving that the idea is fundamentally flawed.
- Investors are wary of solo founders.

Chapter 2

In the End, There Cannot Be Only One

"I am glad you could make it."

I do not know what I expected but a generic WeWork meeting room is not at all what I pictured as an active angel's office.

"We didn't get to really chat at the event so why don't you tell me a little about yourself. Where did you grow up, go to school, kids? The works."

Okay, maybe not such an asshole after all.

"I was born and raised in Baltimore and ended up going to Johns Hopkins."

"Good school. EE?"

"Yes, electrical engineering and comp sci."

"Hard to double major if you are in EE. You must have spent all your waking hours on D level."

"And a lot of my sleeping hours too! You seem to know a lot about Hopkins …?"

"I went there too. Ages ago. Before they let women in. We had to dip quills into inkwells to take notes by candlelight. But I digress. Please go on."

"I had a series of jobs in telecom out of school, gradually moving from engineering to managing engineers to management in general. But I always kept my technical skills sharp, teaching myself the new programming languages as they came out and just generally keeping abreast of new developments. Somewhere along the way I moved up to New York, got married, had a kid, and absolutely refused to move out to the burbs."

"How does your wife feel about you taking the plunge into the startup world?"

"She is very supportive."

"Does she work? Good job, getting healthcare through her employer?"

DOI: 10.4324/9781003542612-3

"Yes and no. She's a real estate agent and they are all 1099 employees so do not normally offer health insurance. Her company set up something with a 'co employer' so she can essentially hire herself and pay herself a salary to give herself W-2 income that she can take healthcare premiums off of. But at the end of the day, the plans I have through work are higher quality and less expensive."

"She is comfortable with zero income for the foreseeable future? Paying for your own health care on the exchange?"

"Well, not exactly. When I raise a little money, I will be able to pay myself a salary and get healthcare through the startup."

"Sure, but what are you living on now? It could take months before you close your round, if you ever do."

"I have not quit my day job yet, if that is what you are asking."

"Oh." Long pause.

"That does complicate things. Investors are pretty leery of founders who have not quit their day jobs."

"Why is that?"

"Well, what are you actually risking? You are asking us to write you a check but you do not really have much skin in the game, do you?"

"Oh." Now it was my turn for a long pause.

"Is that a deal breaker?"

"It's not good. It used to be a pretty hard 'No' when I first started angel investing a few decades ago. Investors are a bit more flexible these days. The cost of launching a startup has dropped dramatically over the years. It was not that long ago that you could not get out of bed for less than $5 million. You had to buy and configure the server yourself, and find a place to physically host it. Anything you wanted your website to do, you had to code from scratch. It was really the wild frontier. But now with Amazon Web Services making hosting so much easier, the ton of other services that you can plug into via API, and GitHub with already written code that you can repurpose, it has gotten a lot easier. It is at the point where for a lot of things, you can build and launch the startup for basically pennies. And a lot of sweat equity. So, investors are a little bit more flexible. What we are looking for in this case is that you have made as much progress as humanly possible under the constraints of a day job. If you have got good early traction and we are convinced that you will actually pull the plug and come on full-time, it is not the end of the world. But it is a harder sell. No two ways about it."

Key Takeaways

- Founding a startup often means going without a steady paycheck, health insurance, and other things most employees take for granted.
- It helps to have prior savings and/or a spouse or other relatives that can support the founder through the earliest stages.
- Investors have a strong bias against entrepreneurs who are not working full time on their startup but as the cost of launching a startup has dropped dramatically over the years, they may make exceptions at the earliest stages if founders can make good progress towards building their startup and validating their business in their off-hours.

Chapter 3

A Good Elevator Pitch Pushes All the Right Buttons

"Whatever, Marcus. It is what it is. Let's hear your elevator pitch."

"But you heard my pitch the other night?"

"That was a pitch, but not an elevator pitch. An elevator pitch is a 20 to 30 seconds long, ultra concise recap of what you are doing and what makes you awesome. And before you object, it *is* important. Not only do you need to nail it if you are ever going to raise money from investors, but I find that founders who can't boil down what their startup is doing into the elevator pitch do not actually truly understand what makes their startup great."

"Twenty to 30 seconds? I can see how last night's tie guy could do it but my business is *complicated*. There is no way to get it all down to 30 seconds."

"First off, you are wrong. Flat out wrong. I have seen far from complicated ideas effectively communicated in a 30 second elevator pitch. Second, the goal of an elevator pitch is not to get 'it all' into the pitch. The goal is simply to get investors' interest. It is the core of your startup that gets him or her coming back and thinking, 'Well that is interesting. Let me give this a minute or two of my attention.' If an investor leans in with a question – and as long as that follow-up question is not some variation of, 'What the hell do you actually do?' – the pitch worked."

"So the elevator pitch is a teaser?"

"Oh God no. I *loathe* teasers. Don't make me think. If I wanted to think, I would read a murder mystery. You have got 30 seconds – at most! – before my attention starts to wander. Without talking like the guy at the end of a drug commercial, you need to convey, in as powerful a way as you possibly can, the key

 DOI: 10.4324/9781003542612-4

points that maximize your odds of my wanting to engage more deeply. Because at the end of your pitch, I am either going to be thinking about your startup or thinking about how to get away from your startup."

"So, what are those key points?"

"Gee, I thought you would never ask."

One finger goes up.

"Company name. I know, it sounds silly. But I can't tell you how many founders actually forget to put the name of their company in their elevator pitch."

Another finger.

"What the hell you actually do … in plain words that grandma can understand. One sentence, no jargon. Even if I know the lingo, why make me use the few remaining brain cells that I have not drunk away to think about what the words you use mean when you would rather have me thinking about what you actually do?"

Third finger.

"Who are you selling to? Specifically. You do not just sell to an industry; you sell to a particular person in a particular type of company. You do not just have users; you have a very particular persona."

Finger number four.

"What makes you a quantum level better than what is already out there? Are you first to market? What makes it defensible?"

Hand wide open.

"What is your traction? If you do not tell me your traction, I will assume you have none. Do you have revenue? Pilots? Beta testers? Partnerships? Name drop the big names. You get the idea."

Thumbs up on the other hand.

"Finally, your Ask. If you are raising money, how much do you want, what milestone will it get you to, by what date? Or are you asking for advice? Introductions? Something else? If you do not ask, you do not get … at least not what you actually want."

Hands down on the desk.

"You can vary the order a bit if you want but those are the broad strokes.

"What? What's with that look?"

"Next time, can you warn me before I need to start taking notes? You were halfway done with your count before I even realized I needed to open my notebook."

"Oh, do not sweat it. I have a deck I can send you later that I used to use back when I was young and generous and volunteered to talk to startup accelerator programs. For now, here is all you need to remember."

My company, *NAME* provides *WTF YOU DO*, to *CUSTOMER* (BE SPECIFIC!). Unlike the other companies in this *$$$$* market, we are the only company that *YOUR SPECIAL SAUCE*. We are already at *TRACTION* selling to *CUSTOMER NAME DROPS*. We are raising *$$$$* to get to *MILESTONE* by *MM/YY*.

Figure 3.1 The Elevator Pitch, Madlibs style

"It's like Madlibs. You are old enough to remember Madlibs, right? You just say what I wrote on the board, substituting in the details. Go for it."

"Yeah … I think that was big at sleepaway camp. I only went once but I remember the other campers getting mailed Madlibs from their parents.

"But I do not have traction yet. What do I say there?"

"If I remember correctly, you are pre-launch, right? That means you have built a lot of the product already, doesn't it?"

"Yes, we are about a month away from launching our alpha."

"Then you can say that. You could also talk about how many customer surveys you have done or any partnerships you signed, say, for difficult to get data or technical integrations."

"No partnerships worth mentioning and we have not done any customer interviews."

"No customer interviews? Then how do you know anyone wants what you are building?"

"Well, I want it. I bet a lot of people like me would want it. I have talked to a bunch of people about it informally and they all think it is a good idea."

"Hmph. That is weak. Investors are going to tear you a new one if you say that. We need to work on that but let's stick with the elevator pitch for now, especially since I think where we will end up on the product is not where you are right now anyway. I guess for traction, just go with being one month away from launch. If you need to, you can dress it up a bit by talking about how much time it has taken you to get to this point."

OK. I can do this. I just need to fill in the blanks. Why am I feeling so jittery?

"My company, CallJar, provides automated call transcription to large sales teams. Unlike the other companies in this $1.7T global telecom services market, we are the only company that, uh … ensures privacy … uh … and compliance with … privacy regulations? We have been working on the alpha for the past 16 months and expect to launch next month. We are raising $500,000 to get to $500,000 ARR within a year."

"Not too shabby for the first attempt. A little shaky in the middle and I am not sure you have the right target at all but let's take that apart piece by piece.

"… 'automated call transcription' is a bit bland but at least it is clear and concise. And I will take clear and concise over confusing poetry any day.

"… 'large sales teams' does not feel like the right target to me. Those are elephants you are hunting. You have got to work your way up to those. It could take you a year or more to land those accounts even when you have a solid track record. My gut tells me you want a different demographic. But let's come back to that in a moment.

"Where did you get the $1.7T global telecom services market from?"

"Gartner Research."

"Ah, top-down nonsense. Irrelevant. But you need to figure out at least two or three other things before we can build up to this. So let's move on.

"… 'ensures privacy and compliance with relevant regulations.' Mmm. We can do better but it will do for now.

"Traction is okay and without diving any deeper I can't tell if you are raising the right amount or if your target is at all realistic. So let's go back to what you do."

Key Takeaways

- An elevator pitch is a 20–30 second statement that entrepreneurs use to describe their startup (primarily) to investors.
- The goal of an elevator pitch is to engage potential investors and convince them that it is worth scheduling a meeting with the startup.
- An elevator pitch cannot and should not attempt to answer all the investor's questions.
- A good elevator pitch should include the company name, what the startup does, what makes it special, who it sells to, how large the market is, its traction to date, and what it is asking for (typically funding).
- Ideally, a good elevator pitch uses simple, jargon free terms that grandma can understand.

Chapter 4

Tell Me Where It Hurts

I am still digesting Jason's deconstruction – more like destruction – of my elevator pitch but, apparently, he is on a roll.

"Tell me, in simple terms, what the pain point is?"

I thought we had covered this.

"Basically, the phone call is broken. You speak to someone, cover a lot of important ground, and then it just disappears into the ether. There is no permanent record."

"Okay, listen. I really wish you kids would stop with this 'x is broken' mantra. I file that under 'cute crap startup founders say because they think it sounds cool but it actually has zero semantic value.' My phone works just fine. It does what it is intended to do. It does not do what it was not intended to do. There is nothing broken about. Now the problem might be that there are other things you want to be able to do that my phone just cannot do. So be specific. What drives you nuts about a regular phone call? Lay out for me the exact scenario that caused you to bang your head against the wall over and over until you finally said, 'Godammit, I need to build this thing!'"

"Uh, okay … When I am talking to developers, I am usually sending messages back and forth via Slack or email or some other messaging platform. If we ever need to go back and figure out what we agreed on, it is all right there. But I also interface a lot with the end users. Mostly they prefer to hop on a phone call or a Zoom. It is actually a lot more productive in some ways; we cut out a lot of back and forth on questions and half understood statements that need clarification. But when we are done, there's no record of the conversation. So, I started taking pretty detailed notes with pen and paper only that slowed the call considerably. Plus, I could not read my own handwriting half the time! What's worse, they would sometimes call when I was driving or running around in general. I couldn't

    DOI: 10.4324/9781003542612-5

really stop to write anything down and was stuck relying on my memory. My memory is pretty good but inevitably things slip through the cracks from time to time. And inevitably an end user would later say that they asked for something and even though I was 99.99% sure that they had not, that they were remembering the conversation incorrectly, I didn't have anything to point to to prove it one way or the other. At best, we lost time or had a bit of unnecessary rework. But if the project was behind schedule or running into snags, we got bogged down with finger pointing and blame casting. Of course, the dev team would get screwed more often than not."

Clapping his hands, "Bravo, that was an A+ statement of your pain point."

I take a silent, mock bow.

"But, Marcus, do you know why it was so good?"

"Jason, I am beginning to suspect that I have no idea."

"Socrates said, 'Awareness of ignorance is the beginning of wisdom' ... although like so many things, Benjamin Franklin tends to get credit for it. That guy had a great PR person. But I digress.

"The way you described your pain point was perfect because you hit all three dimensions of pain: intensity, frequency and prevalence.

"Best case, digging out a pen and paper to take notes is mildly annoying and slows down the call so you can take legible notes. Of course, a lot of the time you are scribbling so fast that you can't even read your notes later if you need them. Worst case, though, you can get fired for someone else's screw up. All in all, it is a pretty intense pain point.

"It is also something that happens every day. Unlike, say, college admissions which are brutally painful and high stakes but that really only happens once in a person's life, we get phone calls all the time. Management gurus often recommend impromptu phone calls because they are faster and more efficient, but they do have that drawback. So, it is not only something that happens frequently, but that ideally would happen even more frequently if it were not for these drawbacks. So, check box number two.

"Last but not least, you laid out a fairly common scenario that applies to a lot of people. While an intense pain point that you deal with a lot is something you would passionately want solved, if it really only affects a small number of people, you are going to get screwed on the market size. That means it could be a great product ... for someone else to build. But not one for you to build yourself and not one for me to put my money behind. Fortunately, that is not the case here. Pretty much everybody has this problem to one extent or another."

Leaning back, Jason continues, "Keeping that pain point firmly in mind, what's wrong with the revised elevator pitch we just hashed out?"

"Honestly, my head is spinning. Can we skip the Socratic Method just this time?"

Chuckling a little Jason says, "I guess I was making you sip from a firehose. Okay, I have a meeting in five minutes so this will be the last point for now.

"Close your eyes. Visualize the large sales force you mentioned in your pitch. What do you see?"

"Well …"

"No! Close your eyes."

"You meant that literally?"

"Absolutely."

"Uh, okay." Pause. "I am visualizing." No smart comment from Jason? I guess I will just keep going. "There is a guy – or woman – sitting at his desk, working the phone. Talking to prospect after prospect, trying to close a sale."

"Does he have a computer in front of him?"

"Of course."

"How about a pad of paper? A pen?"

"Well, sure. I guess. It is his desk after all."

"What kind of phone does he have? How is he holding it?"

"Pretty much a regular kind of desktop phone, only he's probably got a headset on so his hands are free."

"What does he have open on his computer?"

"I do not know. Probably Salesforce or some other CRM software."

"And what is he doing during the call? After the call?"

"He is probably logging the call, entering key information into Salesforce or some other CRM during the call … oh.

"I think I see your point. That is pretty much exactly the opposite of the pain point I just described. Those guys have the time and all the tools they need to capture the information in real time. But CallJar can still help. Every sales-person I know complains about logging calls and the extra work it takes to put everything into the system. It would be a lot faster if they could just focus on the call and have the information automatically extracted from the call and put into Salesforce."

"CallJar does this?"

"It will. I have not built that yet. Right now, it just transcribes the informa-tion but we could build an AI to recognize certain key information and automat-ically feed it into predetermined fields. It would take a little bit of doing to train the AI to look for free text that corresponds to the specific data fields that the customers are looking for, but it is doable."

"Doable for a few hundred thousand dollars and 12 to 18 months?"

"Uh, no. It would probably take a couple million dollars and a couple of years." And then it hits home and I get a sinking feeling in the pit of my stomach. "I am not going to get a few years, am I?"

Jason shakes his head. But he's smiling.

"So, if I am screwed, why are you smiling?"

"Because you are smart and I think you'll figure it out. But enough for now. Go home. Go out for a run. Throw out the mental image of a large sales force and focus on the pain point you just described for me. Think about the kinds of people you know who have that exact scenario happen to them. Every day. Come up with a couple of personas, professions, who live that pain point. Then go back and fix your elevator pitch and we'll find a time to meet again."

Key Takeaways

- Successful startups solve specific pain points.
- There are three dimensions to pain: intensity, frequency, and prevalence.
- Intensity is how much it hurts.
- Frequency is how often it hurts.
- Prevalence is how widespread the pain is.
- A truly painful problem scores highly on all three dimensions.

Chapter 5

Let's Get Personal

I hate the first few minutes of my morning runs. It's cold and the path along the Hudson River is windy. The view is great, though, and whether I go north or south, I know exactly where my turnaround points are so it is one less thing to think about.

But my body is definitely complaining. I know it will basically give up in a moment; "Oh, you are serious about this whole run thing? I guess I am not going to change your mind so I might as well stop bitching and moaning."

If only they made clothes that were warm for the start of the run and magically got lighter once I warmed up. Maybe I could run for five minutes on the treadmill in my building's gym and then go outside? Seems like a pain in the butt …

Focus! Think about what Jason said. So ironic. I listen to podcasts when I run because if I listen to music it is not enough to take my mind off work and I end up thinking about all the emails I need to send and the projects I am working on. Now that I turn everything off so that I can focus exclusively on work, I can't stop thinking about anything but work.

Focus. I need to come up with the persona of a CallJar user. Delete the image of an enterprise salesperson as his or her desk. Do I need to add "or her" in the privacy of my own mind? Still struggling with "their" as the indefinite singular …

Dammit. Must focus. What does a CallJar user typically look like …

Okay, something is coming into focus. I am picturing someone always on the run. Running from meeting to meeting. Trying to squeeze in calls while driving. Better yet, getting a lot of unexpected inbound calls. Especially ones that they think are time sensitive. Got it.

Wow, that is a surprisingly clear mental image. Now who is she? And why is she specifically a she?

Hmm …

Well, damn. That was blindingly obvious in retrospect.

 DOI: 10.4324/9781003542612-6

Key Takeaways

- Creating a customer persona is a way to define who a startup's ideal customer is.
- Visualizing an actual person as the customer going through his or her typical day can highlight when the startup's solution is or is not a good fit for that particular potential market.

Chapter 6

The Perfect Persona

Subject: Thank you

From: Marcus Williams

To: Jason Murath

Thank you again for your time the other day. Definitely gave me a lot to think about.

So, I went for a run like you recommended and it came to me … and then I felt really stupid.

My wife Julia is a real estate agent. She is on the go all the time, constantly getting and making phone calls, fumbling for pen and paper to write down things like the location the client was looking in, the size of the house they want, their price range. She would have killed for CallJar.

What do you think?

Sincerely,
Marcus

Subject: CallJar follow up>> Thank you

From: Jason Murath

To: Marcus Williams

Bingo!

I was actually thinking contractors but realtors work equally well … and you can probably think of several more examples too if you keep at it.

 DOI: 10.4324/9781003542612-7

Let's go with "on-the-go professionals like realtors, contractors, et al." in your elevator pitch for now (and do not sweat the market size for now). Send me the revised pitch.

Then think about your product and simplify it to the bare bones, the MVP that you need to make their lives so much better. That is what we'll talk through next.

Use this link to grab a time for us to meet again …

Yours,

Jason

Subject: CallJar follow up>> Thank you
From: Marcus Williams
To: Jason Murath

I grabbed a time to meet again on Monday.

How about this:

My company, CallJar, provides automated call transcription for on-the-go professionals like, for example, the 2 million real estate agents or the 800,000 small general contractors in the US. Unlike other call transcription companies, we are the only company that is both fully automated and ensures full compliance with privacy regulations. We've been working on the alpha for the past 16 months and expect to launch next month. We are raising $500,000 to get to $500,000 ARR within a year.

I was not sure what the revenue model would be for the new target market so I just went with the number of professionals for now. I hope that is okay?

Also, I feel like that may understate the market a lot. I think ultimately everyone can use CallJar but on-the-go professionals are just the likely first adopters. But I am not sure how to make that distinction in the elevator pitch.

I hope we can discuss this on Monday.

Sincerely,

Marcus

Btw, why did you change the subject line?

Chapter 7

Think Small. Think Minimum Viable Product

"So how was your weekend, Marcus? Do anything wild and exciting?"

"You know, just living the dream." Chuckling. "With a ten-year-old, just getting him into a snowsuit and to the park before he needs to pee is a win. We even got a few runs down the hill on the sled so life is good. Of course, I had pretty elaborate plans for making a snowman, teaching him how to make snow angels, going on a trip for hot cocoa ... but no plans survive contact with young children. And in the end, he had a ton of fun and I got some really great photos so no complaints overall."

"First child, right? I remember those days ... And come to think of it, that is actually not a bad metaphor for what I want to talk about this week.

"Did you understand what I meant in my email about MVP?"

"I assumed you meant Minimum Viable Product, not Most Valuable Player."

"Exactly. Now let me ask you a follow up question. Do you think the product you have in mind is truly the MVP?"

"If you are asking me the question, I am going to go out on a limb and say you do not think it is."

"Even if it was the MVP before, your target persona has just changed dramatically so it is worth revisiting, wouldn't you say?" Looking over his shoulder at the marker board behind him, "Why don't we walk through the pieces of your product and then we will see what parts we need and what parts can come later?"

"I am not sure how granular you want me to get," I say as I start writing:

1. Automatically record incoming and outgoing phone calls
2. Separate audio streams by party

 DOI: 10.4324/9781003542612-8

3. Automatically transcribe each stream
4. Offer draft transcript to each party for correction/revision
5. Get permission from each party to share
6. Merge streams into unified transcript
7. Share transcript with both parties

I am not even done writing the last line when Jason jumps in.

"What happens if the other party to the conversation does not give permission to share?"

"In that case, we only send the user their half of the conversation."

"And what happens if the other party does not respond at all?"

"We were thinking that we would give it two weeks and then, if there is still no response, we assume that their answer is no and send out only half the conversation."

"So, I do not get anything for potentially two weeks?"

"Well, we expect most people would respond right away."

"Based on what?"

"Well, um. If you got a text message right after the phone call, wouldn't you respond right away?"

"Maybe. Maybe not. Probably not, actually, if I am as busy as your target market is. My point is, there might be something in that conversation that I need right away. And if I can't touch it for two weeks, that is a pretty big fail. I have to take notes just in case. Kind of makes the entire product useless for me doesn't it?"

"I guess we could tighten it up to a few days."

"Even a few days is a long time. And what happens if the guy on the other side of the conversation agrees afterwards? You send out another copy of the conversation? Now I have got two versions of the conversation floating around in … what? My inbox? In the app?"

"We send it by email. I figure that is where you are searching for stuff anyway so you might as well put the transcript there so it is all in one place."

"Oh. I like that. I hate having to search in multiple places, to have to remember if something was in an email or Whatsapp or text. But that does not solve the problem of how long you have essentially embargoed critical information. I still have to write things down just to be sure I have it available right away.

"Let me flip this for you. Do you even need both halves of the conversation? Maybe all I need is my half of the conversation."

"What? Not recording the other half at all? What if something important is only on the other side of the conversation?"

"What did you just do?"

"What do you mean, Jason?"

"I asked you a question and you passed it right back right at me, didn't you? In general, if you are a real estate agent or a general contractor, or pretty much anybody who is trying to get critical data out of a client in a conversation, isn't it best practice to repeat it? 'Okay, if I heard you correctly you are looking for a three-bedroom apartment for under $2 million between 72nd and 96th streets. Is that correct?'"

"I guess. I mean, I would do it. My wife does it all the time. It gets to be a habit."

"It's more than habit. It's best practice. And if you had an app that only recorded your half of the conversation, wouldn't you be extra careful to repeat critical information? After all, if you do not repeat it in this scenario it does not get captured."

"I guess so."

"In that case, wouldn't the *minimum* viable product be only to record the app user's half of the conversation? If you hook into the microphone only, you can pretty much cut down your list to only steps 1, 3, and half of step 7."

"That would make things a little easier from a technical perspective. Speech separation with just one audio source is not perfect. If we were only recording the microphone, we would not have to try to figure out when the app user was speaking versus the other party."

"But wait, as the infomercial goes, there's more! Now you don't need permission from the other party. You just send the other party half of the conversation as a courtesy. The other party gets an email saying, 'hey bud, here's what I just said. I did not record anything out of your mouth out of respect for your privacy. But if you think this is cool, why don't you download the app and get it yourself.'"

"Hmm ... that might also help make it more viral. Plus, if both parties have the app, I guess I could figure it out and offer to stitch the two sides of the conversation together after the fact. I probably still want to let app users correct their drafts before sending. Channeling my wife here again, she would want to see the transcript of what she said before it got sent to her potential client."

"Okay, sure. That is the kind of thing you figure out by testing, by going out and talking to real people to figure out how they would use it and what they would need before they would actually rely on your app and ditch the pen and pad. Maybe you need the ability to edit it soup to nuts. Maybe all you need is the ability to add a note at the top of the transcript that says, 'quick heads up. This was an automated transcription. It got a few things wrong so when it says X it really means Y.'"

"Interesting idea. But if I take out the word-by-word correction I do not get the feedback loop that helps train the model."

"Is that a need-to-have or nice-to-have? Could you get most of that some other way?"

"I guess I do not need it from the beginning if the speech to text algorithm is good enough. I guess also I could have the user just read off a couple of standard phrases and use that to help calibrate their voice signature."

"Now you are talking! Even though we have only met a few times, I am willing to bet cold, hard cash that you have super detailed product specs. I want you to go through those specs with a red marker and cross out the features you do not need anymore. Then I want you to take a yellow highlighter and go over all the stuff that you can build later. When you are done, I want to see a super stripped-down product. I want to see the bare minimum that might, maybe, satisfy just enough people to make this valuable. All that stuff in yellow, put in phase two or three. The goal though is to get this down to the point where you can ship product in a fraction of the time and start building from what users actually do, the features they actually use, rather than from what you think they want. I want to find the fastest way to get from inside your head into real customers' hands."

"But how will I know if I cut too much? What if I pull something out that I do not think they need but they actually do?"

"Then you build it. But build the minimum first, then test in the real world, then add only what you need. That is the essence of the lean startup ideal.

"Oh, damn. I must be slipping. Are you building this for Android or iPhone or both?"

"Both, of course. Lots of people have iPhones and lots of people are on Androids."

"So, you *eventually* need to offer to both platforms but do you need to offer it to both platforms right away? Doesn't that double the amount of work you need to get your MVP into real live users' hands?"

"Actually, more than double. Android tends to be a little more open, more permissive. So, the things I can do there I cannot do on iPhone. I basically have to build the app two different ways to get to the same goal with each platform. If I build only for Android, I can probably get the MVP out in a third of the time. But won't that be a bad experience for the other party? Half of the value is that, when the other party gets the email, they download the app. If I do not have an iPhone app, over half those leads go to waste."

Why is Jason taking out his wallet?

"Marcus, I will bet you however much money I have in my wallet right now against however much money you have in your wallet that you have a detailed spreadsheet model of your business that includes dozens of variables like email open, clickthrough, and app download rates. And I am making this bet even though you probably have less than $10 actual cash in your wallet because you pay for everything digitally.

"Am I right? I can tell by the look on your face that I am right. Don't even bother denying it.

"So, I want you to think about that model a little differently. What does the seed stage investor care about more? The absolute number of users that you have or whether the critical assumptions that you are making in that model are correct?"

Let me think about that. "Well, as long as I have enough users to be a valid sample size, I guess it is proving the assumptions that matter is more important, isn't it? I mean, after all, everyone tells me at the seed stage, 'I am just selling the dream.'"

"Exactly! I am not going to invest in you because you have 200 users instead of 100 users. But if your business model lives or dies on having a better than 2% conversion rate and you can show me that on your first 100 users your conversion rate is 7%, *that* moves the needle for me.

"And I have another secret for you. You do not actually have to convert them to prove the metric."

"Okay, I'll bite. If they do not actually convert, how have I proved anything?"

"Let's say the other party gets the email and clicks through to learn more. He is excited about the product and goes to the download page. There are two buttons: iPhone and Android. He clicks on the iPhone icon and then a message pops up saying, 'CallJar for iPhone coming soon! Please give us your email address and we will let you know as soon as it is available for download.' Anyone clicking either the iPhone or the Android button would count as a conversion for me. I do not think a great many of them would bail once they were in the App Store. After all, the process looked pretty real to them; they thought they were going to download the app. So, I will give you full credit for the clickthroughs even though there never was an app to download."

My head is starting to spin.

"Okay, Marcus, okay. Take deep breaths. It actually sounds harder than it is because I talk so fast. Think a bit more about what your MVP actually is. Flowchart it for me. If it helps, flowchart phase two and three and color code it so you see what you are adding at each stage … and implicitly highlighting what you are ripping out to get down to the MVP. But all I need for now is the MVP.

"I will take a look, make some comments. You can then use that to update your implementation plan and come up with the revised time you'll need to develop it. If the number is low enough, maybe we'll hold off fundraising and bootstrap a little more to collect the kind of metrics you'll need to have a better chance of raising a round at a better valuation later.

"But for right now, just send me the flowchart and we'll take it from there. Okay? Any questions?"

"No, thanks for … Wait. Actually, yes. Why did you change the subject line of my emails?"

"Because your subject line sucked. Do you have any idea how many emails I get with a subject line 'Thank you'? I should be able to look at the subject line and at a glance know exactly what the email is about. Plus, a good subject line makes it a lot easier to find what you need later. Instead of changing it entirely, I kept your original subject and just inserted a prefix with the context I needed so that you would know it was part of the same email thread.

"Sometimes, as the conversation evolves and we start talking about something different than the original email, I will even change the subject line again, usually adding another prefix to it. It is kind of like breadcrumbs when you think about it; that way you always know where you are in the conversation."

Key Takeaways

- MVP stands for Minimum Viable Product.
- Entrepreneurs should strive to build only the MVP at first because it minimizes the time and resources needed in order to put their product on the market.
- It is more efficient to release an MVP and then improve on it based on feedback from actual customers than to build a more functional initial product only to later find out that customers do not value many of its features.
- To get down to the MVP, an entrepreneur needs to lay out the components of the startup's product and eliminate or defer any features that are not absolutely necessary for the first customer-usable version of the product.
- While designing an MVP, startups often discover critical information that causes them to make meaningful changes to the product they envisioned.

Chapter 8

New Product Flow

Subject: CallJar revised MVP post call workflow

From: Marcus Williams

To: Jason Murath

See enclosed

Sincerely,
Marcus

PS How's that for a subject line?

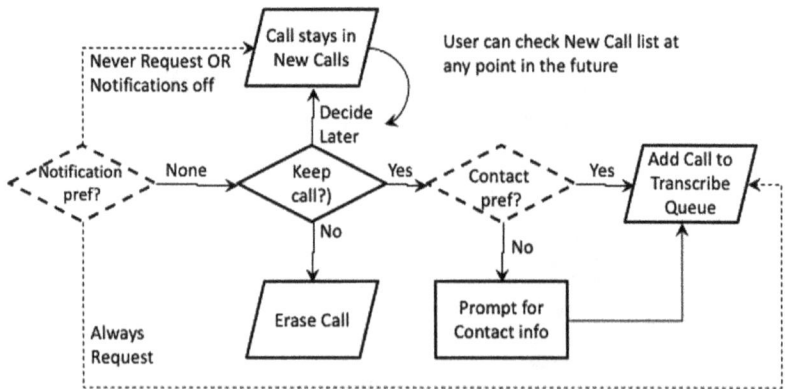

Figure 8.1 CallJar post call workflow

DOI: 10.4324/9781003542612-9

Subject: Re: CallJar revised MVP post call workflow
From: Jason Murath
To: Marcus Williams

Good flowchart (and excellent subject line).
I marked up it up – see enclosed

Next steps:
Mock up the screens – phone, app, texts, webpages, whatever – that the app user would see during the most common use cases. Sketches only, God help you if you pay a penny for a designer at this stage. But make them detailed enough that you can put them in front of a potential user as if they were exactly what he or she was seeing, without any commentary from you to explain them.

Then take those mock-ups and talk to at least ten, preferably 20, on-the-go professionals who are either real estate agents or small general contractors. Show them each screen and watch silently and see how they interact with each mockup to see if they understand the concept and the execution. Run those conversations just like we discussed and, when you are close to done with those interviews, use my calendar link to grab a time for us to discuss.

Yours,
Jason

Chapter 9

Eating up Customer Feedback

"Thanks for taking the time to chat with me about this, Steph."

"Anything for Julia, Marcus."

I have met so many people in the same Starbucks over the past few weeks that I feel like I should be paying rent. Given what they charge for a cappuccino these days, it might even be cheaper for me to get a membership at a coworking space and drink their coffee for free.

I know that Jason recommended meeting a potential customer in their office, to see them in the actual work environment, to pick up on a lot of the more subtle nuances. But Stephanie is out of the office most of her day anyway and CallJar is really there for that on-the-go experience so somehow meeting in a Starbucks just felt right.

Steph had gotten Julia interested in being a real estate agent and had been her mentor for her first couple of years in the industry. She treats technology like a tool rather than a shiny toy: when it is useful, she uses it. When it is not significantly better than what she already has, she passes. Most importantly, she is not shy about speaking her mind. Even so, I lead in with Jason's advice.

"I want to get your blunt and even brutal feedback on something I am working on. I promise you, you are not going to hurt my feelings. I am considering quitting my job and putting a good chunk of money into building what I am about to tell you about. So, if you see any flaws or drawbacks or gaps, you are doing me a huge favor by giving it to me straight rather than sugar coating it. Do not be afraid to break my idea. If you break it and I can't fix it, you may be saving me years of my life."

She laughs.

 DOI: 10.4324/9781003542612-10

"Not a problem. I am not that nice under the best of circumstances. I promise not to spare your feelings."

At Jason's emphatic urging, I had resisted the temptation to immediately start coding the new MVP. Except for a few deliberately crude mock-ups, I did not build anything that I might need to change later in light of customer feedback.

I already know what she does in the organization and how long she has been doing it so I skip over that part of the conversation. I know the depth of experience with software solutions so I do not need to level-set the conversation to figure out how comfortable she is with tech either. I skip right to the scenario that is the core of the pain point I am hoping to solve.

"Julia lives on her phone. She does her best to schedule her outgoing calls for a time when she can be at her desk, notebook open, pen in hand but it always seems like twice as many calls come to her while she is running off to a different showing or meeting with a new prospect or taking our son to a doctor's appointment. We could be in the middle of dinner when a call comes in and she pushes the plates aside with one hand and starts digging through her purse with the other hand, hoping to get her notebook out before she forgets anything important from the beginning of the conversation. Is that how it seems to you as well or do you have a different system for capturing the key information from your calls with clients and prospects?"

"God, I wish I could say I did. I get half a dozen inbound calls on a slow day and I am pretty much always in the middle of something else. Now that I have a team under me, I can delegate a lot of the outbound calls, especially for qualifying new prospects. But the inbound ones are just completely unpredictable. I don't know a single broker in my office who is not struggling with the same thing."

Well, that worked out nicely. Not only did she confirm that she had the same problem, she confirmed that it is also widespread and frequent. Check, check, and check to all three dimensions of pain. Fortunately, I have been getting that feedback pretty consistently over the past few weeks.

"So, I am working on an app that automatically records and transcribes calls for on-the-go professionals like real estate agents. Unlike other call transcription services, this would be the only one that is both fully automated and ensures full compliance with privacy regulations."

"Oh? Interesting."

"I would like to show you a few mocked up screenshots of what the app will look like. The mockups are purposely rough because I do not want specific design elements to confuse things. I am going to put them in front of you with minimal context because I want to simulate what it would be like if you came across this app on your own. You know, as if you didn't have the company founder looking over your shoulder ready to answer questions." That always gets a little laugh. "What I would like you to do is to just verbalize what you are thinking. I can't read your mind so just say out loud what your first impressions are when you see a particular screenshot. If you are confused, think it through out loud. Again, I am going to try not to step in with any advice unless you are absolutely stumped. Please go ahead and touch the screenshot as if you were pressing a button and I will then hand you the next screenshot that would come up. Makes sense?"

"Seems simple enough. Hit me."

"Okay, let's begin. Your phone rings and you answer the call. Everything proceeds exactly the same as it does right now. Your phone's screen looks slightly different."

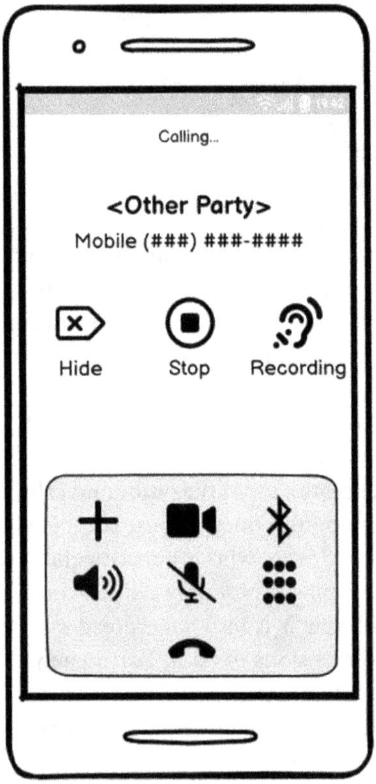

Figure 9.1 App screen for call in progress

She takes out her reading glasses. That has happened a few times. I think I need to make the overlay text a little larger. Or not. Once she knows what everything is for, she won't need glasses moving forward.

"Looks like my normal call screen with something on top of it. I see a notification that the call is being recorded. Did your app tell the other caller that it is being recorded?"

"No." Maybe I erred a little too much in the direction of no context. "As part of installing the app, you would have been told that the app will record only what you say, not anything said by the other party. The app does not inform the other party that anything is being recorded until after you decide if you want to keep the call."

"Is that legal?" I simply shrug a little and cover my mouth. "Ah, cute. You are not here to answer questions like that. Okay, since this is a work tool, I am thinking I would probably need to look at the FAQs to understand that.

"Hmm. My only options are to stop or hide something. I am guessing that the first one means stop recording and in that case anything that I have said before hitting the button will automatically be deleted. I am not exactly sure what 'hide' does though and I am a little afraid to touch it during my call in case it disconnects me. I guess I could just test that with my husband but I am not really comfortable with experimenting during a call with a real client. I guess I prefer a little more context about what these things do before using the app."

Fair enough. I had gotten similar feedback from some of the other interviews. I was trying to minimize how much space this took up but I can change the buttons to say 'stop recording' and 'hide overlay' if necessary. Or I could have a very quick tutorial style walkthrough that explains what each button is before their first call. As a general principle though, I do not like to make a user sit through tutorials; it is just a much better experience if they can jump right in and pick it up as they go along.

"So, I am going to do nothing for now and just keep talking as if nothing different were happening."

I take the current mock up away from her and give her the one with the post call notification:

Figure 9.2 App screen for call ended

"So it looks like I have the option of keeping the recording or discarding it, right? Oh yeah, you are not here. I would bet that if I hit discard, the recording is deleted and the demo ends so ..." Steph leans forward and taps the save button. She totally ignored the ' ...' more options icon or did not even realize it was a third option. Interesting. But I am focused on validating the concept so I let that go and I show her the next screen.

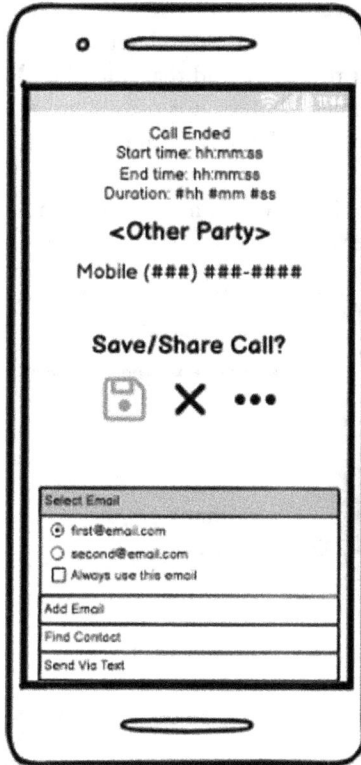

Figure 9.3 App screen for save call

"Huh? What's all this? Why are you asking for email?" Long pause. "And could you make this text any smaller? Jeez ... I give up. What's going on here?"

I am not sure what to do here. About half the test group gets confused here. The other half got it and a few even commented on how efficient the interface was. But the point here is to get overall feedback on the concept, not detailed design recommendations. So let's give her a bit more context.

"When the call is over, if you keep your part of the conversation, the app is going to send that half-transcript to both you and the other party. So, when you save a call with someone, the app is asking you how you want to send the other party that half-transcript."

"Do I have to share the half-transcript with the other side or can I just keep it to myself?"

"The way the app is currently built, you must share. Some states have 'dual party notification' laws on call recording and, even though we feel that only recording your half of the conversation sidesteps these requirements entirely, we feel that full transparency is the way to go." It also means that every time the app is used, someone else finds out about CallJar, but no need to go into that.

"I am not sure how I feel about not having a 'this call is being recorded' notification. Would my client be annoyed to find out after the fact that I had recorded the conversation, even if they were told that only the stuff I said was recorded?" After a pause, she continues, "I guess it is okay. Plus, if I were *really* concerned, I could just tell my clients what I am doing at the start of the conversation. Okay, so what happens next?"

"When the transcript is ready, you have the option of reviewing it before it is sent to you and the other party. If you want to review it, you see this."

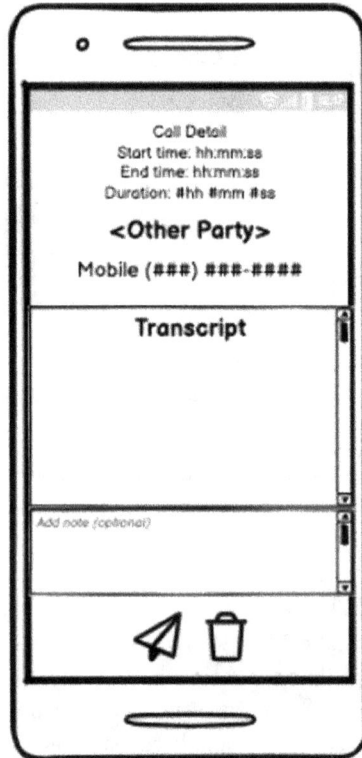

Figure 9.4 App screen with call transcript

Tapping the center area.

"If I tap here, can I edit the text? You know, to correct a typo."

"Not in the first release. Ultimately, you will be able to tap any part of the message to hear the audio and correct the text as needed. In the email you both get, you will be able to tap any phrase in the half transcript to play the original recording as needed." I caught myself before I continued. Let's see if she figures it out.

After a long pause, Steph continues hesitantly, "So I guess I use the section below to tell my client that the transcript was automatically generated and call out any mistakes I see before sending. The note should really go on top of the transcript so my client reads it first, before the transcript."

"Good point. In the email you both get, the note is on top but I can see how that would not be obvious from this screen. I think I will move the notes section to above the transcript so it is more obvious. Here is what the recipient sees."

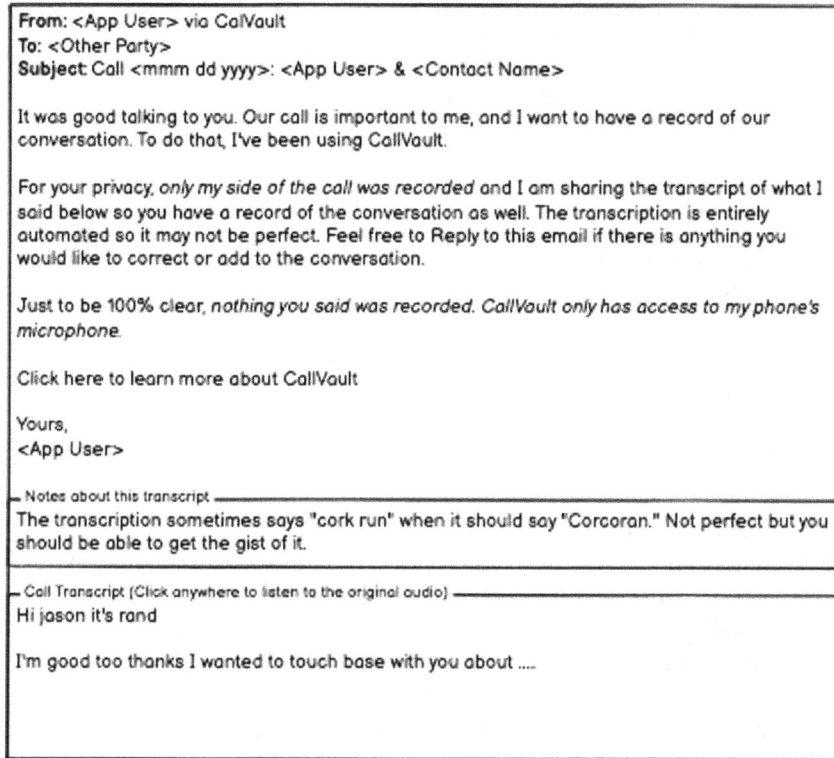

From: <App User> via CallVault
To: <Other Party>
Subject: Call <mmm dd yyyy>: <App User> & <Contact Name>

It was good talking to you. Our call is important to me, and I want to have a record of our conversation. To do that, I've been using CallVault.

For your privacy, *only my side of the call was recorded* and I am sharing the transcript of what I said below so you have a record of the conversation as well. The transcription is entirely automated so it may not be perfect. Feel free to Reply to this email if there is anything you would like to correct or add to the conversation.

Just to be 100% clear, *nothing you said was recorded.* CallVault only has access to *my phone's microphone.*

Click here to learn more about CallVault

Yours,
<App User>

└ Notes about this transcript ──────
The transcription sometimes says "cork run" when it should say "Corcoran." Not perfect but you should be able to get the gist of it.

└ Call Transcript (Click anywhere to listen to the original audio) ──────
Hi jason it's rand

I'm good too thanks I wanted to touch base with you about ....

Figure 9.5 Email with call transcript

"Oh? That is not bad at all. I guess the note I added is that section below the signature?"

"Exactly."

"And it looks like the email came directly from me. Does it show up in my Inbox or my Sent folder?"

"Good catch … and a great question. I think it goes right to your Sent folder. How do you feel about that?"

"I think that is best. I get a lot of email and I will only need to look at a few of the transcripts. Skipping my Inbox cuts out the clutter and I will always know where to look when I do need the transcript."

Steph frowns. "Where does all the text above the notes and transcript come from?"

"You set that up once when you download the app and we use it for every email. We will suggest the default text but you can change it to whatever you want."

Steph nods, frown gone. "Good. This way I don't have to type, 'This is an automated transcription so please excuse any errors' each and every time I record a call."

Taking the mockup away from Steph, I ask, "So now that you have a sense of how this works, does it work for you? Does it solve your problem?"

Cautiously, she answers, "I think so …" and then continues with increased certainty, "Not having to take notes manually, either on paper or on my notes app is a win, assuming the transcript is reliable, of course. But now I need to go through that emailed half transcript to pull out the key info to run my search for that client. I can probably skim the email and find that data pretty quickly. I might even use the Find function to search for specific information. Hey! I do not suppose you could boldface anything that sounds like a number or address?"

Not a bad idea at all. A lot of the other customer interviewees have asked if I could integrate with their CRM, automatically extract the specific data and pop it into a client profile. But when I dug deeper, they each had things set up differently so I would need to build APIs and then handle custom setups, etc. etc. If I can make it easier for them to find most of what they need on their own, that would probably count as the "minimum" in MVP.

"I think we can do that. We are already using different Natural Language Processing libraries to format anything that looks like a telephone number, time, or dollar amount the way you would expect them to look and we convert all other numbers into comma delimited digits instead of having them spelled out as words. Bolding them too should be pretty simple. I think there are NLP libraries that handle addresses too. Would that cover everything?"

"That's most of it. Telephone numbers, price range, numbers of rooms, square feet … Neighborhood would be nice but I guess I will just have to skim the transcript for that. Unless they are kind enough to know the zip codes they want me to search. For a lot of the co-ops I need to know things like what kind of pets they have, if they want to be able to sublet, yada, yada, yada but it is usually only one curveball like that, if any, and those are the kinds of things I tend to remember anyway so yeah, bolding numbers and anything address-like would do it for me."

"That is good to hear. Now let's say I told you that I was not going to build this at all. Are there any other solutions out there that do anything similar to what I just described? Would you use those other solutions or not? How do they stack up to my solution?"

"You know, for a while I actually had a call recording app on my phone …"

Uh-oh. This is new.

" … but it didn't really help all that much because when the call was done, I had to listen to the entire recording to find the bits I was looking for. It would have been so much easier to have it in writing so I could just skim through it. I thought about sending it out to be transcribed but at that point, it was just easier to take notes. Not to mention that the transcription was not free. I did ultimately manage to do away with a pen and paper, though. I have at least one earbud in at all times so instead of having to hold the phone to my ear, I take the call wirelessly and use the notes app on my phone while on the call. When I am done, I just email the notes to myself or to my assistant to get into our CRM system."

Hmm, I guess I have to add "notes taking app" to the competition slide. "How well does that work for you?"

"Eh. It's a bit of a kluge and a distraction from the conversation. Not ideal but definitely better than fumbling through my purse for a notebook and pen. But what you are building would be much better. Assuming it doesn't cost an arm and a leg, that is."

Since I was just about to test pricing, I could not have asked for a better segue.

"I am still working that out. There will probably be a free version to get started on but anyone using it professionally would likely want the pro version which I am thinking would cost $10 per month."

"Oh, I would pay that in a heartbeat."

Don't get too excited. Remember what Jason told you: No one what to tell you that your baby is ugly and no one wants you to think that they are "a cheap bastard." They will almost all say that they would "probably buy" or "definitely buy." So I follow up with the real question.

"Think about your colleagues and coworkers. Do you think they would pay $10 per month for this service?"

"That is a good question. I think that any of the more active agents would pay that – and probably more! I would probably not even blink twice about buying it for my entire team. I would probably want to feel like we got some kind of bulk discount because, well, that is just how people are, but the value is there. On the other hand, there are a lot of new agents and a lot of agents that are kind of marginal. They are often the 'optional' worker of the couple. They do this part time to pick up a few extra bucks while working around the kids' schedules. They may not be doing enough business to feel like they want to part with even $120 a year on this. If you have a free option, they will likely stick with that and make do."

"Hey! Have you spoken to any of the Realtor associations?"

"Huh?"

"Most real estate agents are members of The National Association of Realtors – except in New York City, that is, where we belong to REBNY, the Real Estate Board of New York. Beneath the NAR are the state associations and below them, the local associations. The state or local associations will often have preferred vendors that they promote to their members. Occasionally, the associations will even buy services in bulk to give to their members for free."

"I did not know that. That is really interesting …"

I know I am trailing off mid-sentence but my mind is racing ahead. The curveball Jason pitched me that got me to switch focus from large sales forces to on-the-go professionals is still so recent that I had not gotten a chance to rethink what my Go-To-Market strategy will be. Candidly, I am a little concerned about how to get in touch with hundreds of thousands of small professionals. That kind of direct-to-consumer marketing is not the world I come from. I know business-to-business style marketing, not business-to-consumer. But being able to sell to a large organization, or even just being able to pitch it to them for them to put me in front of their members, that is firmer ground. Heck, anything with a membership implies that there is a member list. And if I can get my hands on a member list, I can market to them. But I need to put the brakes on this train of thought because I have got Steph sitting in front of me wondering what kind of mental vacation I just went on.

"Steph, I can't thank you enough for taking the time to sit down with me and go through this. You had some great suggestions on both the user interface and on marketing strategy that I am still digesting. I hope it is alright if I follow up with you later if I have any additional questions or want an introduction to any of the realtor associations you mentioned?"

"Anytime, Marcus."

Key Takeaways

- The best time to meet with customers is early, often as soon as the founder has the basic concept.
- You do not need a working product to have a customer feedback meeting.
- Customer feedback meetings can validate that the pain point the startup is solving for is as painful as it thinks.
- Customer feedback meetings can also identify gaps in the product's feature set and/or places where the user experience (UX) is not clear so it can be fixed *before* beginning to build the product.
- Customer feedback meetings are also a good opportunity to validate proposed pricing.
- Customer feedback meetings may also surface additional useful insights into how to build or market the startup's solution.
- One technique is to create a mockup of the product or service (e.g., printed versions of app screens) and silently watch how the customer interacts with it.

Chapter 10

Fully Fed

Subject: CallJar customer feedback meetings
From: Marcus Williams
To: Jason Murath

Jason,

Just finished my last meeting, bringing it up to an even thirty. I could go on but the things I am hearing from the real estate agents have been pretty consistent – and positive.

By and large, most of the conversations went pretty much according to plan. A few of the more quirky personalities were all over the place and I had to be flexible about the order in which I went through the questions but you prepared me for that pretty well and ultimately I got what I needed from even them.

Plus, I got some good ideas about how to Go-To-Market with the new target market.

To be honest, though, there are still a lot of unknowns that are keeping me up at night. But I am comfortable enough to start coding what we need to get the product to MVP so we can start fundraising.

Sincerely,
Marcus

DOI: 10.4324/9781003542612-11

Subject: RE: CallJar customer feedback meetings

From: Jason Murath

To: Marcus Williams

Don't start coding just yet. There are one or two things I want to run through with you first to be as sure as humanly possible that we are on the right path

(OK, I know you are not going to listen to me and you are going to want to start coding anyway. Fine. Just stick to the basic stuff that you need to do no matter which way we end up going on pricing and no matter which of the features we are still on the fence about are in or out.)

We are going to probably need to meet at least once a week for the next couple of weeks while we work on this together so we should probably just pick a standing weekly meeting time. I am free from 4:00 to 6:00 p.m. on Mondays and Wednesdays for at least the next month so pick whatever time works for you and throw a recurring meeting on my calendar.

Yours,
Jason

Subject: Coding>> CallJar customer feedback meetings

From: Marcus Williams

To: Jason Murath

(See what I did with the subject line? Are you proud?)

So, I confess that I have been coding all along. I even have a partial working "alpha" version of the product working on my phone to test different elements of the process.

Just to give you a sense of what I am working on, here is a very abbreviated rundown:

1. Automatically begin/end recording when an inbound or outbound call begins/ends – done
2. Stop / delete call recording in progress – done
3. Separate audio by speaker – skip (likely not nec for MVP)

4. Post call keep/delete – in progress (for the alpha, I just manually delete unwanted calls from the folder on my phone)
5. Auto upload audio to server – in progress (for the alpha, I manually upload the recordings every few days)
6. Auto transcribe newly uploaded audio – in progress (for the alpha, I manually run the speech-to-text engine. I have settled on which ASR (Automatic Speech Recognition) model I am using but it still needs to be trained/optimized)
7. Clean up/enrich transcription (punctuation, line breaks, capitalization, formatting numbers, etc.) – next in queue (I need to test a number of different options to see what works best)
8. Review/add comment / for other party – later
9. Choose/add email/phone for delivery to other party – later

Obviously, there are a lot more features on my list but most if not all of the remainders are likely not needed for the MVP

Note: follow the above is for Android only. Some of it was done for iPhone before we settled on initially going to market with Android only.

Sincerely,
Marcus

Chapter 11

De-risking the Model

"Want to see how the product is shaping up?"

"Not really."

"I am not really sure how to respond to that."

Jason chuckled. "Truth is, I am actually dying to see the product but I know that if I start to dive in now, by the time I come up for air, an hour will have passed and we have a few more important things to do first."

"That's fair. What did you have in mind?"

"I want to talk to you about your model. Have you created a financial forecast for CallJar?"

"I did. It was fairly detailed but that was under the old model when I still thought we were going after large sales forces. I have not had a chance to go through it again now that we've shifted focus."

"I think you should refresh the model now. It is going to be an iterative process. We have not fully fleshed out a lot of the important details, like your Go-To-Market for instance, so you won't be able to fully build out your five-year financials but that is not really what I am interested in right now. Right now, I am looking to see what we *know* as opposed to what we *assume*. I want to move as many from the latter category into the former as quickly and cheaply as we can. Then I want to go through the remaining unknowns to see which of them might kill us."

"Well, that sounds fun and cheerful."

"Did anyone tell you startup life was going to be fun and cheerful?"

"No, I guess not."

"Good. Then let's move on, shall we?

"This is not going to be some BS, protracted, fill in the blanks, paint by number exercise. This should actually be relatively quick and to the point.

"I know you like 'conceptual frameworks' so try this one on for size:"

  DOI: 10.4324/9781003542612-12

Jason starts scribbling on the marker board:

Expected Value ($) = Exit Potential ($) * Odds of success (%)

"The expected value of your startup equals the potential exit value times the odds of success."

Holding his hand up, "Before you object, yes, I know I should include a discount rate and the number of years I expect to get to the exit to get to a true present value but let's keep it simple because regardless of how many years it is and what discount rate you choose, what I am about to tell you still holds true.

"You have no control over the exit value of your startup. The market sets it and you simply do your best to capture that full value. The only part of that equation that you control is the probability of success.

"There are a whole lot of unknowns when you start a startup. If you model your startup correctly, you can represent these unknowns in the variables that go into the model. Some of these variables, like how much you spend on advertising for example, you control. Other variables, say office rent, you know with reasonable certainty. Still others, you neither control nor know. For those variables, you make assumptions. Basically, you guess.

"Not all of those assumptions are created equal. Most of them don't matter. Even if you are off by 20–30%, the bottom line does not change much. For example, if you need to pay salespeople a $120,000 base instead of a $100,000, it is probably not going to make or break your company. It's a rounding error.

"A few of those assumptions, though, do matter. They may matter a lot. Even being off just a little bit could mean the difference between success or failure, between you having a viable business or just an interesting but unworkable idea. Typically, there are no more than a handful of these critical assumptions. Often, it comes down to one.

"Even after all these years of angel investing, it is still shocking to me how many founders do not know what the critical variables are for their business. Especially since it is actually fairly easy to figure them out. You build your model as a spreadsheet. You put all the variables, known and assumed, on a separate tab. You start changing each assumption a little bit, up or down. Then you look at what happens to your revenue and your income five years out, ten years out. Did it move substantially? If it did not, it is not a critical assumption and you can ignore it for now.

"Once you have the critical assumptions that do really move the needle, that is the real risk. That is what is dragging down your probability of success. Anything you can do to prove out those assumptions, to give you and potential investors comfort that your guess is accurate, reduces the risk inherent in your startup. If you de-risk your startup by proving out an assumption, the probability of success goes up. And when that probability goes up, it brings up the expected value of your startup at that point in time.

"At the earliest stages, there are still going to be a lot of risks. That is why a company that could ultimately be worth hundreds of millions of dollars or more will raise a seed round at a valuation of, say, $7 million. As the startup gets more mature and starts to make sales and bring in revenue, it proves that it has product-market fit. So, the risk goes down, the probability of success goes up. The startup can then go on to raise a Series A round at, say, a $25 million pre-money valuation. The potential exit value has not changed at all, only the odds of success have changed because one of the big assumptions, product-market fit, moved from assumed to proven. Still with me?"

"Yes. Seems pretty simple so far."

"Really? Okay smart-ass, what does this mean you have to do?"

"Build my model, check out all the variables and see what the real values are."

"Wrong and wrong in two different ways. The first one, is not all of your assumptions matter. Unless it is a single phone call or web search or something equally quick, I do not want you spending time on stuff that does not matter.

"The second problem is that it is not always easy to prove an assumption. What if your critical assumption is how viral your app is? How do you know if one happy customer tells two of his friends or ten of his friends? Other than actually building the product, you may not be able to prove that assumption. As an investor, I won't ding you on that. What I am looking for is that you have de-risked as much as you possibly can, as efficiently as you possibly can, before asking me for my money.

"Here is a real-life example. Ages ago, when I ran a startup accelerator program, I had a company with a freemium subscription model. You know how that goes, right? There is a free service but if you want the premium features, you have got to pay. Demo Day was coming up in a few weeks and they desperately needed to know what the conversion to premium would be so they could show that to the investors in the audience and line up meetings while they had everyone's attention. But they were from Costa Rica and it was taking them a bit more time than normal to get a merchant account. So, you know what they did? They added a page listing all the premium services and what it cost to upgrade along with a 'Buy Now' button. The button took the user to a purchase page that looked 100% real. They even went so far as to collect the credit card number. But when the user clicked 'Submit,' a message popped up saying, 'Congratulations! Have one month free on us. We are so confident that you will enjoy our product, we have not charged your card yet.' They did not have an SSL certificate so they did not even store the credit card number. When the month was up, they asked for the credit card again. It was a less-than-optimal user experience at that point but the important part was that they had solid, unimpeachable data on what the clickthrough rate was and what percentage of users would pay to upgrade to premium. They were able to move that variable in their model from assumed to proven in time for Demo Day."

"Very clever. I do not have my MVP up yet so I do not think I can test that right now."

"True. But you could do a 'Wizard of Oz' prototype with the call transcription."

"Okay, I will bite. What's a 'Wizard of Oz' prototype?"

"You fake it. Do it manually behind the scenes. 'Pay no attention to the man behind the curtain.' You do not actually do automated transcription. You have the audio sent to a human being and make it look like a machine did the transcription. That way you can test a lot of the other variables before building the speech recognition engine."

"We are actually using an open-source speech recognition engine. The underlying tech is getting that good. It's how we train the engine and how we use it that is the real value add here. Whether the automated translation we can deliver is 'good enough' is pretty much the most important assumption I need to prove."

"Hmm. I guess you are right about that. But the transcript doesn't have to be sent immediately. You could do the translation automatically then hold on to it for a short while to review it manually to see how good it is. You could even use that to train the model to the specific user. If it is only an hour or so delay, I bet that would be acceptable to the end user and, as far as they were concerned, they would just get a really good transcription. After the first ... dozen? Two dozen calls? The model would be well personalized to that user."

"Wouldn't that be cost prohibitive? Wait, maybe not. I guess it depends on the length of the call, the cost of the manual review, how many minutes of manual review I need to hit for a certain level of accuracy ... I was planning to have the user train the model as he corrected the transcripts but if I am leaving user correction out of the MVP, I can use this to calculate the cost of getting to different levels of accuracy. But until I am sure about my pricing and have some idea what the actual conversation rate from free to paid user will be, I won't know if I can actually sustain that. The formula is pretty simple but there are so many unknowns that it is assumption on top of assumption on top of assumption. I am not sure if I would have much confidence in the answer."

"That is actually a really good example. Take those variables one by one and you'll see that you can get a lot of that data without spending much time or money. You should be able to get a bunch of your friends, ideally with a variety of accents, to give you a bunch of audio samples. You could give them scripts or let them freestyle, whatever. Make them all roughly a minute, two minutes, five minutes long whatever. Hire some guys in the Philippines to manually transcribe them. Then run your speech to text algorithm against them six ways from Sunday. Run it first without any training to make sure that it is 'not so bad' out of the gate that your users bail right away. Then run the algo with a few minutes of manually corrected transcripts. Then run the algo with a few more minutes. Rate the accuracy at every point and figure out when you think you have hit 'good enough' for the long run to give you a sense of how much time your users are going to have to put in before they get there."

"Interesting. Plus, the individual user training time goes down the more we train the model across all users. I like the elegance of having our users correct their own transcripts and having that feed the engine that makes the transcripts better for future users, and so on until the out-of-the-box quality is as good as it can possibly get. But this might be a good way to jump start the process."

"Actually, that is an interesting dynamic worth talking about. I assume you are familiar with economies of scale? This is something I refer to as data economies of scale. If somebody were to come along in a few years and replicate every line of code you had, the quality of their transcription would still be worse than yours because they do not have the tens of thousands of hours of user corrections feeding into and refining the model. So why would anyone use their product over yours? It's a built-in 'unfair competitive advantage' or 'moat' that investors love to see that becomes even more unfair over time.

"When there is this kind of dynamic at play, it pays to treat things as a land grab. It can pay to lose money for some of those early users to get that initial advantage so that your product gets better than the competition, faster than the competition.

"Anyway, I am about to be late for another meeting. Take a crack at the model. When you have it down to your critical assumptions, let me know what they are and we will see if there is anything we can do to test them quickly and cheaply to de-risk CallJar more before moving on to the next step."

Subject: CallJar model/de-risking

From: Marcus Williams

To: Jason Murath

Jason,

It's a little after 3am but I finally finished rebuilding the financial model. I will be a zombie at work tomorrow but once I was in the flow, it felt better to just push through and finish than to pull my head out of the game midway and try to get back in later.

I did the sensitivity analysis you suggested. Honestly, I just pumped the value up and down by 10% to see what happened to the revenue and income in year 5. The variables that made the most difference were:

1. $ Price
2. % Upgrading to paid
3. $ Customer Acquisition Cost
4. # Referrals
5. $ Cost per minute of transcription (computational)
6. $ Cost to train algo per new user (manual review)

No huge surprises there.

I have done all I can do to validate the $10/month price point in the customer interviews and I think I have a fairly good handle on the compute time and cost for the automated transcription.

No idea how to test #2 or #4 at this point. I am going with 3% for the upgrade rate because I read somewhere that 2–5% was the right range for this sort of thing.

I am assuming two referrals per user happening in the 2nd month. Why two? Idk. One seemed too low and at three or four, the numbers got very large absurdly quickly. So, I went with two … just like the old shampoo commercial.

#3 is really worrying me. I am just taking a complete leap of faith on CAC because I still do not know what the best way to acquire the initial users. Google ads, Facebook ads, buying (and spamming) lists of email addresses (real estate agents, contractors), bulk sales to Realtor or trade associations, etc., etc.

Any thoughts?

Sincerely,
Marcus

Subject: CallJar model/de-risking

From: Jason Murath

To: Marcus Williams

Marcus,

Don't sweat #2 or #4 right now. The goal is to test whatever we possibly can before launching. If there is no possible way to test something without actually launching it, do not beat yourself up. The assumptions you make are reasonable to start with and we will have to see how it plays out after launch. There is a certain amount of irreducible risk here …

(And yes, I do remember that commercial.)

Re: CAC – it's still going to be a SWAG but maybe I can put some more "Scientific" into this Scientific Wild Ass Guess.

Get on one of those website builders and create a fake site. Get a different domain for it. But make the home page look real.

Then throw a few bucks into Google AdWords. Play around with a few different ads – different copy, different calls to action, etc. Don't worry, Google will test the different ads against each other for you to see what works best. Select the keywords you want to target. And then sit back and see what happens. At the very least, you should get some decent data on your cost per click. Then do the same with Facebook ads, maybe even LinkedIn, Instagram … I think you can pass on TikTok but you never know. It will likely cost you a few hundred dollars per platform.

Google around and see what it would cost to buy lists of email addresses belonging to real estate agents, contractors, and any "other on-the-go professionals" that you can think of.

Or maybe you just scrape email addresses off company websites, property listings, etc.? Probably violates the MLS terms of use but if you are subtle, you can probably fly under their radar for a long time because they get so much other traffic. They aren't called *Multiple* Listing Services for nothing.

You could even send out a few hundred test emails to see what the clickthrough (and ultimately download) rates are. That said, A/B testing subject lines, email copy, etc. is tricky. You start to need some pretty large numbers to test all the permutations so if you do a test email, my advice is to keep it simple. Once you have your baseline, you can always optimize the email campaign to get better.

Btw, once you have the fake site, you can go beyond just testing CPC. Build out the site a bit more and put a "Get the App" button on it. If anyone clicks, give them a "coming soon." (Before you ask, don't worry about what people will think. The numbers are low and you are sending them to a bogus site so your brand won't be affected.) See how much it costs to get you a download. You will still have to come up with a reasonable assumption for how many users who download actually set up the app but you have minimized the guesswork.

No easy way to test out bulk sales other than actually doing them. Sorry.

While you are working on that … New topic:

I have attached another presentation: Perfecting the Pitch Deck. Give it a read and come to our next meeting ready to talk about your Problem and Solution slides. Please, please, please do *not* spend any time (or money) making it look pretty; just put the content in the right places for now.

Yours,
Jason

Key Takeaways

- Good entrepreneurs de-risk their startup as much as possible before spending money.
- Founders can model how their startup works in a spreadsheet.
- The goal of modeling the startup this way is not primarily to forecast future profit. The goal is to be able to identify critical assumptions.
- As such, the model should be detailed enough to show how income and cash flow are impacted by different actions that the entrepreneur takes (e.g., spending more on marketing) and what happens if certain assumptions (e.g., clickthrough rates) are incorrect.
- By varying the assumptions a bit, an entrepreneur can identify the handful of assumptions that can make or break the startup.
- Once the critical assumptions are identified, there are often free or very inexpensive ways to test those assumptions as much as possible before raising funding for the startup.

Part II

Prepping your Pitch Deck

Now that you are comfortable that you have built a product the market wants and you have de-risked it as much as possible, you may be ready to raise. Here is what you need to have in your investor pitch deck.

DOI: 10.4324/9781003542612-13

Chapter 12

Ordering the Narrative

"I have got the Problem and Solution slides like you asked but I am confused. Shouldn't the Team slide come first?"

"Okay, let's take a step back. Let me see if I can get this deck on the monitor ..."

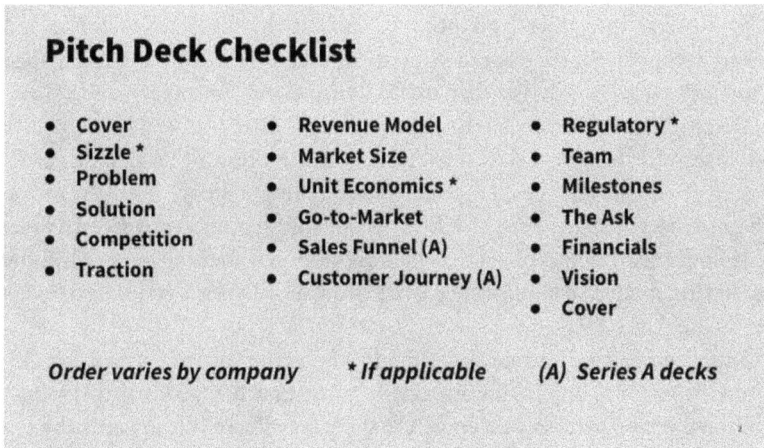

Pitch Deck Checklist

- Cover
- Sizzle *
- Problem
- Solution
- Competition
- Traction

- Revenue Model
- Market Size
- Unit Economics *
- Go-to-Market
- Sales Funnel (A)
- Customer Journey (A)

- Regulatory *
- Team
- Milestones
- The Ask
- Financials
- Vision
- Cover

Order varies by company   * If applicable   (A) Series A decks

Figure 12.1 Pitch deck slide checklist

"That was quick."

"I figured you would have questions so I had the deck open and waiting to go ... and God help you if you show up to an investor pitch without your deck open and whatever pages you might need pre-loaded on tabs on your browser. Investors hate having to sit around while you sign in or, God forbid, register as a new user. But I digress.

DOI: 10.4324/9781003542612-14

"First off, there are no rules. Investors all have their own preferences, pet peeves, personal styles. This list is simply what I, in my not-so-humble opinion, think most investors will want to see. Depending on your particular startup, you may need some additional slides. Maybe they'll go in the body of the deck, maybe they'll go in the appendix. But this is a good starting point.

"Some of these slides only apply to slightly later stage startups. For instance, I would not really expect to have a Customer Journey slide in a seed stage deck; a startup that has little or no revenue just has not been around long enough to have data on how long it takes to go from the initial, small pilot to convincing enough people in the organization to spread their solution far and wide. Even a company with a few million dollars in revenue and three or four years under their belt is only starting to understand how to best land and expand.

"Other slides just depend on the nature of the business. Most e-commerce businesses do not really need a regulatory slide. Virtually all healthtech companies do. Depending on how many questions you get about the legality of recording conversations, it might make sense for you to have one about that."

I was actually planning to ask Jason about this today. "I do get that question fairly often."

"My general rule, based on nothing more than uncommon sense, is that you need an appendix slide for any question that over 20% of your prospective investors ask. If over half ask that particular question, move the slide from the appendix into the main part of the deck.

"The second thing to keep in mind is that the order of your slides can vary from startup to startup. Remember: you are telling a story. If you want to hit the theme that you are taking off like a rocket ship, you frontload your Traction slide. If you want to emphasize that you are doing something so much different and better than anyone else in the market, you move your Competition slide up earlier in the deck.

"On the other hand, some slides tend to be earlier or later in your deck. For example, Problem is almost always one of your first few slides and it would be odd to have your Financials or your Ask slides anywhere but towards the end of the deck.

"Also, some slides, like Problem and then Solution or Revenue Model and then Market Size, naturally go together.

"The only absolute constants are your Cover slide and End slide … which can most often be identical. Of course, it is actually a little bit shocking how many people get those slides wrong."

Key Takeaways

- There are very few hard and fast rules governing the order of slides in a startup's pitch deck.
- The important thing is that the pitch deck tells its particular startup's story as effectively as possible.
- More established startups are more likely to have a Sizzle slide and to put their Traction slide earlier in the deck. Earlier stage startups may not have a Sizzle slide and may put their Traction later in the deck or omit it entirely.
- Phenomenal founders (e.g., multiple large prior exits) might put their Team slide early in the deck. Most other decks will have Team closer to the end of the deck.
- Some slides, like Problem and Solution or Revenue Model and Market, typically go together.
- The Problem and Solution slides always come early in a startup pitch deck.
- As a general rule, any topic that over 20% of a startup's prospective investors raise should have a slide addressing it in the appendix. If over half of the investors ask that particular question, the slide belongs in the main section of the pitch deck.

Chapter 13

Judging a Deck by its Cover

"Really? How do you screw up a Cover slide?"
   Jason advances the deck to an example of a Cover slide.

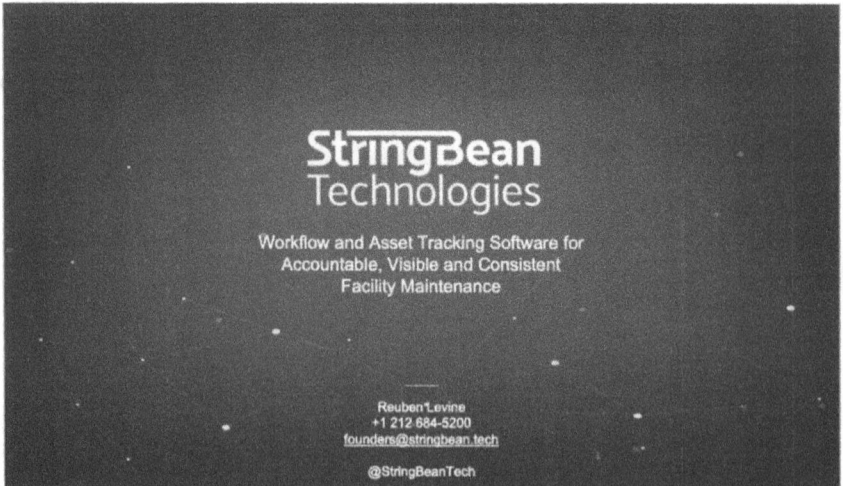

Figure 13.1 Cover slide example

Source: Stringbean Investor Deck, www.stringbean.tech

"Here, take this example. Nothing crazy fancy about it but actually has all the right elements.
   "Logo front and center – duh.

DOI: 10.4324/9781003542612-15

"More importantly, the tagline is clear and concise. Some founders get it into their heads that a Cover slide is meant to be airy and inspirational. Rat pellets. For example, the original text here was 'Changing the world, one building at a time.' What the hell does that even mean? Why would you ask anyone to pay attention to a slide and give them zero chance of getting any useful information out of it? So, spell it out concisely, in plain English, prose, not poetry, using words grandma can understand. The tagline can't tell the entire story but at least it gets the investor thinking in the right direction. What does Stringbean do?"

"I am guessing it is software for office or manufacturing plant maintenance?"

"Bingo! See the difference?" Without waiting Jason continues, "Okay, let's keep it moving.

"Founder name, email and telephone number are all there and easy to find. Notice the +1 country code for the US to the telephone number for foreign investors. Not critical – most foreigners assume Americans are morons about this sort of thing anyway. But if you were, say, based in Mexico and pitching to US investors, a clearly marked country code matters.

"Also, he set up Founders@ as an alias. You can configure that to go to multiple founders so if one is busy, another can jump in and not keep a potential investor waiting. I also tell founders to set up Gmail to automatically label or star any emails coming to that address so they know it is from an investor and they can prioritize it over the random inbound questions or solicitations that an info@ or support@ or help@ address gets."

"Makes sense. I use Outlook though."

"Okay boomer."

"What?! Wait."

"Oh, don't get your non-gender specific undergarments in a twist. I am just teasing you. But seriously, no one in the startup world uses Outlook. And in any event, you can set Outlook up to auto label incoming email too."

"Just a second, Jason. The URL is missing."

"Is it? What's this company's website?"

"Stringbean.tech."

"How did you know?"

"I saw it in the email address. Oh, I get it. Since it is in the email address, I do not need to repeat it separately."

Tapping his nose, Jason replies, "Exactly. The less cluttered the page, the more the reader actually sees.

"Lastly, the Twitter handle – I refuse to call it X – is optional in my humble opinion. If you are presenting on stage, it is good to have. If audience members really like a point you make, they can take a photo and tag you in the tweet. But a VC at his or her desk is not going to screen grab and tweet. So in this case it is the fielder's choice whether to include your handle as far as I am concerned."

Key Takeaways

- It is actually possible to screw up a Cover slide.
- The Cover should include …
- … the startup's logo or a screenshot of the product.
- … a concise and informative tagline to get the audience to start thinking about the solution immediately.
- … and the email address to make it easy for investors to contact the startup if they are interested.
- Phone number is optional.
- The startup's website is in the email address so is not necessary.

Chapter 14

Hold the Sizzle

"I see. What comes after the Cover slide, Jason?"

"If you have a Sizzle slide, it is always the second slide. But you are not going to have a Sizzle slide."

"Why not?"

"Because you have no sizzle. At least not yet. Here, take a look at a Sizzle slide:"

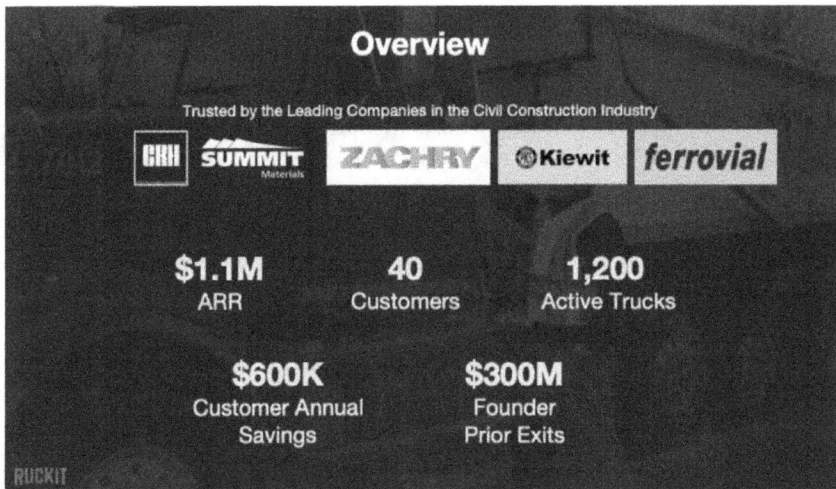

Figure 14.1 Sizzle slide example

Source: Ruckit Investor Deck (acquired by Command Alkon)

DOI: 10.4324/9781003542612-16

"A Sizzle slide is there to call attention to a few, key points, the things that you especially want the investor to know and pay attention to, the things that cut through VC ADHD by telling them, 'Bro, this is what you should be excited about.' This startup wants to stress that it has good revenue from a lot of customers, including large, 'name brand' companies. They also wanted to call out that the two main founders had already sold successful businesses.

"But this kind of traction or prior exits is uncommon. Truth be told, it is actually fairly rare for a seed stage startup to warrant a Sizzle slide.

"Unfortunately, some startups turn this into an overview slide. Bad idea. Investors see the summary points and start asking questions. The founders then end up getting sucked into talking through their entire deck on that one slide. Better just to jump right into the deck and tell the story the right way."

"I guess that makes sense."

"Now you asked about the Team slide. Ironically, that is the one slide that either goes right up there at the beginning of the deck or pretty close to the end, but never in between. Let me ask you this: were you secretly the fourth person at Google?"

"Uh … no?"

"Okay, so Team goes close to the end."

"I assume you are going to elaborate on that?"

"I thought you would never ask. Let me get Socratic on you. What is the goal of a pitch deck? Why are you using it to talk to investors?"

"To get them to write me a check?"

"Exactly! So, either your team is the main reason they are going to write you a check or it supports the other slides in the deck. If you or your team were early founders of a very successful unicorn or you have unique skills, abilities, or connections that perhaps a only dozen people in the world have, an investor might look at that Team slide and say to themselves, 'I have to back this team no matter what they are building.' But if you are *merely* a good-to-great team, an investor's decision is going to hinge on other content in the deck. In this case, the Team slide is telling the investor that you are the right team to execute on the strategy you just laid out. So, you need to have Team at the end. After all, if you have not yet laid out what you are going to do, the investor has no way of deciding whether or not you are the right team to do it. So, 98% of the time, the team slide goes towards the end."

"Thanks, now I see it. Everyone else I asked only said, 'I like the Team slide here.' No one else ever had any logic behind the preference."

"The deeper you go, the more you will realize that there is a lot of fluff on my side of the table. Some of us who have been in the space a long time and have given these things a lot of thought. Other guys have come up in the industry fairly quickly and simply parrot what they've been told. Or worse, there are schmucks who got lucky or who pried some cash out of a rich uncle or their trust fund friends and think that they are the Albert Einstein of angel investing. It takes years before an early-stage startup ultimately exits and those punks go around spewing nonsense for years before they, and everyone else, finally figure out that they have zero clue what they are talking about."

"Don't hold back there, Jason. Tell me how you really feel."

"Fine, I will get off my high horse now. But only if we can move onto your Problem and Solution slides."

Key Takeaways

- A Sizzle slide can be a good way to present the few, key reasons an investor should pay close attention to the startup.
- A Sizzle slide is not an overview. It is not intended not to summarize the entire pitch.
- A startup typically highlights revenue, high profile customers, and meaningful prior exits that the founders have had on the Sizzle slide.
- Sizzle slides are optional. Very early-stage startups often do not have them.

Chapter 15

Solving the Problem

"So this Problem slide is not perfect but it is pretty good. To give you a little context, this startup had a kind of vertical windmill so you could use it in dense environments, like on top of buildings.

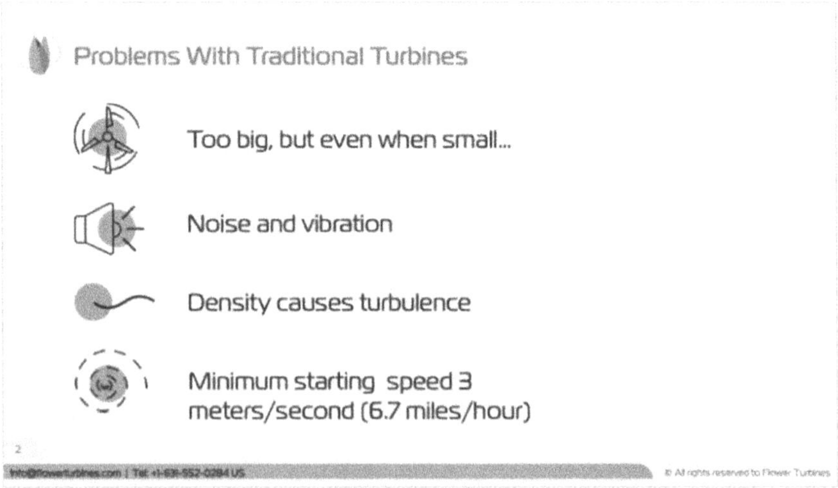

Figure 15.1 Problem slide example

Source: Flower Turbines Investor Deck, www.flowerturbines.com

"The Problem slide is clean and jargon free. Within about five seconds of reading it, you can tell exactly why you cannot use a traditional windmill on top of your office building. I don't love that he did not spell out exactly who has this problem.

 DOI: 10.4324/9781003542612-17

He could have solved that pretty easily by titling the slide 'Traditional Turbines do not Work in Dense Urban Environments' but he was not sure that that was going to be his only market so he wanted to keep it open ended for now.

"If you are pitching a specialist who knows the space well, you can often breeze right through your problem slide. For example, I once ran an edtech accelerator program and told the startups that, if they were pitching an investor who specialized in edtech, to just say something like, 'I do not have to tell you how much universities struggle with student retention' and offer to skip past the problem slide. The VCs actually thanked me for that later.

"But you cannot count on a generalist investor always knowing your industry that well so you need to spend time here proving that the problem really exists, that it is actually really painful and widespread. Spelling it out for him or her, ideally with precise, well footnoted, numbers can make all the difference.

"In some cases, you might even need a two-part Problem slide. This happens a fair amount for marketplaces where you need to show the pain points from both the demand and supply sides.

"Or in especially complicated industries, you might need a first slide to explain the overall industry conditions that make something like your solution necessary. Then the second problem slide drills into the specifics of why that is such a hard problem to solve. Usually that level of specifics can wait until your Competition slide but sometimes, if you do not explain it up front, you lose the investor's interest before you have even left the gate. For those startups, I usually recommend using just one Problem slide, then go to the Solution, and then go immediately to Competition to show how much better they are than what is currently out there. But there are no hard and fast rules here. It all depends on your specific startup and the current state of the market you are looking to disrupt."

"Jason, did you just say disrupt?!"

"Oh God, I think I just did. Ugh. I hate it when everyone says words like disrupt, or X is broken, or any of the other jargon that startup founders parrot because they think it makes them sound cool. I must be slipping … But I digress.

"In this case, there is not a hole deep enough for investors to hide in where they would be unaware of the push to generate as much wind energy as is economically feasible so why bore them by being Captain Obvious? No need for a two-part problem slide here.

"Also, a large part of what made this startup special is the technological breakthrough so it made sense to get to the good stuff asap. Show them the product first and then flesh out the other topics on the Competition or Market slides later.

"As long as you get there in a logical, concise way, you pick the path to take that shows off your startup in the best light."

"Duly noted. May I ask a question?"

"Always. You don't need to raise your hand or anything like that."

"You were on a roll. I didn't want to ruin your flow. Where do you talk about how you came up with the idea?"

"Ah, the 'Genesis Story.' That depends. If you have a genuine connection to the problem, something that telegraphs to an investor that this is not just a business but a personal mission, it is worth mentioning it. For example, one entrepreneur I know was in med school when his mom came down with breast cancer. He was talking to the radiologist about the treatment to understand how they calculate how much radiation to administer and what angle they administer the radiation from and he was basically told it was 'more art than science.' Not at all what you want to hear when your mother is the patient. With all the data in the EHRs – sorry, Electronic Health Records – about the treatments and outcomes, he was certain there had to be a better, more scientific way to come up with the optimal dose and delivery. So he took a leave from med school to found his startup."

All I can say is, "Wow."

Jason nods. "Agreed. Very powerful story. It really made me feel the pain viscerally and I knew instantly that, no matter how hard it got, he was going to keep banging his head against that wall until the wall came down. By contrast, the guy who pitched me on an anonymous waiter feedback app did not need to tell me about how he got cold soup but was too spineless to say anything. He could have just skipped right to the Problem slide. Truthfully, he could have skipped the whole damn pitch. I wish I had those thirty minutes of my life back. But I digress.

"I don't remember exactly where the radiology guy told his story. I think he hit it on the Cover or Problem slides as a lead into the pitch. All other things equal, the Problem slide is the better place for it because I hate it when someone opens up a presentation and then pauses on the Cover slide for a five minute trip down memory lane.

"By the way, the backstory was not in the deck. It was all in the voiceover. It can be a little hard to translate a good Genesis Story into bullets or images. Also, a lot of the time the founder was basically the target customer so it is pretty simple to lead into the Problem slide with something like, 'My family owns a mid-sized general contracting company so I grew up in the construction world and one of the biggest problems we had was …'

"It also works when you get to the Team slide. 'I am not only the president of the Hair Club for Men, but I am also a member.'"

"Huh?"

"You do not remember the Hair Club for Men TV commercials?"

"No."

"I definitely need some fresher material. Whatever. Let's move on to the Solution slide."

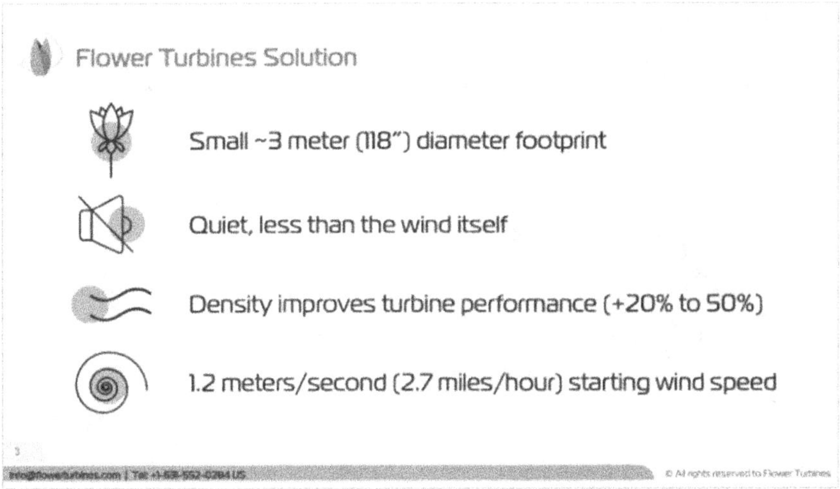

Figure 15.2 Solution slide example

Source: Flower Turbines Investor Deck, www.flowerturbines.com

"One of the big problems I see in pitch decks that I am sent is that the Solution slide does not actually solve the problem that was just set up. That is why I like this slide so much. It is basically the mirror image of the problem slide. The attributes are mapped one to one with the issues the founder had just raised and then quantified. He even initially quantified the noise level in decibels but sometimes a common reference point is better than a precise number.

"By the way, Problem and Solution are typically separate slides but they do not have to be. Since it almost never makes sense to have any other slide between Problem and Solution, you could even combine them into a single slide. It can get a bit crowded but sometimes you can make it work like these guys did.

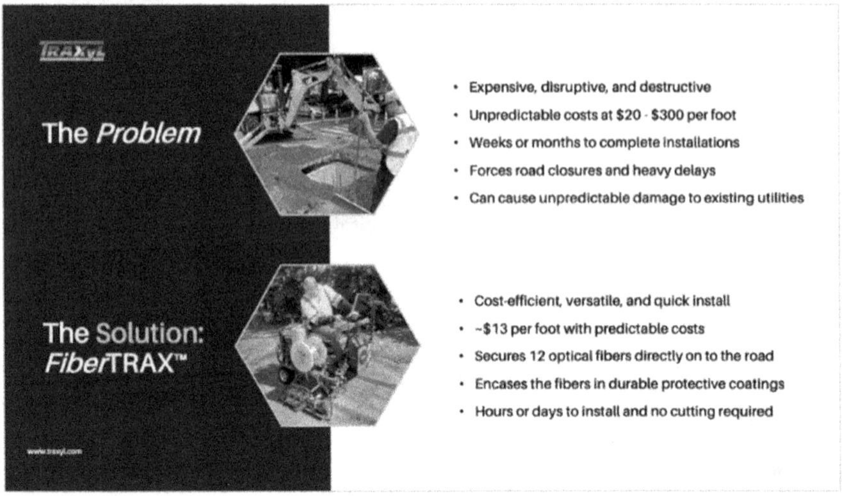

Figure 15.3 Problem Solution combo slide example

Source: TRAXyL Investor Deck, https://traxyl.com

"Okay, let's see what you have for these slides."

It took me a good two minutes to finally negotiate the sites and passwords necessary to get the monitor to give up Jason's laptop and embrace my own. Sometimes, I wish for the bad old days when I could just take a cable out of my bag and plug it into the monitor.

Problem: Phone calls are efficient but leave no footprint

Figure 15.4 CallJar Problem slide

Jason is leaning so far back on his chair that I am starting to worry.

"Not bad. The 'leaves no footprint' part is a bit arty-farty for my taste but I think anyone you send this to will get it, if not right away, as soon as they read the rest of the slide. It might be nice to quantify the problem a bit more. I do not know if you can find data on how many hours per year on-the-go professionals lose taking notes … eh, that probably would not add much. Forget I mentioned that. You could add the cost per word for manual transcription and the error rates for non-personalized, out-of-the-box speech to text. Maybe you turn "x¢ per word" and "y% error rate" into the icons you use.

"I am a little concerned about the 'not always legal' phrasing."

"What I mean is that 11 states have "two-party consent" laws, meaning that both sides of the conversation need to know that the call is being recorded. If you are calling to or from one of those states, you need to explicitly tell the other party that you are recording the call. And since you can't always know where the other party physically is when taking the call …"

"Okay, let it stand for now. Let's see the Solution slide."

I advance to the next slide.

Solution: Automated, privacy compliant, one-sided call transcription

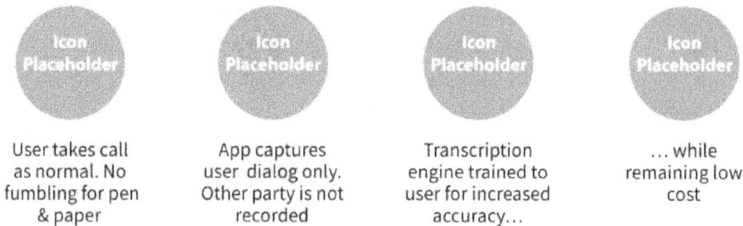

Icon Placeholder	Icon Placeholder	Icon Placeholder	Icon Placeholder
User takes call as normal. No fumbling for pen & paper	App captures user dialog only. Other party is not recorded	Transcription engine trained to user for increased accuracy…	… while remaining low cost

Figure 15.5 CallJar Solution slide

"Does capturing only one side of the conversation avoid two-party consent?"

"I think so. Obviously, the laws were not written for this situation so it is not explicitly allowed but my lawyer thinks it is a strong case. Do you think we need to get regulatory approval before launching?"

"Hell no! You could grow old and die before anyone gets back to you on this. If they ever did. Regulators generally do not like to rule on hypothetical situations so two guys in a basement can maybe, possibly, eventually build something. This is one of those 'better to ask forgiveness than permission' situations. Like Uber, in a way. If this takes off, the public will embrace it en masse before the regulators even start to consider it and as a practical matter it will be hard for them to take it away when no one is complaining. Equally important, at that point you will have money to fight it out if necessary. Or to lobby for the law to be amended. Worst case, you can just add an automated message at the start of all calls."

"An automated message is exactly the creepiness factor that I was trying to avoid. I thought it might deter adoption."

"Maybe. Maybe not. More likely if you add it now, before CallJar is well known. If it takes off, the public will already know that CallJar is the non-creepy version of call recording. Hell, at that point a big lawsuit could actually be good marketing for you.

"What I am a bit concerned about is whether the reader will connect the dots from only recording one side of the conversation to being legal to record with a notification to keep it not-creepy. You might need to get a bit more explicit about that."

"I could just talk to that when I present the deck."

"Yes, but what happens when the associate you pitched forwards your deck to the partner? The partner reads the deck without your voiceover. It needs to stand alone."

"I see. I will work on that."

Jason nods and continues. "Also, it would be nice if you could quantify the improved accuracy and reduced cost on this slide. Truth is, you really just need to show that you take the transcription from 'just inaccurate enough to be too annoying to use' to 'accurate enough' and that the cost goes from 'a lot' to 'cheap enough to be viable given your business model.' You may or may not need actual numbers to make those claims convincing.

Jason frowns. "My biggest concern is that the reader won't really get what CallJar is doing from just looking at the solution slide. You are going to have to add some screenshots to make it clearer.

"Why are you smiling like that? You got gas or something?"

"No. Because of this …" and I bring up my next slide.

Jason's eyebrows go up a notch. "Nice. Screenshot after the Solution slide can go a long way to getting the investor on the same page as you. You are planning to replace these with actual screenshots I presume?"

"As soon as the designer is done with them. And before you ask, I also included this next slide so the investor understands what the other party sees."

How it works: The user experience

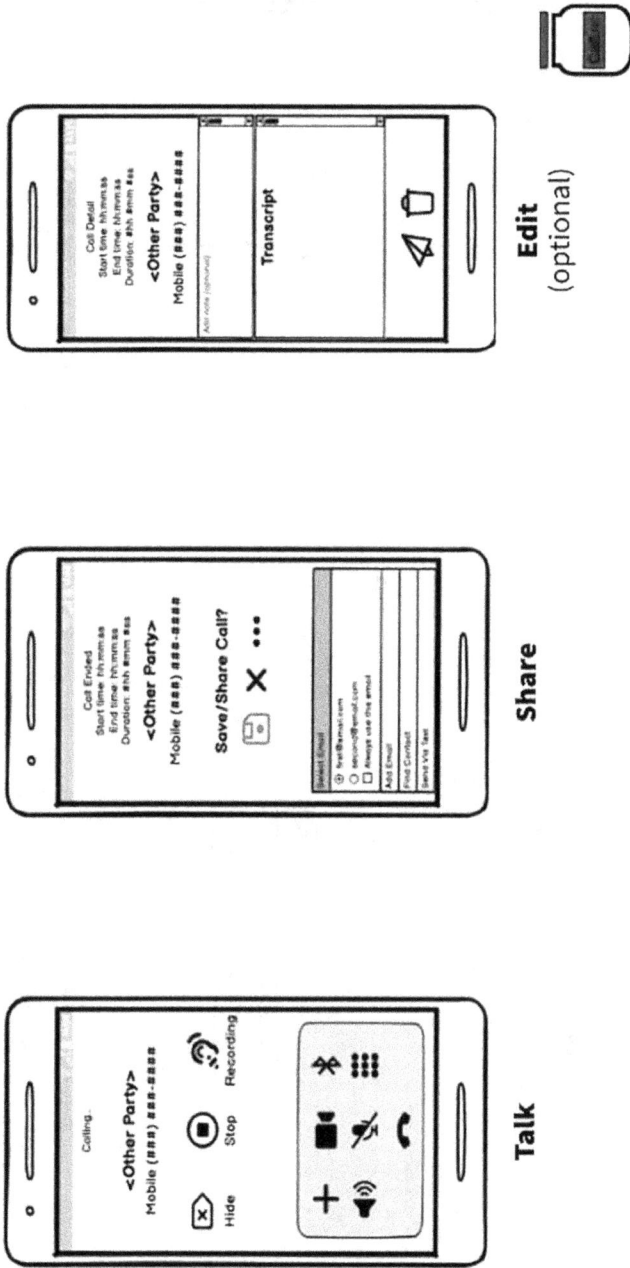

Talk

Share

Edit
(optional)

Figure 15.6 CallJar app user screenshots

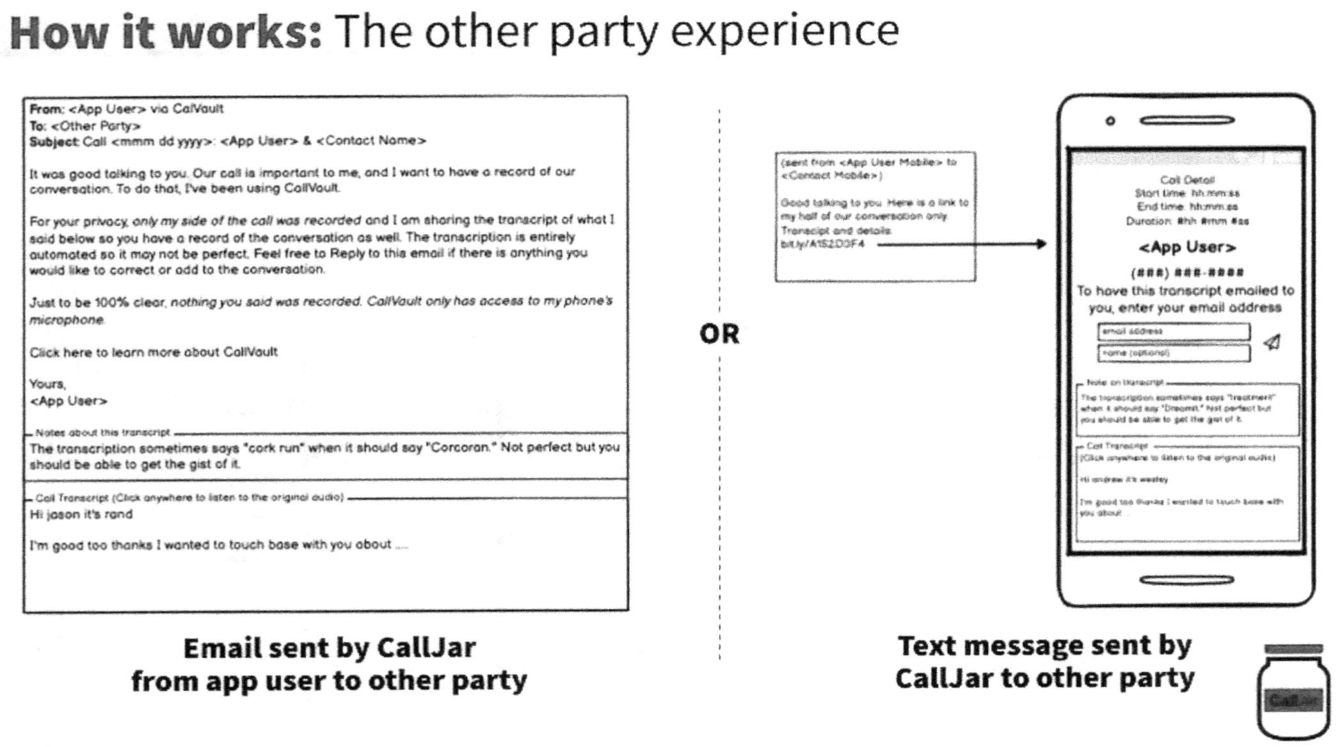

How it works: The other party experience

Email sent by CallJar from app user to other party

Text message sent by CallJar to other party

OR

Figure 15.7 CallJar other party screenshots

I slow down a bit to give Jason a chance to scan the slide. When he nods, I continue, "Is it okay that I skipped a few of the screens? The steps I skipped are necessary to the user experience but didn't really add anything to the story so I took them out. Or does the deck have to have the actual, exact flow?"

"Nah, don't sweat it. When you are presenting, you will offer to do a quick demo instead of the screenshots anyway. The screenshots are only for when someone is reading it without you in the room. It is okay to be 'truthy' here. As long as you are not misleading the investor on anything meaningful, it is fine to simplify to make it easier to digest. You could even crop or edit out non-relevant parts of the screen if you want to make sure the investor is laser focused on what matters. Investors rarely notice that level of detail and even if they did, user interfaces change so rapidly in the early stages of a startup that they would simply assume that it evolved since the deck was written."

Jason's eyes drift to the time in the top right corner of the screen. "Goddammit! I am going to be late to my next meeting. Ever since Covid moved so many meetings to Zoom, now, when I have an actual honest-to-God, face-to-face meeting, I am out of practice. I keep forgetting to set my calendar reminders to give me travel time."

As he is packing up, "Let's call it here for today. Next time we meet, let's do your … Hmm. You do not have any real traction so let's save that for later in the deck and continue with Competition, Revenue Model, and Market Size. Sounds like a plan?"

"Works for me. And thanks!"

Key Takeaways

- The Problem slide explains exactly what pain point the startup is tackling.
- This slide is ideally graphical, jargon free, and quantifies (with footnotes) the extent of the pain.
- In some cases, the Problem may require two slides. (e.g., marketplaces where it is necessary to show the pain on both the demand and supply sides.)
- When pitching investors who are very familiar with the industry, the founder may only need to touch lightly on the Problem and then move on to the Solution.
- The Solution slide lays out and quantifies the benefits of the startup's solution.
- Problem and Solution can sometimes be combined into a single slide if desired.
- A startup's 'Genesis Story' is the reason the founder had for creating the startup.
- The Genesis Story is only useful when it is directly relevant to the solution or the founding team. In many cases, it is best to omit it to free up time for more important topics.
- The Genesis Story is not a slide. It is typically a voice over for the Cover slide or as a prelude to either the Problem or Team slide.

Chapter 16

Co-founder Wanted

Subject: CallJar – potential co-founder?

From: Marcus Williams

To: Jason Murath

Jason,

I have been thinking about what you said to me about being a solo founder and I completely agree. There's just a ton of work and it would really help to have somebody that I can bounce ideas off of to see if they sound as good when I say them out loud as they do in my head.

The part of the business that I am weakest on has got to be marketing. So I have been talking with a guy I met through work about CallJar. He has a lot of experience in enterprise sales and knows the telecom space pretty well. He is interested in what I am doing and might be willing to jump ship.

Can we move our Friday morning meeting to his office? It is only a few blocks away from your WeWork.

Sincerely,
Marcus

DOI: 10.4324/9781003542612-18

Subject: Re: CallJar – potential co-founder?

From: Jason Murath

To: Marcus Williams

Marcus,

That's great news. I would love to meet him.

I was planning to cover Competition so having your potential marketing co-founder with us for that discussion makes a lot of sense.

Please update the address on the calendar invite and I will meet you there.

Yours,
Jason

"Jason, this is Cory."

At first glance, Cory is my photo negative. White where I am Black, blond where I am clearly not. I have better teeth but somehow the minor imperfection just makes him look even better. Yeah, I will admit it. I am a bit jealous.

Jason puts his phone face down on the table and says, "Nice to meet you, Cory. Funeral or job interview?"

It is not often that I see Cory thrown off his stride. Is it petty of me to admit that I am enjoying it a little?

"Sorry?"

(Oh, yeah. Did I mention that Cory is Canadian?)

Relenting a bit, Jason chuckles. "In the startup world, if you show up in a suit and tie it means you either have a funeral or job interview later that day." Smile fading, "It's actually pretty awkward when you say it and it turns out actually to be a funeral, though."

On firm ground again, Cory smiles ruefully. "Unfortunately, big corporate dress code trumps tech dress code, at least in the sales department." Looking sideways at me, "I hear they issue programmers a full wardrobe of khakis and polo shirts along with their ID badges. Undershirts optional, yet oddly recommended.

"Want some coffee, Jason?"

"Sure. Is it as good as the WeWork coffee? WeWork coffee is surprisingly underrated. Their business model was wishful thinking and their investors lived in a state of perpetual suspension of disbelief, but they got the coffee right."

When Cory suggested we meet at his office, I was a little concerned on his behalf. I was worried that us showing up to meet with him would raise awkward questions for him. But I need not have worried. This place is a ghost town. I don't know about the coffee, but they definitely took the WeWork aesthetic to heart; I do not think there is a single interior wall not made of glass. You can see into every office and conference room. They are all empty.

Jason notices it as well. "Having a little trouble with the 'Return To Work'?"

"Management's given up even calling it that anymore. Too coercive for the gentle millennial snowflakes' sensibilities. Employees just flat out refuse to come back five days a week. To be fair to the millennials, though, it is the more seasoned people too. Finally, they figured, if you can't beat them, join them. Now two days a week remote is a perk they advertise on all job descriptions. The only problem is, everyone chooses Friday as a remote work day and most choose Monday as their other remote work day. So, the company is really paying for offices that are used three days a week."

"Yeah, it looks like they missed the boat on making lemonade out of lemons," Jason says. "In theory, if your employees are spending two days out of five at home, you could reduce your footprint by 40% and save a ton of money on rent. But that only works if you can more or less distribute those days off evenly throughout the week. And if you can get everyone to embrace hot desking. Most companies can't so they are going to end up with roughly the same real estate footprint. At least, scheduling meetings won't be meaningfully harder."

"What do you mean?" asks Cory

"If everyone is in the office Tuesday through Thursday and out of the office Monday and Friday, you know to schedule any meetings that you want people to be there in person for the middle of the week and anything you schedule on Mondays or Fridays is a Zoom.

"If the company actually got it quote unquote (Jason is actually making air quotes and it is a little embarrassing to watch) right and got everyone to come in on different days so they could actually reduce their footprint and save money on rent, things will get really complicated. It would not be enough for you to know who is free. You would also have to know where they are on that particular day. Scheduling meetings would be really complicated."

Cory looks thoughtful. "I hadn't considered that. You are right. Shared calendars do not manage location, at least not how it would have to. We would need a whole new system."

"Exactly! And on top of that, you need some ability to track who is in and who is out to make sure that whatever policy you have at the corporate level is being followed. I looked at a few startups that are trying to tackle the problem and it was actually pretty hairy."

Jason flips from dividing his attention 80/20 towards Cory to mostly facing me and continues. "More generally, it is why a lot of the startups who sell themselves on efficiency savings, fall short. It is one thing to say you can create a 20% or 40% efficiency gain but it is not always a sure thing that is going to lead to hard savings. If you have software that a large, centralized call center can use, they can take the 20 call reps that they have down to 16 or even 12 people if you make them that much more efficient. But if those same 20 people are distributed, one person each, across 20 different properties – and even more importantly, being paid out of 20 different budgets – saving them a good chunk of their time may not result in any savings. You just can't fire 20% of a person. But I digress."

Cory didn't miss a beat. "Marcus has been telling me a lot about you and your meetings."

"Great. Then we can skip talking about me and go straight to you." Holding his hand up, "Sorry, I know I am being a bit rude but I am tight for time today."

"No worries. This is kind of a job interview anyway, isn't it?"

"Yup, 'fraid so, Cory."

"My biggest weakness is that I work way too hard. And mint chocolate chip ice cream. Zero self control."

"Perfect. Then the rest of the questions are mere formalities.

"Why don't you tell me what about CallJar makes you want to take a pay cut and take on a lot more risk. How does your past experience mean that you are going to knock it out of the park here and make me very rich?"

"Well, Jason, I live on my phone. So, the problem CallJar solves is my day to day. Plus, I am a big believer in the potential of voice. Sometimes, I am sitting in front of my computer but instead of typing out an email, I pick up my phone and dictate it. Then I close the email, go back to my laptop, fish the email out of Drafts and give it a quick proofread before sending. Klugey as it is, it is still faster – and easier – than typing. Somewhere around two years ago, speech-to-text got so good that I make about the same number of typing mistakes as it makes transcription errors so it is a wash time-wise."

Cory pauses for questions but Jason waves him on so he continues. "I have been in software sales my entire career. I learned the ropes at Avaya selling cloud communication systems so I understand the telecom tech stacks pretty well. Salesforce had just IPO'ed and they recruited me just before the PE guys took Avaya private. I had a good run there and still have good connections there for when CallJar is ready to build out its enterprise solutions. I hopped on the VoIP bandwagon and joined Nextiva in 2012. In 2020, OwnBackup raised a Series C. They do cloud data protection for companies using Salesforce so their in-house recruiter found me and made me an offer I couldn't refuse. I was pitching Marcus's company and he got pulled into the technical due diligence process and we've been in touch ever since."

"That is pretty impressive, Cory. What's your ACV?"

"I work mostly with larger customers these days so the Average Contract Value is pushing six figures per year. That said, it usually takes a few years to get there so we typically 'land' a smaller deal of plus or minus $25,000 in the first year, show the value, and then 'expand' over the next two to three years to whatever the full potential value of the customer is."

"How do you get your leads?"

"When I was first starting out, we would literally go down the Fortune 2000 list and try to beg, borrow, or steal company directories to figure out who within the company was the person we should be selling to. We would cold call them and stalk them at conferences. It got a lot easier when LinkedIn came along. Now we have a pre-sales team – I have trained up several of them – who build the lists and pre-qualify the leads. We also get some in-bound leads from marketing."

"Gotcha. And what was the smallest company you ever worked for?"

"Interesting question. I think probably in the low two hundreds. They were all fast-growing companies so even the ones that were small grew pretty fast."

"Thanks." Turning to me. "I have got all I need."

Turning back to Cory, Jason continues, "Stick around. We are going to talk Competition."

Key Takeaways

- Good co-founders complement each other's experience (e.g., one founder is technical and the other has strong sales experience.)
- When evaluating a potential co-founder consider depth of industry experience
- For co-founders with sales experience, probe to see if they have sold to customers that are similar to the startup's initial target customers.
- Also get a sense of the type and size of the companies the prospective co-founder has worked at.

Chapter 17

There's No Competition

I can't help but smile. "Jason, I have a surprise for you."

"Well, I do like a good surprise. I'll bite. Whatcha got for me?"

"This:

Competition

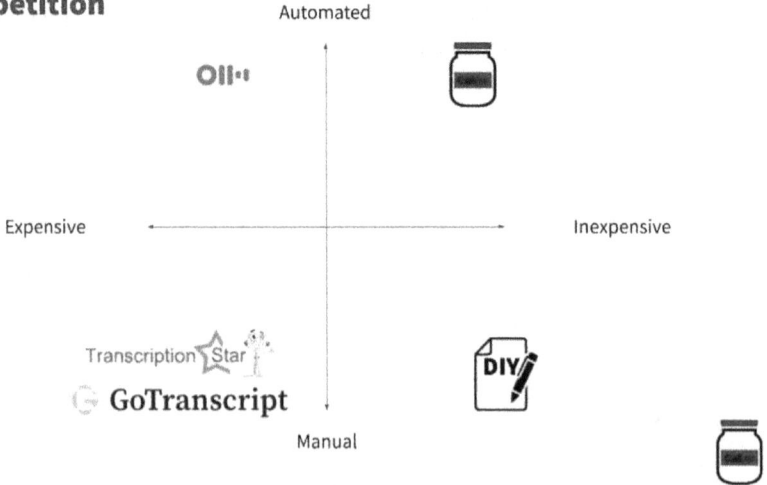

Figure 17.1 CallJar Competition slide

"What do you think?"

"Love the initiative. The slide, not so much. But at least it is not that petal diagram BS."

  DOI: 10.4324/9781003542612-19

"Uh, thanks, I think. Why not and what's that?"

"A 2x2 matrix doesn't really tell me all that much. For one thing, the startup that is pitching is always at the top right. Actually, that is not strictly true. Sometimes I see it a little lower or to the left but with an arrow to the upper right." Switching to a high pitched, cartoony voice, "Hey Mr. Murath. I know I suck a little now but I will be awesome in a year or two! And of course my competition will stay exactly where they are now. You betcha!"

Back to his normal voice, "Plus, the startups typically choose dimensions that are subjective like 'clean intuitive design.' Have you ever met a startup that said 'Our UI kinda sucks but we are going to win anyway'? Of course not. And the competition – if it even noticed the new upstart at all – probably looks at the startup's design and snickers, 'Yeah, we tried that. Thought it looked cool but it just confused the customers.' Large companies often A/B test the hell out of every little button and link. Sometimes, simple and boring outperforms.

"Inexpensive is a popular axis too. Most of the time, when I ask them what happens when the competition matches their price, they look like a deer caught in the headlights. At least in your case, you have an actual cost advantage over manual transcription services. That is a real advantage. If they want a price war with you, have at it! They are bringing a knife to a gunfight. That said, all other things equal, I would rather compete by offering a much better service and charge a premium than compete on price.

"But the bigger issue is that no product is just two dimensional. Your customers have more than two things in mind when deciding what to use. Where does the privacy advantage come in? Where is the 'not-sleezy' element? The user-training of the speech engine?"

"Yeah, I was going back and forth on whether to use 'privacy compliant' as the vertical axis. I guess I could try to make a 3D matrix …"

"Give it up, Marcus. There are more than three benefits and you are not going to hand out those funny red and blue paper glasses to investors so they can view your Competition slide in 3D. Here is how you need to do it …"

"Wait. Before you go there, what was the flower graph you were talking about?"

"Oh, yeah. Hang on, let me find an example online … Got one. Looks familiar?"

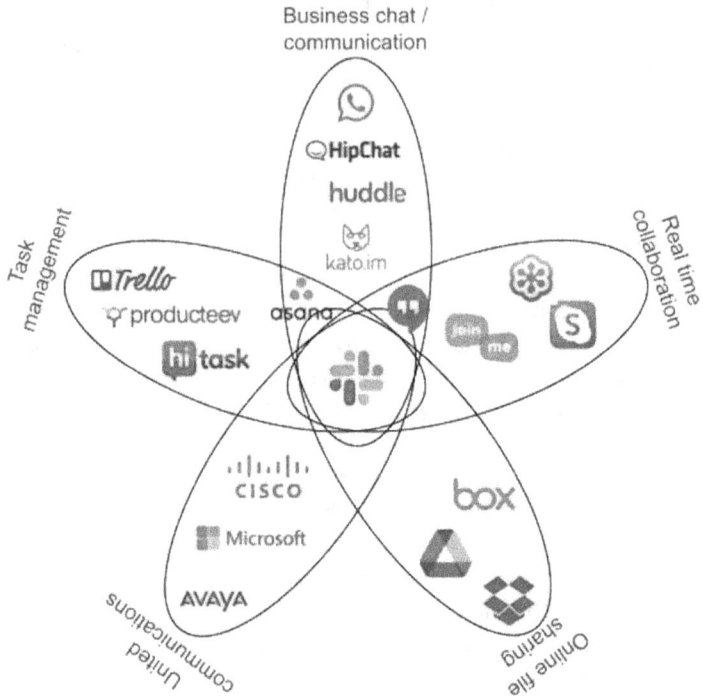

Figure 17.2 Competition slide Petal Diagram

"Of course. Everyone knows Slack. Interesting way to show that it combines all those elements into one package … although I think saying that they do Task Management is a stretch."

"Marcus, pull out of the weeds. This is not about Slack. It's about communicating effectively. You are using this slide to tell an investor why it is that customers are going to drop those other lame products to use yours. And what do customers make those decisions based on?"

"That was not a rhetorical question, Marcus."

"Sorry, you were on a roll and I didn't want to interrupt."

Jason turns to Cory. "Well, how about you? What do customers make a purchase decision on?"

Cory leans in, "Ultimately it comes down to price and features. Once you have got into their business deep enough to understand their pain points, it is all about how well the features you have meet their needs at a price they can afford."

"Very close. They choose based on benefits. It is partly semantics, I admit. How the features meet needs is basically the same thing but I have found that without a bright red line, startup founders can often lose sight of the distinction. And it is a critical distinction. The bottom of the fighter jet being painted blue is a feature; it being harder to see from the ground so the enemy can't shoot it down is the benefit."

I always cringe a bit when people talk about the military in ways that make it clear that they know nothing about the military. "I do not think that is how it works, Jason."

"Of course it doesn't. But why ruin a good analogy with facts? And I was on a roll, dammit. Where was I …?

"Oh, the petal diagram. That image tells me that Slack combines elements of all those other software but it does not say which elements of that software. What does it keep? What does it not include? For its particular customer set, is it providing a unique combination of benefits that are going to make it win in the market? I can't tell any of that from a petal graphic. It raises more questions than it answers.

"The solution to the problem is the humble table. You put four to eight benefits that you provide in the far left column and then you list your competition across the top row with you at the far right. Then you have a bunch of check marks or gaps in the columns under each competitor showing where they compete strongly against you and where they come up lacking."

Cory chimes in. "That is basically how we start to close the sale. Once we have established that the person we are talking to has the need for what we are selling and the budget to buy it, we do a feature – sorry, benefit – line up to knock the competition out of the consideration set."

"Exactly. And of course, you have rigged the game so that you have a solid column of check marks and the rest of the chart looks like it comes from a country with bad dental care. Obviously, investors will not take that at face value but now they can look at that list and sanity check it based on what they know about the competition and whether they agree with your assessment of the other companies' strengths and weaknesses. Plus, if they think there are any benefits that are missing from your list they will ask you how you stack up on those benefits. It is simply a much more informative way to get across your competitive positioning and opens the door to a much more substantive conversation with the potential investor you are trying to pry a check out of.

"Here, let me show you what I mean:

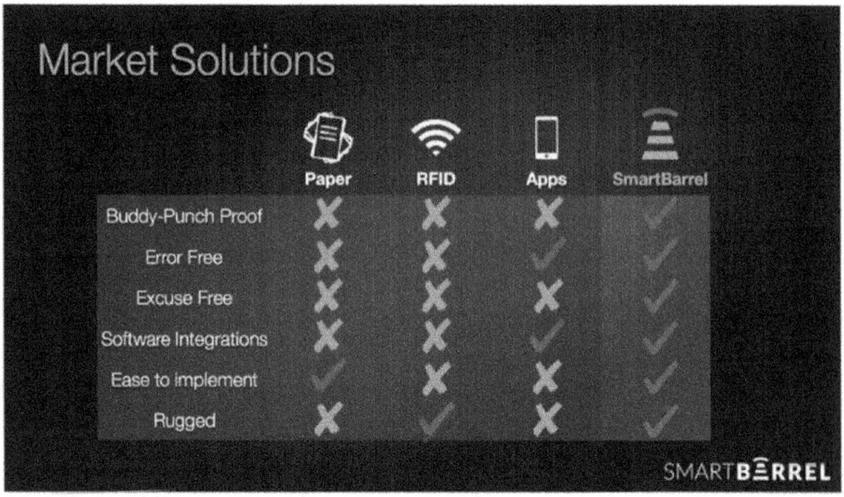

Figure 17.3 Competition slide example

Source: SmartBarrel Investor Deck, https://smartbarrel.io

"See? Straight and to the point. This startup made a construction site check in kiosk so making it rugged and impossible to game was critical. 'Software integrations' is a bit vague – it would have been better to list the top or top three software that it integrated with by name. Ditto 'Ease to implement' should be more precise. 'No setup required' or 'Just open and use' would have been better but you get the idea.

"The other clever thing this founder did was talk about the types of other solutions rather than specific companies. In his case, there were a bunch of apps or RFID tag solutions out there but none of them were very big. Rather than list a dozen startups that no investor had ever heard of, he grouped them by approach. That way when the investor does due diligence and finds, say, another punch-in app, he sees that all the app-based solutions basically suck in the same overall ways.

"By the way, his main competitor is the same as yours: paper. Often 95% of the potential customers fall into the low-tech workaround or do not-really-use-anything bucket but a lot of startups forget to lead with that on the Competition slide. They end up missing the opportunity to stress to an investor that they are attacking a big, open green field opportunity.

"Here is another example that I like:

Competition & Integrations

DIRECT COMPETITORS

	B AUTODESK BIM 360	SYNCHRO SOFTWARE	fieldwire	Touch plan.io	onTarget	IPSUM
Lean	◗	○	◔	◕	◑	●
BIM 4D	◕	●	◕	○	◑	◕
All-in-one	◕	◕	◑	○	◑	●
Analytics	◔	◔	◔	◔	◕	◕

POTENTIAL INTEGRATIONS

PROCORE	PlanGrid	SKYCATCH	HOLD BUILDER	RHUMBIX
Docs/Log	Plans/Log	Drones/BIM	360 Pics/Quality	Labour productivity

Figure 17.4 Competition slide example

Source: Outbuild (fka IPSUM) Investor Deck, www.outbuild.com

"I do not love the benefits column here. Way too vague. But he does do two interesting things.

"For many startups, the competition sorta, kinda, does all the same things they do but in a much more basic, half-assed way. So simple check marks or Xs don't work. So, this founder used Harvey Balls. A fully filled in circle means that a particular player rocks that benefit; an empty circle means that they do not do it at all. You can also give your competitor a quarter circle to tell the investor, 'Yeah, I know that when you go to their website you are going to see that they claim to do this but when you dig a little deeper and talk to customers you will see that their feature is shite.'"

Cory smoothly inserts, "I like their candor. Giving themselves ¾ circles on a few of the benefits. It telegraphs confidence to admit, 'Honestly, those guys are a tad better than us on this one, small feature but overall, we crush them.'"

"Solid point, Cory.

"Also, take a look at the bottom of the page. When a startup plays in a very complicated space, the investor may have some trouble figuring out where the competitive landscape begins and ends. In that case, he or she might think the startup competes with big players that it does not actually compete with. You absolutely do not want an investor to think, 'these guys do not stand a chance against Procore. I will pass' when you actually do not compete with Procore at all. So, this startup took the bull by the horns and added Procore and the other most common 'wait, don't you compete with XYZ?' names and added them to a 'potential partners' section. Now, instead of seeing the competition, jumping to the wrong conclusion, and passing, the investor knows to at least ask. Again, a pitch deck is all about engaging an investor in a productive dialogue.

"By the way. I invested in that one. A few years later, Procore invested in them too. Procore is now pushing the startup's solution to its customers so the founder was spot on here."

Cory bows his head ever so slightly. "Nice."

"Thanks. Damn. That is the front desk telling me my 2 p.m. is here. Let's pause it here on that high note and pick this up again next meeting. I am back Thursday night for the Hacker's Roundtable pitch night. Are you going to be there?"

"Sorry, can't. My wife lets me take one night 'off' to work and I took two last week so I need to make up the family time this week. But if you have time to kill before the pitch, I would not mind squeezing in a second meeting this week. Buy you an early dinner?"

"I can't let you buy me dinner."

"I am not that hard up for cash, Jason. I still have a day job, you know."

"Yeah, I am painfully aware of that. I just do not want my angel investment money going towards buying me dinner. The Hacker's Roundtable is at 7 near Grand Central. I will buy you soup at Mendy's at 5:30."

"Your money?"

"Yeah, it is time for you to quit your day job. Can you make $50,000 last six months?"

"It will be tight, but yeah."

"It's supposed to be tight. I will send you a vanilla Convertible Note with a $4 million cap and a 20% discount tomorrow to review. Okay?"

I am grinning so hard it hurts. "Absolutely okay."

(I'll figure out what a "vanilla Convertible Note" is later.)

I am halfway out the door before it occurs to me. "Wait. Why soup?"

"Because soup is not a meal."

Key Takeaways

- The purpose of the Competition slide is not just to list competitors but to also show why the startup is going to beat the competition.
- The common 2x2 matrix style Competition slide is limited because there are typically more than just two dimensions to consider. Also, startups often use subjective (e.g., good design) or easy to change (e.g., inexpensive) dimensions for the axes of this graph
- The less common petal diagram Competition slide can show how the startup combines functions of several different types of companies but does not specify which functions of each it does or does not incorporate nor whether it does those functions better from the perspective of its particular customer set.
- A simple table with benefits and competitors efficiently conveys how and why a startup is better than its competition.
- The Competition slide can also proactively address companies that investors might mistakenly think compete with the startup.

Chapter 18

Co-founder ... Not

[Text message]

Jason: Love Cory. Sharp guy. Seems solid. Needs to fix that front tooth.

Jason: Hire him ... in 3 years.

Marcus: Wait, what?

Jason: Call me.

Marcus: What's wrong with Cory?

Jason: Nothing. He's just not the right guy to co-found CallJar. Let me explain. One, he has never worked at a small company. He has always had the scaffolding of a working company around him. He has never had to assemble his own desk that you ordered from IKEA because it was the cheapest furniture you could find. He has never had to set up a merchant account because, well it is just the two of you and you are coding. Two, he has only sold products that were reasonably mature and well defined. CallJar is going to be a moving target for the first few years. You will be evolving the product while testing the sales script at the same time. Lastly, the biggest issue is that he has never sold small ticket price services to SMBs – sorry, Small and Mid-sized Businesses. When you are selling five and six figure contracts, you can afford to hire someone to do outbound sales, to take months to

DOI: 10.4324/9781003542612-20

nurture a lead. You are selling to SMBs, sometimes even to individuals. You will be making as little as $100 per year on some customers. You cannot afford an outbound sales approach for small tickets like that. You need someone who knows how to generate inbound sales, to drive traffic to a site and to optimize the site so they can sign themselves up with as little human hand holding as possible. You need more of a marketer and growth hacker than an enterprise sales person. At least for the first few years, that is.

Marcus: Damn. I see your point. It is so obvious in retrospect. I wasted weeks looking for the wrong kind of co-founder.

Jason: Don't beat yourself up. It's like those pictures you stare at and they look like nothing until then suddenly turn 3D and the image jumps out at you. I have just been staring at these images for a long time and my pattern recognition is better trained. Please let Cory down easy, though, because I meant what I said. When and if you do roll out the enterprise version of CallJar, he could be a kick-ass head of sales.

Key Takeaways

- Someone who appears at first glance to be a good potential co-founder may, on closer inspection, be a poor fit.
- Deep industry experience is good but may not be enough.
- Even if a co-founder has experience selling in the same industry, if the type of customer is different (e.g., very large corporate sales vs. small companies or individuals) or the average customer value is much larger or smaller (e.g., $10,000+ annual contracts vs. $100), that experience may not be relevant.
- Potential co-founders who have only worked at established companies may not be comfortable working at small, rapidly evolving companies where the product is still a work in progress.
- Potential co-founders who have only worked at medium or large companies may not be able to function effectively at a startup with little formal support (executive assistants, HR departments, etc.).

Chapter 19

The Price Is Right (a.k.a. The Revenue Model)

"How's your tummy feeling now, Kofi?"

"I am all good now, Dad."

I am standing on the platform holding Kofi's hand, waiting for the 1 train. He had woken up with a stomach ache so we let him sleep a little late this morning. He was feeling fine an hour later but Julia has an apartment showing so I am taking him to school. Truthfully, I don't mind. His school was on the way to Jason's office and this gives me a little more one-on-one time with him. Ten minutes here, 15 minutes there. Some of my fondest memories are the random, quiet moments when it is just us talking about his shows, basketball, the new sneaker drops, or whatever random thing that he feels like talking about.

"Dad, I wish I owned the subway."

"Well, that would be pretty cool … Wait, what?"

"I said, I wish I owned the subway."

"Uh … Okay, buddy. Why do you wish you owned the subway?"

"Because then I'd be RICH!"

"How do you figure?"

"There are miles and miles of tracks. That has got to be worth something."

"I guess … But you can't rip up and sell the tracks so how much track you have does not make you rich. It's what people pay to use the subway that makes you money. And do you know what's cool about that, buddy? For the same fare, I can ride six stops to take you to school, ten stops to my meeting, or all the way out to Coney Island. One stop or 31 stops, it is the same $2.90. Isn't that cool?"

DOI: 10.4324/9781003542612-21

"That totally sucks."

"Huh? Why's that buddy?"

"Why would I let you do that? These are my tracks and my trains. Do you know how much gas it takes to get to Coney Island? No way, man. You want to ride far, you got to pay more."

Well, this is not where I thought the conversation was going. He is a bit young to talk about reducing carbon emissions by subsidizing public transit but heck, let's run with it.

"The subway trains run on electricity, not gas, but that is a fair point. You have to pay for the electricity, you have to pay the conductor to drive the train …"

"And the cleaning crew. The more your cheap asses ride, the dirtier the car gets."

"Kofi, 'asses'? Really? Is that how you talk at school?"

"Sorry, dad. But you got to pay by the stop on my subway."

"You know buddy, they actually do that in some places. The Metro in Washington DC is like that. Before smartphones, you had to swipe your card when you got onto the metro and then swipe again when you got off and how much you paid depended on how far you traveled."

"That is smart. Why don't we do that?"

"I am not sure, buddy. I think it is because the DC Metro is newer. When they built it, the machines that could read and write to the magnetic strip on the fare card were not too expensive so they built the system that way from the start. The subway in New York City is over 100 years old and they didn't have electronics back then. Heck, I remember taking the subway as a kid and you had to pay with a token. So once the technology came around, we would have had to rip up the old turnstiles and add new turnstiles on the way out."

Hmm … He's ten. Is he old enough to follow this if I take this deeper? Let's see.

"But I have a question for you, buddy. Where do you think it is cheaper to live? In the middle of the city or on the edges?"

"Duh, the edges. All the cool stuff is in the middle."

"So, the poorer people live on the edges?" He nods, so I continue. "But most of the jobs are in the middle. So the people with the least money have to travel the furthest to go to work. On Kofi Transit, they would have to pay more to get to work than people who can afford to live in the middle like us. Is that fair, buddy?"

Oops. I may have pushed it a bit too far. As cute as that face he's making is, it looks like he may have blown the gasket. I should probably let him off the hook-

"Dad, I don't pay for the subway, do I?"

"No, young kids are free. When you get a little older you will have to pay. Except, actually when I come to think of it, when you are going to school. Once you get old enough that you don't ride the school bus anymore, your school will give you a free metrocard. It will work just for rides to and from school, so you will still have to pay to ride the subway if you want to go to a friend's house, for instance."

"So why can't I do that? I will give everybody two free rides a day. One to get to work and the other to go home. If they want to use my subway more than that, they have to pay for every stop."

"That is not only pretty sharp, it is actually exactly what I am doing. You remember that I am working on a new startup, right?" Kofi nods so I continue.

"It will cost me a little bit every time they use my startup so I don't want to go with an all-you-can ride, flat monthly fee. I was going to charge for each stop, or in my case, for each phone call. But my startup does something new and people generally do not like paying for something new until they have tried it. I was thinking about giving new users one month free and then making them pay ..."

"Like the mean cheese guy at the supermarket?"

Chuckling. "Well, he was pretty nice for the first four free samples you wanted. When you went back for the fifth piece you were definitely pushing it."

"But it was soooo good."

(For the record, I am pretty sure we are the only family in NYC with a ten-year-old boy who insists on us making his cheese sandwiches with hickory smoked gouda.)

"The problem with the free trial approach is that software is not cheese. Sometimes one month is not enough. Sometimes it takes people longer to get used to it, to figure out how to use it best, to really see the value in it. So, if you cut them off too soon, you lose someone who could have become a great customer."

"Hmm. I have an idea. Why not give everyone the first month totally free. Then every month after that, give them just a few free calls. If they want more calls, they have to pay. But every month they get a quick taste of the cheese to remind them how good it is."

"Damn, you are a pretty smart kid. That is actually what's called 'freemium' pricing. You get a little for free and if you want more – you want more calls, or you want to unlock some of the other features, whatever – then you pay to upgrade to premium. I was leaning towards pricing my startup this way. I was not sure but buddy, you just convinced me!"

That put a smile on his face. Standing there, holding hands with Kofi, swaying a bit with the train while we are each thinking our thoughts. Good times.

"Hey dad. It's expensive to own a car, right? I mean, you got to buy gas and you have to go out every night to park it, right?"

"It's not just gas. You also need to pay for insurance. And yeah, alternate side of the street parking is a pain in the butt but paying for parking in the city is even more expensive. That is why I got rid of the car last year. It just was not worth it when you can take the subway or buses or an Uber pretty much anywhere you want to go. We just rent a car when we need to go somewhere outside the city."

"So not having a car is cheaper and easier?"

"Yep."

"So, if I let people ride Kofi Transit, they can sell their cars and save a ton of money and time, right?"

"Yeah, I guess that is true."

"So, people shouldn't complain that I am charging them by the stop because I am saving them all that money. Maybe, instead of paying me by the stop, they should just pay me half of the money they save on gas and insurance. Oh! And when they sell their cars, I want half of that too!"

Sweet Jesus. I hadn't even thought of share-of-savings pricing until I saw the Revenue Model slide in Jason's deck and Kofi just figured it out on his own. I don't know whether to be impressed or scared. Or both.

I would have loved to do share-of-savings pricing but I could not figure out a way to make it work for CallJar. On the other hand, I would not have thought you could do that for a subway either.

Maybe I should let Kofi run CallJar.

Key Takeaways

- There are many different ways that companies can charge for their products
- Usage based pricing is a good way to align the revenue a startup gets with the value the customer receives.
- All other things equal, usage-based pricing that tracks closely to the cost to deliver the service are better revenue models.
- Freemium pricing gives customers a limited quantity or reduced functionality version of the product for free; customers can pay to upgrade to the premium version for more.
- Freemium pricing can be a good way to get customers familiar with and hooked on a service.
- Sometimes a startup can charge its customers a percentage of the new revenue or cost savings their product generates for the customer.

Chapter 20

Go-To-Market or Go Home

"… and that is how I settled on the pricing."

"Marcus, that is one sharp kid. If he were five years older, I would tell you to make him your CMO."

I laughed a bit. "Wouldn't that look good on his college applications?"

"I was only half-joking. I have backed a 16-year-old co-founder before.

"But I digress. I want to talk about your Go-To-Market."

I squirm a little uncomfortably. "Yeah, about that. I am going to need some help on the Go-To-Market. I do not know where to begin."

"The beginning of wisdom is the knowledge of your own ignorance."

"Who said that?"

"Me. I just did. Ben Franklin said it before me but he was just ripping off Socrates. If Socrates stole it from someone else, it looks like he got away with it. But that doesn't make it wrong. But I digress again and I am on a tight schedule.

"Most people screw up their Go-To-Market slide. They only answer How. A good Go-To-Market slide answers three related questions: Who, Why, and then How.

"Who are you targeting first?

"Why are they the thin end of the wedge that you will use to pry open the market?

"How are you going to reach your initial target customers?

"Here is an example of what I mean:

 DOI: 10.4324/9781003542612-22

Go To Market

Who	Materials Producers	General Contractors	Trucking Companies
	Primary Focus	**Secondary Focus**	**Opportunistic**
Why	Both shipper and receiver of materials. $10B companies.	Receiver only but $1B+ companies.	Carriers are fragmented and regional
	Greater market power & network effects		Acquired primarily through network effects & WOM
How	Scale by region / subsidiary	Scale by project	Inbound only. No direct sales
	SEO, social ads & email marketing	SEO, Social Ads & Email Marketing	Companies that already have free Ruckit Accounts
	Asphalt & aggregate conferences	Construction conferences/ events - ConAgg etc.	Word-of-Mouth
	Target transportation manager, GM	Target project controls director	

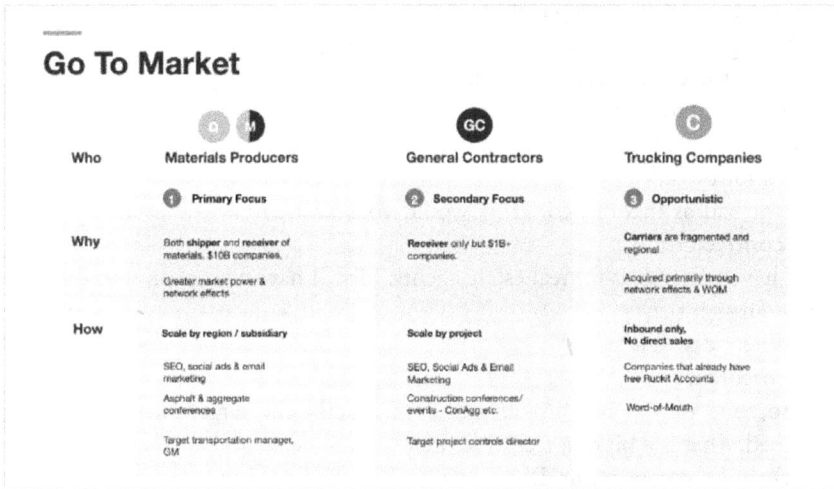

Figure 20.1 Go-To-Market slide example

Source: Ruckit Investor Deck, (acquired by Command Alkon)

"These guys were a little further along than you are and they had a complicated three-sided market so they wanted to show what their priorities were across the entire marketplace.

"So let's focus on any one column and you'll get the idea. This company helps companies who ship asphalt and other aggregates, the companies who receive them, and the trucking companies who actually transport the material. While the real magic happens when all three parties are on the system together, there is still a lot of value for any one party even if they are the only ones using it.

"This startup chose to focus on material producers first because they both receive raw materials such as gravel and ship finished product like asphalt. That meant that they could use two out of the three product modules. So that answered the Who and the Why.

"The How is pretty straightforward. Outbound sales, going to conferences, the usual things you would do to sell these kinds of enterprise services. They did have a really clever T-shirts, though. 'If you don't use Ruckit, it's your own damn asphalt.' That one still cracks me up …"

I could not help smiling. I think my company would fire me if I were a t-shirt like that to conferences.

"Okay, Marcus. Time to get Socratic: Who are you targeting first?"

"I am up in the air between real estate agents and small general contractors. They both live on their phones and, while there are large brokerages and large builders, for the most part they work either individually or in small teams."

"Good. You have two possible Whos and already started to answer the Why. Why is it good that they are mostly small teams?"

"Well, there isn't really anything aimed at them and they do not have a large IT department to try to implement an enterprise software solution. So, the theory is that version 1.0 of CallJar, even with all its limitations, will still be a big leap forward for them."

"Not bad as theories go. How would you reach either real estate agents or small contractors?"

"I have a few ideas for real estate agents. First, I have a bit of an in there since Julia is an agent …"

"Where does she work?"

"Corcoran."

"So, one of the big brokerages? Not exactly the target market you just described. That is a bit of a record scratch."

"Yeah, I see your point. But Corcoran doesn't have any solution in place yet so It could count."

"Meh. But Julia's immediate network will peter out pretty quickly. I would only count on it for some early test users and testimonials. What else do you have up your sleeve?"

"Most real estate agents belong to the National Association of Realtors which has local associations around the country. New York City is a bit different but REBNY – the Real Estate Board of New York – is basically the same thing as a Realtor association. I was thinking that I might pitch the associations and try to get them to pitch it to their members in exchange for a special members discount and/or a commission to the association. Sometimes an association even buys the service outright to give to its members for free."

"That is not bad. What else?"

"Well …" I am a little hesitant to bring this up but I push forward. "Whenever an agent is representing a seller, they put the property on a Multiple Listing Service. Buyers' agents can search the MLS for properties to show their clients. You can usually see the Seller's agent's email address on the listing. You can also often see the same info on other sites like StreetEasy. It is against the Terms of Use but I was, well, I thought, maybe …" Deep breath. "I was going to scrape those email addresses and just spam them."

"If you are that concerned, you can probably scrape the emails off the agents' websites … although I will bet someone has already done that and you can buy the list pretty cheaply. As long as you comply with CAN-SPAM laws, there is nothing wrong with spam. You just need to do it right. Which means having someone on your team who knows that kind of email marketing is mission critical.

"How would this work for contractors?"

"The closest equivalent of the NAR I can find is the Associated Builders and Contractors. They have about 22,000 members and 69 local chapters. I can try the same strategy with their local chapters. There is no equivalent of the MLS for builders and contractors but I guess they have websites and there are email lists out there that I could buy."

"How many members does NAR have?"

"1.5 million."

"1.5 million vs 22 thousand? Fairly easy access to email addresses vs 'I guess there are'? All other things equal, I think we have a winner."

Key Takeaways

- Startups need to choose an initial customer segment to focus on first.
- The initial customer segment should be customers whose pain is particularly acute, for whom the value of the startup's solution is especially high, who are more open to trying a new solution, and/or who the startup already has good exposure to.
- A good Go-To-Market slide conveys more than just who the initial target market is.
- It also explains why that initial target was selected.
- It then lays out how the startup plans to reach those customers.

Chapter 21

Co-founder Wanted (Redux)

Subject: Presenting at Talkcelerator

From: Jason Murath

To: Marcus Williams

Marcus,

My friend Tim Wozensky runs Talkcelerator and he guilted me into talking to his latest cohort of startups. I figured I would run them through the same 'what goes into a pitch deck' material that we have been working through. Why don't you come over? Pay extra close attention to the Market Size slide so we can cover that right after the lecture.

Plus, there is someone there that I would like you to meet so come a little early …

Yours,
Jason

 DOI: 10.4324/9781003542612-23

Subject: Re: Presenting at Talkcelerator

From: Marcus Williams

To: Jason Murath

Jason,

Sure, why not? I have never been to an accelerator. I would love to see what it is all about.

Please send me a calendar invite with the details.

Sincerely,
Marcus

I don't know exactly what I was envisioning but in retrospect, I think it is pretty much this.

Other than an unmanned reception desk immediately in front of the entrance, the accelerator looks like one big room. Some couches and low tables flank the kitchen / break room just behind the reception desk. To its right, an open bullpen of ten – no, 12 – desks, each with two to five chairs around them. A little under half the chairs look like they are actually occupied.

Wrapping around the outer edges of the bullpen are a series of offices, breakout rooms, and phone booths. Most have glass windows looking in. Not quite WeWork chic, but perhaps a slightly earlier iteration. Most of these are occupied … although two of the guys in one breakout room are asleep with their heads on the desk.

Beyond the kitchen and couch area, wrapping a little bit around and out of sight to the left, I can see rows of seats all facing off to the left. I guess that is where Jason will be presenting.

I was just about to dig my phone out when a woman in a hoodie – yes, a real hoodie! – comes up to me.

"You are probably Marcus."

"Yes, I am Marcus …?"

Tilting her head over her left shoulder to point to the bullpen, "You look like these guys did at the start of the program but I know you aren't on any of the teams. If you were a new hire, I figure someone else would have come to get you or you would have recognized someone by now. So, you are probably Jason's friend."

"Elementary, my dear Watson."

"Look who thinks he gets to be Holmes? I am Cheryl, which, incidentally, sounds a lot more like Sherlock than Marcus does.

"Let's get a room. A conference room. Damn, that came out all wrong."

I could not help but laugh at that.

Cheryl heads straight for the room with the sleeping entrepreneurs and raps on the glass sharply. "Nap time is over children! Speaker in 20 minutes. Wipe your drool off the table on your way out."

They mostly smile and, on the way out, one throws over his shoulder, "For what it is worth, we were up at 4 a.m. for a team call with the CTO and developers in Kyiv."

"Great. Go get some coffee. Then bring some out here for our guest. He looks a little tired too."

"I don't …" I started to say but they were already halfway across the room.

"So, what did Jason tell you about me?"

"Ah … nothing? Just that he had someone who he wanted me to meet."

"That would be me. I'm the growth hacker in residence. You know what an EIR is?"

"I know it means Entrepreneur In Residence but I don't know what it means. If you know what I mean."

"An EIR is typically an entrepreneur who has had some success that a VC fund or accelerator wants to keep close. With a fund, it is often a part time, sometimes unpaid gig. The EIR gets to know the portfolio, think about his or her next startup. They either join one of the portfolio companies or launch a new startup with seed money from the fund.

"At an accelerator, it is almost always a paid position. I basically consult for all the startups to teach them how to grow their customer base or communities. The B2C ones anyway; the Biz Dev EIR helps the B2B startups with business development and enterprise sales."

"Interesting. What did you do before?"

"I was the first hire at WhenUVenue. We helped event organizers get clients – you know, couples getting married, lots of bar mitzvahs. We called them 'celebrants.' We also helped the organizers find venues, caterers, and other vendors."

"Interesting. A three-sided marketplace?"

"Yes and no. We mostly sold to the event organizers. They sold their service to prospective celebrants and used WhenUVenue behind the scenes to close the sale and then to manage the entire planning process. We had plans as we grew to start driving celebrants to the site and charge organizers per lead but we never got that far."

"Why not?"

"COVID."

"Oh."

"Yup. So the celebrants were never a 'side' but we had to get venues and vendors on board opposite the organizers. Supply – the vendors – was the easy side of the market. Getting the organizers was the hard part. They are virtually all one or two woman shops, not very tech savvy relatively speaking, and like most SMBs, very price sensitive."

"Yeah, small business can be difficult that way."

"Oh, they are great once you have them. Once they have something that works, they don't have time to keep looking for something slightly better or cheaper so churn was very low. Unfortunately, it takes as much time and effort to convert a $150 a year customer as a $15,000 a year customer. We had to nail the conversion funnel, really make signing up as self-service as possible."

"How did you do that?"

"Very carefully constructed and thoroughly tested drip campaigns. There was pretty sophisticated if-this-then-that branching logic. If an email recipient did not click through within a few days, they got one type of email follow-up. If they clicked through and went to a certain part of the website, we would send them a different email. Ultimately, we had different emails for a lot of different website journey scenarios. Depending on where users got stuck or distracted, we would follow up with an email to nudge them back on track. We were constantly A/B testing the emails. About 20% of the time, we would try a different type of email to see if the alternate email worked better at getting the prospect back on the purchase path. I had to set up the experiments and assess the results, but everything had to be automated or else the economics just could not work.

"We had just about gotten the kinks worked out so that every dollar we put into email marketing spat out at least $5 in revenue – at least $5, that is. We were not around long enough to see where lifetime revenue would top out so we were only counting the first year. Then COVID hit and the event world came to a screeching halt. Jason was willing to bridge us some money to get us over the hump but the other investors were too scared. We ultimately had no choice but to sell the technology to a large venue provider at fire sale prices."

"Well, that sucks."

"Well, you know what they say? Experience is what you get when you don't get what you want. So this was a pretty effing stellar experience. Fortunately, just about when WhenUVenue was collapsing, Jason put me in touch with Tim. So, other than a pretty scary month or two, I was not ever all that worried about missing the rent."

"Well, that's something."

"True that. Plus, I get to get to know a half dozen startups and if any of them interest me and look like they are going to make it, I could be their first hire." Lowering her voice. "To be candid, though, I am not really that impressed with the speech-to-text applications that the direct-to-consumer startups in this cohort are working on. Some of the enterprise software startups are pretty cool but they don't need my skill set."

"Are a lot of the companies here working on speech to text solutions?"

"Uh, just about all of them. You do realize this place is called Talkcellerator, right?"

"Damn. I guess I never made the connection."

"I am so definitely Holmes in this little convo and you are going to need to step it up if you aspire to be Watson."

Laughing ruefully. "I guess I earned that."

"But as Jason would say, 'we digress.' That's why I was so interested in what he told me about CallJar. I drank the Kool-Aid on voice interfaces so I had just about resigned myself to sticking around for another cohort and seeing if the next batch had anything I particularly liked when he told me what you are trying to do. Realtors and contractors are a different market than event planners, although event planners also do live on their phones too. Actually, I think I still have a copy of our old customer list floating around somewhere …

"But when you look at it from the 10,000-foot view, they are not all that different. They are almost all small or midsize businesses and they have a lot of details coming at them on phone calls that they need a record of."

"Yeah, I guess they are pretty similar when you put it that way. How did you get your list of event organizers email addresses? Did you buy the list?"

"Nah. We tried buying lists but they were pretty crap. I found code for a simple spider to crawl websites that we thought were for event planners and to suck out the email addresses. I had to go through the results site by site because the crawler was not all that good at recognizing event planner. There were a lot of false positives and I didn't want the performance of our email campaigns to look worse than they really were because we had a bad list going in. One of the things that I was playing around with before we went bust was seeing if I could feed my manual acceptance or rejection back into a machine learning algorithm to make the crawler better. I was still teaching myself what was out there when we sold the company. Over the past year or two AI tools have gone to quantum leap better so I am itching to give it another shot."

I could not help but nod along with her. That approach could definitely work for CallJar.

Cheryl waves her hands as if to signal that she is moving on to a new topic. "If I join one of the companies coming out of this program, I will be one of the first hires but not a founder. I like the idea of stepping it up a notch. More risk for more reward."

"Jason told you I am looking for a co-founder?"

"He might have alluded to it."

"Did he allude to the fact that we have not raised any money yet? Other than $50,000 from Jason so I could quit my day job, I really do not have anything to pay with."

"That is actually the best part of my current job. It only takes about half of my time and it covers my nut. I can work for sweat equity until we raise a seed round and then come on full time after that. Not to get ahead of ourselves, that is."

"We wouldn't want to do that …" I begin but then notice through the conference room window that everyone seems to be moving to the speaker area in the back of the room.

Cheryl follows my gaze and says, "I guess that means Jason is about to begin. Let's hustle so we get good seats in the back where we can check email while ignoring the boring bits."

Key Takeaways

- Like a venture capital fund, most startup accelerators invest in startups.
- Unlike a fund, accelerators also work closely with startups for an extended period
- Accelerators generally work with batches of startups in a structured program with a fixed start and end date.
- Most accelerators are fully or partially in person and require the startups to work in the accelerator's coworking space for the duration of the program.
- Accelerators often have staff who work with the startups on specific skills such as enterprise sales or growth hacking.
- Paid experts like these may be called Entrepreneurs In Residence. (Unpaid volunteers may be called Mentors.)
- Accelerators also often call in guest speakers to lecture on specific topics.

Chapter 22

(Market) Size Matters

Okay, I admit it. I am answering my email during Jason's presentation.

It's not that it is not interesting and it is not for lack of useful information. It is certainly not the lack of profanity – I think he dropped his first F-bomb eight seconds in. It's just that Jason and I have already covered the material he is talking about right now one-on-one.

The founders in the audience are eating it up though. There is an interesting mix in the room. I expected them all to be college dropouts or 20-somethings. But while several of them are, it looks like the majority of the entrepreneurs are in their 30s and a few are even in their 40s. Jason has them prefacing all questions with their name and ten second description of the startup. It looks like the ones focusing on B2B solutions skew a little older and the ones that are focusing on consumer targeted startups skew younger. And I have to agree with Cheryl – the enterprise solutions seem more interesting and better thought out.

" … and your Market slides."

Damn! I am so deep in my email that I almost missed the part I came to hear. Marcus, you had one job … Let's mark the email I just opened as unread and focus on Jason.

"There are two approaches to your Total Addressable Market, top-down and bottom up, otherwise known as the wrong way and the right way.

"When it comes right down to it, your market size is third grade math. A times B equals C. A is what you are going to charge for the product. B is how many people out there might possibly buy your product. It's that simple.

"Don't tell me the US automotive industry is a $4.8B market if you are selling cup holders. The steel, the rubber, the leather, all of that is irrelevant. All I need to know is how many cup holders are there in the average car, how many cars are

DOI: 10.4324/9781003542612-24

sold in any given year, and how much you are charging per cup holder. It really is that simple.

"It is no different if you are selling productivity software. I only care about how much you are charging for your software times how many people might possibly buy your software.

"Since how much you charge is the first part of this equation, you can't really do your Market slide until you tell me what your revenue model is. As I said in the beginning of this presentation, where you put your Revenue Model and Market Size slides in your deck will vary depending on how you want to tell your story. But almost, almost, almost without exception – heck, without exception period – these two come as a pair. Revenue Model, then Market Size.

"Let's run through a couple of examples of Revenue Model slides. This is probably one of the simpler models and one that might make sense for some of you guys on the enterprise infrastructure side:

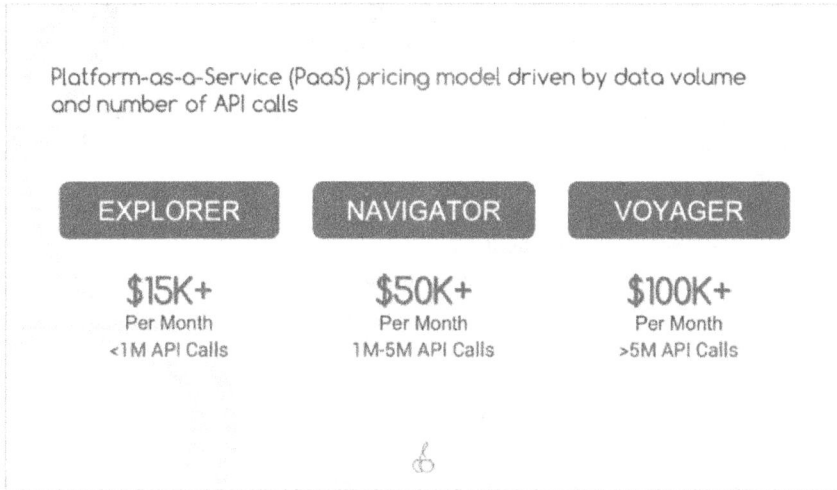

Platform-as-a-Service (PaaS) pricing model driven by data volume and number of API calls

EXPLORER	NAVIGATOR	VOYAGER
$15K+	**$50K+**	**$100K+**
Per Month	Per Month	Per Month
<1M API Calls	1M-5M API Calls	>5M API Calls

Figure 22.1 Revenue Model slide example

Source: Cherre Investor Deck, https://cherre.com

"There are two reasons to price like this. The first is if you have actual hard unit costs. If you are building widgets – by the way, what the heck is a widget? – you have the cost of steel. I assume widgets are made of metal and that each widget needs to be welded so you need to cover the cost of labor and material. For software, the incremental costs are just compute time and can be pretty trivial. In those cases, you are pricing to make sure that what you charge is going up in proportion with the value that you provide.

"Per user pricing is also pretty common so if you go with either a per unit or a per user revenue model, your slide will look basically the same.

"There are two drawbacks to per user pricing. The first is that, depending on how your service works, customers can sometimes cheat the system by telling employees to share accounts. The second is a bit more subtle but also more dangerous. Per user pricing gets your customer to ask themselves whether a particular employee really needs your software that much. The incentive becomes to limit usage of your software so they can save money when what you want is for everyone in the organization to use it until they are so hooked that switching is utterly unthinkable.

"Pro tip: if you want to go this route, try to price on total company headcount rather than per user if you can. Even if you end up making the same money, now the incentive is to get every employee onboarded because they are already paying for them and they might as well get the full value for their money, ultimately bringing down your customer churn rate."

Pointing over his shoulder in the rough general direction of the screen, Jason continues, "This startup could have gone even simpler and charged a flat 1.5 cents per API call but large companies like predictability. They have budgets that are set far in advance. Managers who go over budget get passed over for promotion. Sometimes a department beats their sales target and it still looks bad that they went over budget on some of their costs. It seems a little dumb put like that but large corporations are so complicated that they have to do what they can to reduce that complexity. So, setting your pricing in tiers gives them that little bit of predictability that they need … and makes it easier for you to close the sale.

"Truth be told, simple is almost always best. If your customers tend to be fairly similar in how much they use and how much value they get out of your product, you can charge a flat price and there is nothing simpler than that.

"Alternatively, the price you charge a particular customer can be a complicated combination of pre-set formula and case-by-case negotiation. In that case, just use an average price per customer for your deck and throw the details into the appendix.

"Moving right along … What if you have a complicated product that takes a lot of configuration? Well, in those cases your Revenue Model looks a little like this:

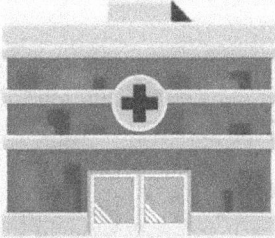

Figure 22.2 Revenue Model slide example

"Hint, hint: if you have a hardware component to your business – sensors, speakers, cameras, robotics, whatever – when it comes right down to it that is basically the same kind of one-time cost as a set up or installation fee.

"Okay, now that we talked about revenue models, we can get back into the Market slide:

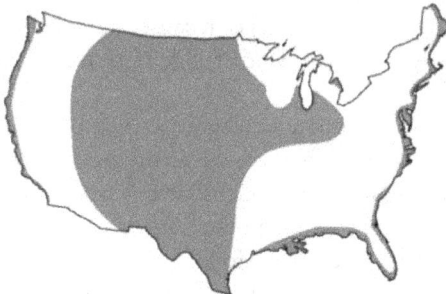

Figure 22.3 Market slide example

Source: Flower Turbines Investor Deck, www.flowerturbines.com

"You can see the third grade math I was talking about right at the top of the page, although in this particular case, the solution was only economically viable in 30% of the country so he had to include that in the equation and added the map to answer the inevitable 'which 30%?' follow up question.

"If your Revenue Model is simple enough, you can even combine the Revenue Market and Market Size slides into one:

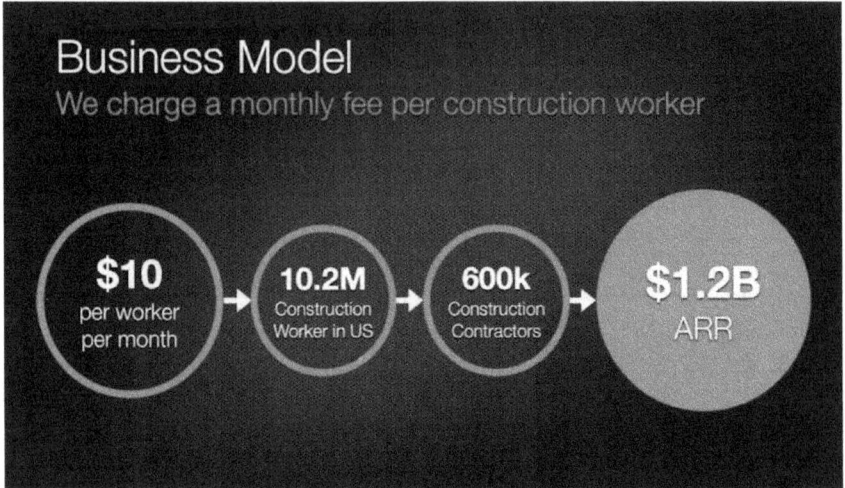

Figure 22.4 Market slide example

Source: SmartBarrel Investor Deck, https://smartbarrel.io

"Ignore the 600K part in the middle – that was just there to show the investors how many companies the startup could sell to – and the A times B equals C equation could not be plainer."

A hand goes up in the audience and Jason pauses and points at the hand's owner.

"What price do we use on the Market slide if we have a revenue model with different tiers or add-on modules?"

"Very good question. You can use a blended average price. If you are far enough along to have actual customers, then use the actual average. You might already be using that average on the Revenue Model slide like the healthtech startup above. If not, as long as the average you use on the Market slide is roughly in the middle of the range you showed on Revenue Model, you will likely be okay."

The founder followed on with, "What if you are pre-revenue and do not know what the average ticket price will be?"

"If you do not have actual sales data to calculate the average from, make an educated guess as to what the average purchase will be and footnote it. As much as possible, you want to base that guess on data. Surveys, conversations, whatever you can do to back it up when the investor asks how you came to your estimate.

"Remember: the slides, your deck, the whole shebang – it is all just a means to an end. The point is to have a meaningful conversation with the investor. You want the investors you speak with to understand how you think about your business, to get their thoughts and their advice, and, when appropriate, to incorporate that into your plans. You want to show them not only what you plan to do but also how you think, what kind of founder you are. If you can get to that point, you have a fighting chance of getting a check out of them."

Related question from a different founder across the room.

"What if you have multiple revenue streams that are priced differently?"

"You build each of them up as a series of equations to get to the subtotal for each revenue stream and then add those up to get the full total. Hang on while I jump to the appendix to find a good example. Ah! Here it is:

Market Size, Business Model

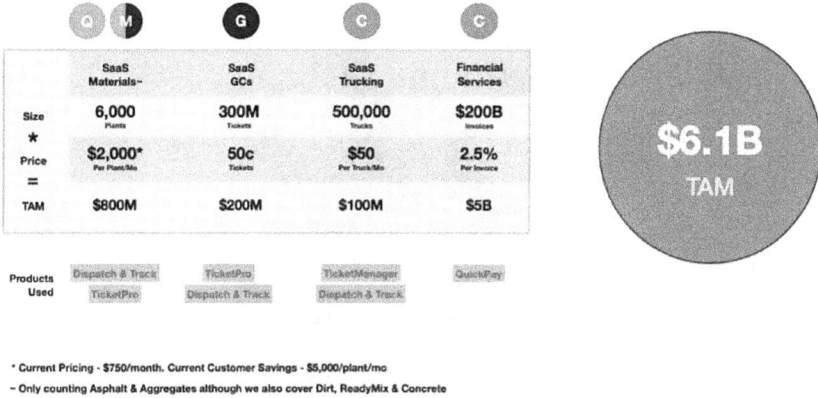

	SaaS Materials~	SaaS GCs	SaaS Trucking	Financial Services
Size ★	6,000 Plants	300M Tickets	500,000 Trucks	$200B Invoices
Price =	$2,000* Per Plant/Mo	50c Tickets	$50 Per Truck/Mo	2.5% Per Invoice
TAM	$800M	$200M	$100M	$5B
Products Used	Dispatch & Track TicketPro	TicketPro Dispatch & Track	TicketManager Dispatch & Track	QuickPay

$6.1B TAM

* Current Pricing - $750/month. Current Customer Savings - $5,000/plant/mo
~ Only counting Asphalt & Aggregates although we also cover Dirt, ReadyMix & Concrete

Figure 22.5 Market slide example

Source: Ruckit Investor Deck (acquired by Command Alkon)

"This startup … well, we are already running late so I will skip the specifics. The important part is how they structured this slide. Each of the products is in its own column with the first row showing how many potential customers there are for that product, the second row showing the price, and the third row is the first row times the second. A time B equals C. Then they add up the subtotals at the bottom of the four columns and have the Total Addressable Market in the big circle at the right of the slide."

Questions are starting to come fast and furious.

"What if you are charging one thing today but expect to charge more later?"

"Also a solid question. Take a look at the footnote on the slide. At the time they wrote this deck, they were charging about $750 per month per plant. But since they had good data showing that the average plant was saving $5,000 per plant per month, the startup felt comfortable using a $2,000 per plant per month price point. When investors asked, in addition to pointing to the savings, they could also say that they had already begun to close customers at this new, higher price point."

"How do you deal with a mixture of subscription revenue and one time set up fees?"

Before Jason could even answer …

"And what about a mix of software and hardware sales?"

"When we get to the Traction slide, I will talk a bit more about how VCs feel about different types of revenue but for now it is enough just to say that you count only the recurring revenue here: software subscription fees, commissions on transactions, etc. Do not count set up fees, service revenue, or one time hardware purchases. Highlight them on your Revenue Model slide so investors know that they exist but make sure that it is clear to the investor that they are not included in your Total Addressable Market calculations. A simple note as on the top right of this Market slide is fine:

TAM: 29 Million Rooms Globally

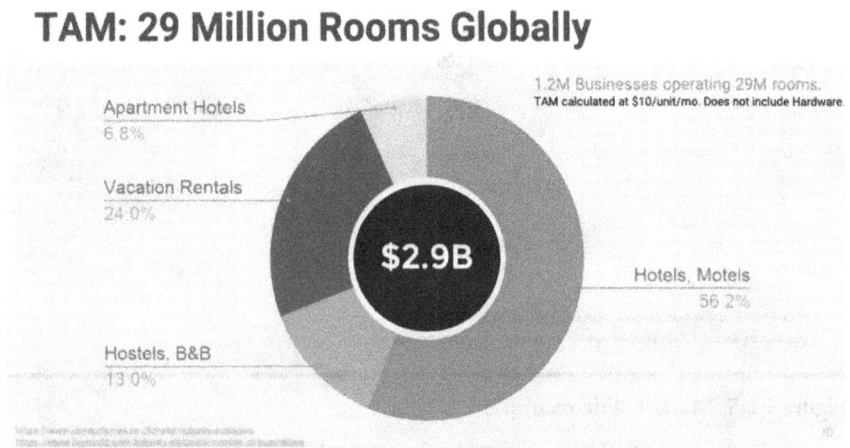

Figure 22.6 Market slide example

Source: Lynx Investor Deck, www.getlynx.co

"I have said it before and I will say it again: There are no absolute rules here. If you feel strongly that you need to include those revenue streams in your Market slide, do it. Just be clear to count them separately."

Without preamble, the guy next to me says, "I don't think that top-down is always wrong."

I had not really looked at the guy much since sitting down. I guess my eyes dove into my phone the moment my butt hit the chair. He is a little older than average but not much older. Other than a slight Slavic accent, I would not have expected him to push back on Jason.

Jason takes it in stride. "Okay, convince me."

"We are backend software for transcription and translation companies. Instead of charging by the word, we baseline how much their current process costs and charge them a percentage of the savings that we unlock for them. We generally save about 35% and keep a third of that, call it roughly 10% of their current spend. So, we see our market as 10% of the total current spend for these kinds of transcription and translation services."

Jason pauses thoughtfully. "You are absolutely correct. It is a bit of a special case. I sometimes see something similar in construction tech where the software provider simply charges a percentage of total project cost. If that is how you price, then, as long as you are starting with only the exact spend that you impact, top-down is the same as bottoms-up. You can't say that transcription companies spend $1T or whatever on software services as your starting point if that includes things like payroll software, servers, and other things utterly unrelated to what you touch. But if you start with just the software spend that you impact, that is kosher.

"Charging on total spend as a Revenue Model is actually more than kosher. It is a fairly good way to avoid the incentive for customers to ration use or cheat the system by sharing accounts the way they might with per user pricing.

"In fact, if you can charge on just the savings, that is even more awesome. It gets around a lot of the hesitation because they are only paying for you 'out of their winnings.' You have to be very confident in your ability to deliver value and to target the right kinds of customers. But if you do it right, it is very powerful."

Hmm ... very, very interesting. I still do not think I can use that pricing model for CallJar but it is something to think about.

"Any more questions on the price side of the slide? No? Okay, let's talk about the other part of the equation: the number of potential customers.

"I will cut to the chase here. For most of you, you are only going to count the US or North American markets. The reason is that you can really only be active in one market at the early stage so for you guys it is just the US and perhaps Canada. It will take you a year or two just to make sure you have a product-market fit and to raise your Series A. Then you will work on nailing your sales process and scaling that up for the next year or two. So, it will be at least three to four years before you will be able to turn your attention to Europe or Latin America or any other market. Then you need to start to understand that market well enough to make the changes to your product and processes needed in order to penetrate those markets.

"But those markets are not just going to wait patiently for you. If there are not already startups in those local markets doing something substantially similar to what you are doing here, over the three or four years it takes you to get ready to tackle those markets, somebody over there will notice what you are doing, see that you are starting to have success, and will copy it. They will have the home field advantage and a one- or two-year head start by the time you are ready to take the competition to them.

"I will give you credit for more than just your home market if you are actually already selling in other markets. It is pretty hard to sell in multiple places at once but sometimes it works. The burden of proof to show that you can do it is on you. But if you are already doing it, then that counts as proof."

A hand goes up in front. (Who actually sits in front?)

"What about adjacent markets?"

"It depends what you mean by adjacent markets."

"Well, our solution helps physicians transcribe their patient notes after an examination. We are building out a robust suite of features around that use case, with deep integration into the EHR – sorry, Electronic Health Record. But after we have tackled that, we feel like we could use the same solution for market research, sales organizations, and other industries. Do we count those opportunities in our Total Addressable Market?"

"You are going to find that a lot of the answers to a lot of the questions that you have are going to begin with the words 'it depends' and in some cases, there is no clear answer one way or the other. My gut tells me in your case, the answer is no. If you are really building deep integration into other systems that are unique to a particular industry, you would be starting from scratch in the new industry years later. And, like the example I gave before with different geographic markets, those industries aren't simply going to wait for you to get around to them.

"You might include the opportunities in other industries in your Vision slide but you would have an uphill battle making the case for including those other sectors in your startup's Market slide.

"If, on the other hand, you are talking about relatively minor tweaks to the product before it can be used in other contexts, then the only thing holding you back in tackling those other industries is your choice of where to prioritize your marketing efforts. If that is the case, I would probably give you full credit for the other markets.

"In that case, I would want to see your logic behind why you chose the sector you did for your initial market on your Go-To-Market slide and understand your timing for tackling those other markets – your Milestones or timeline slide would be a good place to show that – but I would probably judge your viability based on the total opportunity in this case.

"The other place where this can get a bit gray is around new products and features. The more you offer, the more you can charge – usually – so the pricing half of your TAM equation goes up. As long as you are selling related services to the same customers, absolutely count that. If you are selling to different customers in the same industry, maybe you need additional features, security or data integrations to meet the more complex needs of larger customers, then I would still count that. But the less connected the new customers are to your core customer set or the less related the new products or features are to what you have built previously, the more you start to enter separate market territory. Makes sense?"

Nods all around. A tentative hand goes up in the middle of the room. Jason looks at him.

"Question?"

"Yes." With hesitation. "So far all you have been talking about is TAM. What about our SAM and SOM?"

Jason slumps down on the high stool next to the screen and sighs.

"If I had the choice between going back in time and strangling Hitler at birth or the moron who came up with the idiotic Russian nesting doll TAM-SAM-SOM slide, it would definitely be Hitler ... but I would have to think about it for a moment."

Jason sighs again and continues. "For those of you who are innocent of this monstrosity, your colleague is referring to a slide that generally looks like three circles, one inside the other. Hang on."

Jason drags a marker board from off to the side to in front of the monitor and draws what looks like a dying snowman on it.

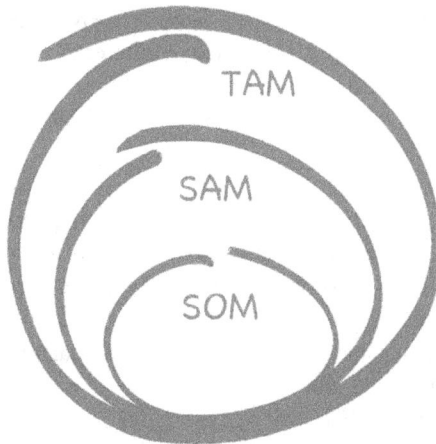

Figure 22.7 TAM SAM SOM sketch

"When I see a market slide like this, I know one thing for certain: at least two, and probably all three, of the numbers on this slide are wrong.

"The top number is usually a ridiculously large, top-down BS number that has nothing to do with the real market. It can be the entire car market when all the startup sells is cupholders, the entire software spend in an industry when that startup is only targeting a small part of it. Sometimes it is a global figure instead of the US. Regardless, it is almost always wrong or irrelevant.

"Occasionally, the second number is right. If the top figure was the global market, the second number could be the US market. Maybe. Typically, it is also wrong. If the global number above it was a top-down estimate and this is the top-down estimate of the US market, it is equally wrong, just smaller.

"Very occasionally, the bottom number is correct. More often than not, the bottom number is the middle number, multiplied by some utterly unsupported guess at what percent market share the startup will get. 'If we get just one percent of the China market, we are rich!!!' Well guess what? Getting any percentage of a market is brutally tough. You aren't being modest by claiming a percentage of it. You are being naive.

"I don't blame you for being all over the board nor for being confused. The other labels mean nothing. What the holy heck does Serviceable Addressable Market even mean? How is Serviceable different from Total? It's as if you are saying to the investor, 'Pay no attention to the number above this. It is utterly irrelevant. It is only what we can service that matters.' Well, if the number above is irrelevant, why do we even bother putting it on the page?

"And how in God's name is Serviceable Obtainable Market different from Serviceable Addressable Market? Now you are telling me investor, 'Oh yeah, that middle number? Also irrelevant.' Again, if the third number is the one that matters, why do we have any other numbers on the page?

"It's really simple guys. Total means total. It is everyone you might possibly sell to and not one person more. Don't make guesses as to how much of the pie you are going to get. That is my job. I mostly want to see that the total market is big enough that even with capture rates that I typically see, it is going to be a good opportunity.

"Very, very occasionally I see a TAM-SAM-SOM slide where the top or middle number is correct and the bottom number is the part of the total market that the startup is going to tackle first. That number is not wrong so much as in the wrong place. I am going to want to talk about that number, why you chose that submarket, and how you are going to capture it … on your Go-To-Market slide. But since it is just part of your actual total market, putting it on your Market slide is just a distraction."

Jason takes a deep breath and slowly lets it out.

"As you may have noticed, I have somewhat deeply held opinions about this …

" … but the pizza is getting cold so let's move along."

Key Takeaways

- A startup's Total Addressable Market ("TAM") can be calculated in two general ways.
- Top-down market sizing is almost always the wrong approach as the industry measured rarely aligns perfectly with the customers the startup is targeting.
- Also, top-down market sizing does not account for how the startup will charge for the service which may be meaningfully different from how the incumbent companies currently price their products.
- Bottom-up market sizing is more accurate.
- Bottom-up market sizing is essentially the price of the product multiplied by the total number of potential buyers.
- Generally, startups can only count their local market (e.g., the United States, North America) for the Market slide because copycat startups arise fairly quickly in other markets.
- If a startup has multiple streams of different kinds of revenue, it should break them out on the Market slide
- As price is an integral component to bottom-up market sizing, the Revenue Model slide had to precede the Market slide.
- TAM SAM SOM is a common way of displaying a startups Market but it is confusing and should be avoided because "Serviceable Addressable Market" and "Serviceable Obtainable Markets" are inconsistently defined and poorly understood concepts and this method replaces a single, definitive number with three numbers where two (if not all three) of the numbers are not actually correct or relevant.
- Per unit pricing is a common and simple revenue model.
- Corporate customers with formal budget processes value predictability so some B2B startups will price by usage tiers (viz., up to X units, between X-Y units, etc.) rather than strictly per unit.
- Per user pricing is a pretty common revenue model but users can sometimes cheat the system by sharing accounts.
- Also, per user pricing incentives customers to limit usage of the software rather than to share it broadly within the organization.
- Pricing based on total customer headcount or revenue is harder to game and encourages customers to use the product as much as possible.
- Startups with simple pricing can combine the Revenue Market and Market Size slides if they so desire.

Chapter 23

The Attraction of Traction

"Traction. If you do not show me your traction, I will assume you have none."

The title of the slide Jason has on screen is, I kid you not, "Types of traction: S&!t investors love (in descending order)." Oddly, no one else in the room even blinks.

"The best kind of traction is revenue. If you have revenue, I do not need to know what awards you have won or press you have garnered ... but hey, if you have it, it does not hurt to flaunt it. The point is that revenue implies that you have product-market fit because customers generally do not pay for a service that does not meet their needs. Plus, paying customers are the best data to support your Revenue Model ... which, as we just discussed, is half of how you calculate your Total Addressable Market."

Jason points to the top and starts talking his way down the list.

"Not all revenue is created equal. We love, love, love recurring revenue from software sales. Software as a Service, a.k.a. SaaS, subscriptions, whatever. Show us that your contracts automatically renew and that you have low or no churn and we are happy as a pig in ... uh, mud. So, the gold standard for traction is recurring revenue, and lots of it, in a short period of time.

"Don't forget that last part. Getting to $500,000 in six months is a hell of a lot more impressive than getting to $500,000 in six years. So it is not just how high on the graph your current number is but also the slope of the line made by all the numbers to date. Makes sense?" The audience is nodding along so he advances to the next slide.

"Here is an example of what a Traction slide looks like if you have recurring revenue:

 DOI: 10.4324/9781003542612-25

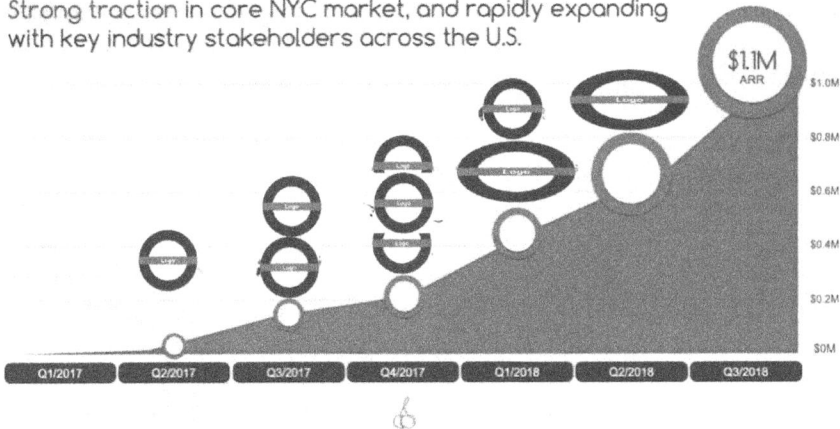

Strong traction in core NYC market, and rapidly expanding with key industry stakeholders across the U.S.

Figure 23.1 Traction slide example

Source: Cherre Investor Deck, https://cherre.com

"There are a lot of things I really like about this traction slide. In addition to the revenue number just jumping out at you, it also shows how quickly they grew to over $1 million from zero. I also like how they added the logos of big, well-known customers. Unfortunately, I had to redact those logos because those contracts are not yet public. But the startup had permission to use them in its investor pitch deck and the street cred that came with those names went far beyond just the dollar value of their contracts.

"But not all startups can generate recurring revenue. So, the silver medal goes to some other kind of revenue, preferably from multiple customers, who are being charged the way you intend to charge for your service.

"And don't skim over the multiple customers part. There is no question that some revenue is better than no revenue, even if it took you a while to get there. I see a lot of decks where a startup is proud of their first $100,000 of revenue but when you dig deeper you find it is coming entirely from one or two customers. That tells me much less about whether they actually have product market fit and about their ability to scale than it would if they had the same revenue from, say, ten customers. For all I know, they have a niche product that few customers actually need. Or perhaps they made their initial sale or two on the basis of personal connections rather than anything meaningful about the product."

A familiar voice from across the room chimes in. "What if we have multiple revenue streams. Do we need to break revenue out by stream on the Traction slide?"

"The short answer is yes. The slightly longer answer is mostly yes. If you have a lot of software modules and breaking it out to that level of detail would get messy, you can consolidate the revenue streams a bit and put the details into the appendix. What I absolutely want to see broken out are different types of revenue. I have said it before and I will say it again: Subscription services for software that automatically recur are like catnip to investors. Anything different, while still valuable, is measured against that.

"Revenue that repeats but is not automatic, such as frequent, small, one-off transactions like in-game purchases of virtual goods, are not bad. The more steady and consistent those revenue streams are, the closer you get to the 'full credit' you would get for automatically recurring revenue. But if your revenue is lumpy and large, and especially if you are making a lot in some months and nothing in others, the investor is going to give those numbers a haircut.

"One time revenues like hardware sales, setup fees, consulting services, etc. get the least love. Some investors will discount one time revenue entirely and look only at the recurring revenue. Others will take one time revenue into account but value it much lower.

"So, if you have multiple types of revenue, you definitely want to break those out.

"Also, if you have sales to two or more different types of customers like the guys I showed you a few minutes ago, we are going to want to see the breakdown there too. We want to know which customer set is more important to you and how hard it is to sell to each customer set relative to what they are worth to you. It is not uncommon for me to see startups spending half their time trying to sell to a customer set that is 5% of their revenue. Most of the time, they are trying to sell to large enterprises before they have the track record or feature set to win that business. Sometimes, it is just not a good customer profile to go after.

"Like I said, your pitch deck exists to engage the investor in a meaningful conversation and these are the kind of conversations we find meaningful. We are absolutely going to ask you about this so you might as well put it front and center rather than make us drag it out of you."

The founder of the startup with software for transcription and translation companies raises his hand and starts talking at the same time. "We started out as a transcription and translation company and developed software to make our lives easier and give ourselves a cost advantage. About six months ago, we pivoted to selling the software to other translation companies instead. Do we count the revenue we made under the old model as traction?"

Jason furrows his brow. "I am afraid not. I love that you are solving a problem that you experienced firsthand and that, having basically been the customer, you know the pain points intimately. But remember that I said 'multiple customers being charged the way you intend to charge for your service'? Before, you were selling a different product – the finished transcripts rather than software – to a different customer – the end user rather than the transcription and translation companies – under a different revenue model. So the prior business tells me nothing about product market fit nor whether your pricing is acceptable to the current customer.

"Don't take it too hard. The truth is, it is sometimes necessary to start as a service provider before selling the product. For example, construction robotics technology is still pretty new and fairly expensive. In many cases, it is too expensive for subcontractors to buy so the startup is banking on convincing the general contractor to replace the subcontractor by self-performing that trade with the robot. General contractors are generally not going to just take a leap of faith so the startup kickstarts the process by using its own robot under a traditional subcontractor agreement. This lets them plug into the established way that a GC does business and demonstrate to the GC that the technology is viable. It is basically a paid pilot and if it goes well, the GC may become comfortable buying or leasing the robot and taking that part of the project in-house. From the investor's perspective, it is not as good as showing that you have a general contractor who is paying for the machine the way you ultimately want to price the product, but at least it shows us that there is enough interest that you have a foot in the door. Then we can call the GC and get a sense for how well the project is going and whether they might convert to the kind of customer we ultimately want them to be.

"Sometimes it happens the other way, though. A company starts out eager to sell software into an industry. The customers prove to be too conservative to adopt the new technology so the startup ends up using its own software to compete against the companies that it had hoped would be its customers. In a best-case scenario, the startup ends up eating their lunch and the investors do well. This is risky from our perspective because the revenue model of a service provider does not scale as quickly as a software provider. But if the tech really is a quantum level better and the founders are nimble and skillful enough to pivot to the new model and make it work, all's well the ends well."

Another voice chimes in from the front of the room, "Isn't it pretty standard to offer your first few customers discounts?"

"Sure, but it also means that you have not actually proven that anyone will pay the full price. So, if you use the full price to calculate your market size and price is an unsupported assumption, the number on your Market slide is also unproven. In a way, it is a kind of Catch-22. You can either get initial customers a little faster by giving them discounts or you can prove out your market size by charging them the full price but take longer to close those first few deals.

"Now maybe that does not matter to your startup. Maybe your market size is so huge that even using your initial pricing, it is big enough. Alternatively, if you can document with your initial customers how much you save for them or how much additional revenue you generate for them and it is several times what you intend to charge, that is typically a good sign that the full price you intend to charge is reasonable.

"Or there are other ways to square the circle. Let's say you want to offer a discount to encourage a customer to do a paid pilot with your startup. What you want to do is to write the pilot agreement for the full amount, give them a discount for the first year, and have the contract set to auto-renew at the full price at the end of the pilot. They will, of course, reserve the right to cancel before it renews but at least you can point to their willingness to pay the full price if all goes well as a proof point that your pricing will ultimately work."

Tim, who runs the accelerator, and who has one eye on the clock prompts Jason, "So, what do you do if you do not have paying customers?"

Jason takes his cue to move things along. "I thought you would never ask. If you do not have any revenue, the bronze medal goes to multiple unpaid pilots with big, referenceable customers or, for B2C startups, a meaningful number of unpaid users.

"Ideally, when you have the customers sign the free pilot contract, you can get them to agree to automatically renew into a paid subscription. You see this a lot with consumer-facing apps that ask for the credit card upfront but tell the customer that they will not be charged until the free trial is over. For both large corporate clients and individual consumers, you typically allow the customer to cancel at any time between now and the end of the trial. But if customers are reluctant, don't push it. It is better to have customers trying the product with no commitment than having them refuse to even try it."

"If it is a free pilot, why do they need to sign anything?" a voice says off to the right of the room.

"Obviously, a binding Letter of Intent is better than a non-binding one, but a non-binding LOI is still valuable. Even though it is non-binding, you should write it with the same level of detail as you would have binding LOI, including what the potential customers expect you to do in what timeframe in order to give them the confidence to place an order, the expected quantity of the initial order they would place, and the price they will pay. This lets you squeeze a little pricing confirmation out of even an unpaid pilot. But I can't stress this too much: spell out what constitutes 'success' before going too far down the path. That way you know what to shoot for and it is easier to convert them to a paid customer when you hit it out of the park. There is also the signaling factor. Large, reputable organizations are pretty leery about what they sign in general. Getting them to sign anything remotely detailed, even if non-binding, shows a measure of seriousness on their part. It also gives the investor someone they know they can talk to seriously about how well the startup is doing and its odds of winning the business. But if a corporate customer cannot even articulate what a homerun looks like to them or is not willing to put it in writing, they are just going to keep moving the goalposts on you and you will never close them as a customer. Don't waste your time."

"There are no goalposts in baseball," says the voice from the right of the room. "What are you? The metaphor police? I am on a roll here."

"Here is an example of what traction can look like when you are pre-revenue:

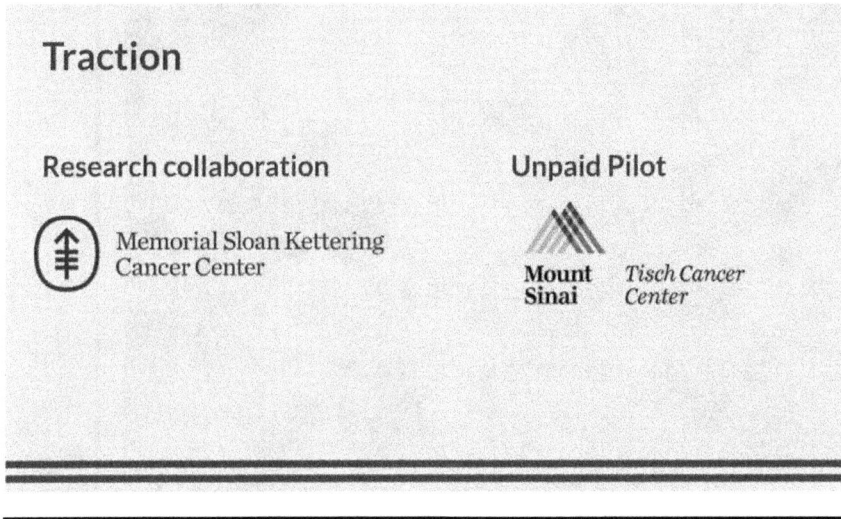

Figure 23.2 Traction slide example

"Super super and I mean super duper important so pay attention guys in the back row. You need to be crystal clear about whether a customer is paying or not. Clearly label or separate the unpaid pilots from the paid customers. You never, ever want to mislead an investor about this. You do not even want them to get inadvertently confused and suspect you were trying to pull one over on them. The moment they begin to doubt your honesty, is the moment the deal is dead. You need to be purer than Caesar's wife when it comes to things like this. Got it? Okay, let's move on."

A new voice chimes in. "Wait. This is all very B2B focused. What would a traction slide look like for a B2C startup?"

Jason looks momentarily stumped. "You're right. All these examples are business-to-business. I should probably add some business-to-consumer examples. Hang on while I bring up a B2C focused deck …"

Jason toggles out of presentation mode and starts digging through his email. Damn, he is on some weird email lists. Note to self: turn off screen sharing if anything like this happens when I am presenting.

"Aha! Got one." Jason says while scrolling through the deck. "And here is their Traction slide:

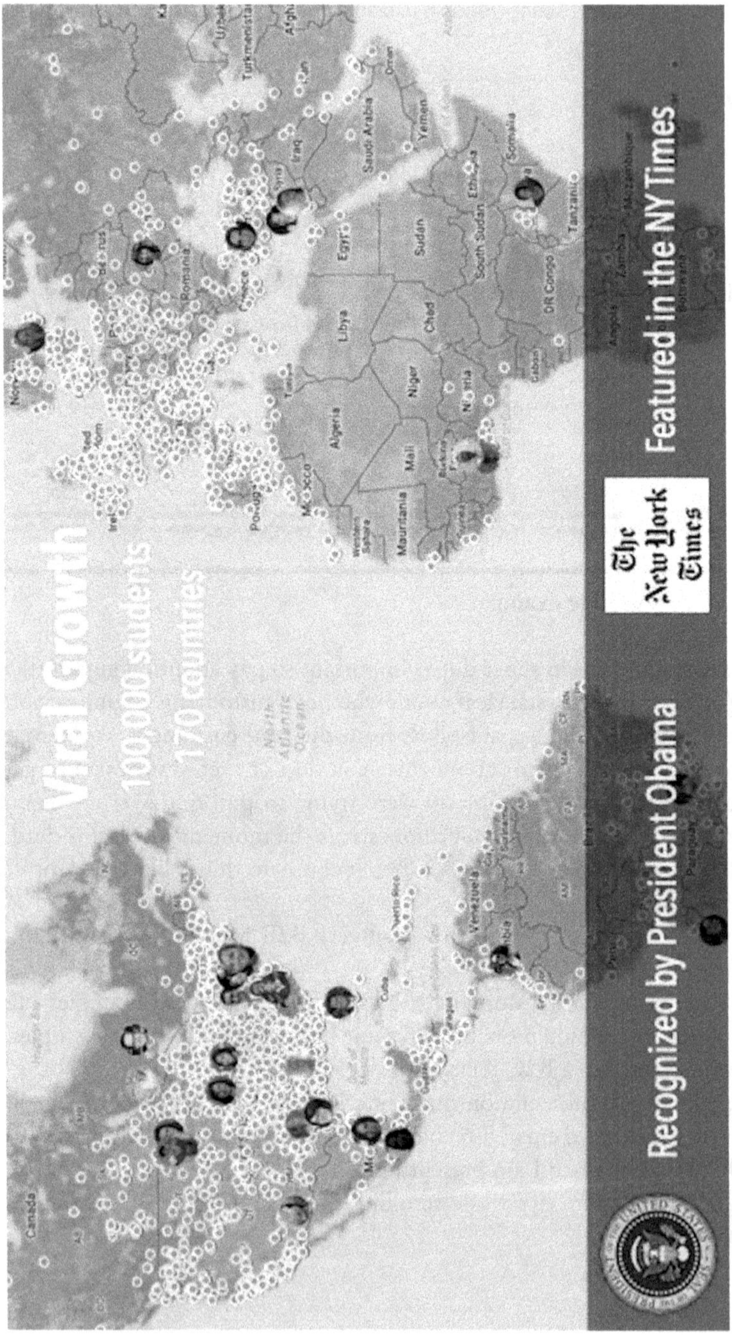

Figure 23.3 Traction slide example

Source: Go Pangea (fka PenPal Schools) Investor Deck, www.gopangea.org

"As you can see, this was several years back. If I recall correctly, this startup had just started generating revenue at the time they wrote this deck but it was so little money that they opted not to put it on this slide. Instead, you can see their user count and this map is a nice, graphical way to highlight their global user base. They do not specify that these are paying users so investors likely assumed that they were all free registrations. Now that they have paid users, I would want to see revenue and a breakdown for paid vs. unpaid users on future versions of their Traction slide.

"Depending on what the B2C startup's revenue model is, they might highlight the number of monthly visitors, the average time on site, etc. If the revenue model is advertising, I would expect to see the number of page views per month too. If it is an app, they will likely also show me the number of downloads. All in all, active – and better yet, paid! – users are what I want to see. The other numbers either show me that the startup is on the right track to getting paid users or are no better than vanity metrics.

"Awards, press mentions – these guys highlight those nicely. What you are telling me with these are essentially, 'Hey, if we have all these, it is a good chance we can close sales too.' Obviously, it helps if the awards or articles are things that your customers value or read. If they are not, they are not good proxies for product-market fit as far as I am concerned.

"If you are very early stage and you do not have any of the above, what else have you got that would give me confidence that you have product-market fit? Have you conducted over a hundred customer meetings? That helps. So, tell me about it. Do you have research collaborations with top tier institutions? Those are generally not easy to get so highlight them. Do you have agreements with potential partners or distributors? Those are meaningful signals to highlight too."

"You forgot to mention patents."

Turning to that entrepreneur, Jason's tone shifts from encouraging to slightly sorrowful. "Patents generally are not worth what you think. If you are a pharma startup and the patent is on a new drug or you have invented transparent aluminum, then yes. Patents are very important. But software patents or method patents are generally pretty worthless. Competitors can typically find a way around them easily with different code or methods that lead to the same results. And large companies often step all over patents, knowing that if you sue them, they can afford to drag the case out for years and run up legal bills that you can't possibly match. Even if you win, it will be years later and your startup will be long dead."

"But my lawyer …"

"… makes money by filing and defending patents. Well, I guess that was a little unfair. As lawyers, obviously they believe in the power of the law and the protection that it provides. They are trained to try to create the strongest protection they can. They are not trained to ask themselves how much it is really worth. That is your job.

"Next time you speak to your lawyer, try this: When he starts talking about the different patents you can file and what you can do to make them as strong as possible, ask him to pretend that he is the lawyer for a large corporation that competes with you. Ask him how he would get around that patent if his client wanted to. Like flipping a switch, I bet you he comes up with half a dozen ways to easily circumvent the protections he was pushing just moments ago.

"The bottom line is you are probably going to want some level of patent protection but do not go crazy about it. And more importantly, do not depend on it as your main competitive advantage."

The reminder for my next appointment just went off so I don't have time to digest that depressing bit of news about patents before slipping out of the back row and heading back to work.

Key Takeaways

- Traction is how much progress a startup has made.
- Early-stage investors are used to being pitched by startups that have little or no revenue so if a startup does not state how much traction it has, the investor will presume it has none.
- Revenue implies product-market fit because customers do not pay for a service that does not meet their needs.
- Revenue also proves that the Revenue Model is acceptable to the market (although it may still be underpriced) and supports the Total Addressable Market calculation.
- Recurring revenue from multiple customers is the kind of traction most valued by investors.
- Frequently repeating transactional revenue is almost as valued.
- One time revenue from set up fees, services, and hardware are valued lower.
- Revenue generated under a prior, different business model is not relevant traction as the product, customer, and/or revenue model has changed.
- If a startup has multiple revenue streams or customer bases, it should break them out on its Traction slide.
- Pre-revenue startups can demonstrate traction with free pilots or free user accounts, meaningful partnerships with large companies, awards, etc.
- Always distinguish clearly between paid and unpaid pilots.
- Even unpaid pilots should be governed by a Letter of Intent that clearly spells out the terms of the engagement, what constitutes success, and the expected quantity and pricing of the expected contract should the pilot succeed. The LOI can be non-binding if necessary.
- Patents can be less valuable than one might expect because it is often easy for competitors to work around them.
- When in doubt as to what belongs in the pitch deck, remember this: The pitch deck exists to engage the investor in a meaningful conversation. It needs to tell the investor what is important about the startup. It does not have to answer all questions.

Chapter 24

Avoiding a Founder Equity #Fail

Subject: CallJar – I really like Cheryl as potential co-founder

From: Marcus Williams

To: Jason Murath

Jason,

I really like Cheryl. We have been talking regularly since you made that introduction. I like both the skills she brings to the table and how she thinks about the problems. She could be a great co-founder and she was not shy about showing her interest.

When I asked her if she was interested in coming on board, she asked me what I was thinking for the equity split. I told her that I hadn't really thought it through and that I wanted to talk to you first. She was okay with that.

What should I be thinking here?

Sincerely,
Marcus

 DOI: 10.4324/9781003542612-26

"I am thrilled that you and Cheryl hit it off. I knew the skill fit would be there but I wasn't sure you would mesh temperamentally.

"So, you want to know how much equity to offer her?"

"Hi, Jason. How have you been? Did you watch the game on Sunday?"

Chagrined, Jason slows down a minute. "Yeah, that. Sorry, when I know I have a lot to cover so I sometimes forget the important stuff. All good on my end. Busy, but good busy. How about you guys? Everyone happy and healthy?"

Chucking, "It's okay Jason. Everything is pretty much as it should be. We can skip right to the fun stuff."

"Great."

(Oh, God. Did Jason actually rub his hand together? I thought they only did that in cartoons.)

"So, there is really no hard and fast rule in equity splits other than that you all have to agree that it is basically fair. You can't start a relationship where one party is bitter from the get-go.

"It's also a pretty bad idea to divide the shares exactly evenly because if you disagree, the company is deadlocked. As a practical matter, you are going to want to make those decisions by consensus. If you constantly overrule your co-founder and run roughshod over her feelings and opinions, pretty soon you are not going to have a co-founder. But investors always need to keep the worst-case scenario in mind. If push comes to shove, deadlock sucks. Some investors won't invest unless one founder has more shares than the other, even if it is just 50% plus one share.

"Fortunately, this is more of an issue when two or more founders start a company together. When a co-founder is joining later, there is less expectation of an equal split. It's tempting in your situation to feel like you own the company and whatever share an incoming co-founder gets would be you giving them something out of your pocket. I am going to urge you not to think of it that way because you run the risk that you will give her too little equity. If co-founders have too little equity, they do not feel fully invested in the outcome. Imagine this: After living on ramen noodles for two years, they get a decent job offer that pays well. If they do not have a lot of equity, are they going to stick around or are they going to jump ship? You want your co-founder to be so emotionally invested that if something breaks in the middle of the night, they are up and trying to help you fix it. Even if there is nothing they can do to fix it, they are up because they can't sleep knowing that something is broken.

"Again, no hard and fast rules. But in my not-so-humble-opinion, if you were to give Cheryl anything less than 20%, you are taking a big risk."

"20% doesn't feel like that little."

"It is not right now but it will be soon. Remember, you want to raise a seed round. The new investors are going to get 20 to 25% of your company when they put that money in. That dilutes you and Cheryl. The moment you raise that money, her 20% goes down to 15 or 16%. And you are not just going to raise one round. Raise a Series A and take another 20 to 25% dilution. Cheryl's stake in CallJar is now down to 11–13%. And if this takes off, you will need to raise more money after that.

"Personally, my feeling is that, if the person you are bringing on board has that big an impact on the potential success of the startup, be generous until it hurts. In your shoes, assuming you are only going to have one other co-founder, I would give Cheryl 30% to 40%.

"I am also assuming that Cheryl will be taking as little salary as you are. Co-founders share the risk, they share the suffering. If a potential co-founder comes in and wants to be paid market rate for his or her work, they can't have it both ways. If they are not sacrificing on salary, they do not get co-founder size equity. To the best of my recollection, Cheryl is single, no kids or older relatives to support, and I think she lives with a roommate. So, her nut is pretty small. She will probably be able to take much less salary than you need, especially if you are able to use her the 50% of the time she is not supporting the accelerator startups. If she can keep that gig until you raise a proper seed round, she can probably go entirely without salary for now. Just have an open and honest conversation with each other about what you can both afford to do and what you feel is fair."

No salary fits my budget pretty well. And she does bring critical skills to the table ... but I do not have time to fully digest what Jason has said before he continues.

"Regardless of how you decide to split the founder equity, you need to set up a vesting schedule."

"I thought that vesting was only for the options that you give new employees?"

"No, no, no! It is even more important for founders. What happens if one co-founder calls it quits after nine months? Without vesting he's got 30, 40%+ of the company and is contributing nothing. The other co-founders are busting their figurative balls and he's just mooching off their sweat.

"No, founders vest too. Typically, they vest just like new employees over a four-year period and with a one-year cliff. If they leave before one year, they go empty handed. When they hit one year, they get 25% of the equity. After that, every month or quarter they vest a little more until, when they finish the fourth year, they are 100% vested. The main difference is that new employees get options that vest and founders get Restricted Stock Units that reverse vest.

In a mock whisper, "Marcus, here's where you jump in with an insightful question."

"Huh?"

"That'll do.

"The difference between options and RSUs is taxes. You pay much more taxes on short term capital gains than you do for long term capital gains and the clock starts when you get the asset. If you get a few options each month and exercise them immediately, the clock for long term gains starts for each batch in the month you get it. For example, if the startup sells at the end of the fourth year after an employee joins, he pays long term cap gains tax rates on most of the options he got but pays short term cap gains rates on the options he exercised within the last year.

"On the other hand, RSUs you get all at once. You have to give some of them back if you leave early but the long-term cap gains clock starts right away for all your shares.

"But other than the tax issues, they work exactly the same."

"I see. Will Cheryl be okay with this?"

"Of course. This is not her first rodeo. Plus, she can't really say no when you are doing it too."

"I am?"

"Only if you want to ever raise money from investors. While it is unlikely you will be the one to quit early – although it has happened! – what if you are hit by a truck? Cheryl is going to need the equity to give the guy she finds to replace you."

"You don't get invited to a lot of dinner parties, do you, Jason?"

"Marcus, the CTO of a startup I invested in was literally hit by a truck."

"Really?"

"Swear to God. Emes."

"Wow. So they gave his equity to the new CTO?"

"Well, he'd been there a little over two years so his RSUs that vested went to his parents – the kid was not married, no children. Hell, he barely shaved. But that was not the problem."

"What was the problem?"

"Other than for the bank account – and thank God for that! – he had all the passwords. They could not get at any of the code. Had to recode the entire product from scratch."

"Damn."

Key Takeaways

- There are few hard and fast rules governing how co-founders divvy up the equity in their startup but there are some guiding principles.
- The equity split should be considered fair enough by all parties so there is no lingering resentment that could lead to lack of commitment or other tensions down the road.
- A founder who is working full time generally gets more equity than a founder who is part time.
- The founder who is sacrificing more (e.g., salary foregone) and/or has rarer, harder to replace skills or connections generally gets more equity.
- All other things equal, the more salary a founder is taking, the less equity he or she receives.
- Setting a co-founder's equity level too low could result in him or her not having enough 'skin in the game' to stick with the startup when times are tough, especially after the startup has raised a few rounds of funding and the founders' stakes have been diluted.
- An exact 50/50 split is undesirable for governance reasons.
- All equity should vest over time in case a founder leaves the startup early so that that equity returns to the company and is available to offer to a replacement.
- Both stock options and Restricted Stock Units can vest.
- RSUs may be preferable for founders because they are more likely to be taxed as long-term capital gains.

Chapter 25

The Regulatory Story

"Okay, Marcus. Happier thoughts.

"How often do you get asked if it is legal to record a phone call?"

My mind is still processing the dead co-founder story and Jason is already peppering me with new questions. But that is just how he rolls and I am beginning to learn how to roll with it.

"Probably about 70% of the time."

"In that case, I think we want a slide on regulatory issues sooner rather than later. You could possibly put it before Competition but I feel like the Competition slide cements exactly what you are doing differently and if you put Regulatory first you might get questions that are not really relevant once they understand exactly what is going on here. So, let's keep Competition before the Regulatory slide.

"I have got a couple examples of Regulatory slides but most of them are healthtech startups talking about whether and what kind of FDA approval they need and where they are in that process. Hint, hint: it is really important to have a Medicare billing code for a lot of healthcare startups.

"On the construction tech side, when you are pitching new building materials you have to have a conversation here about what is approved for which kinds of load-bearing uses or issues around electrical safety. But that also is not really relevant in this case.

"Why don't we start with a blank sheet of paper. Pretend I am an investor and I am asking you 'Is it legal to record a conversation like that?' and you just tell me how you answer it."

"Sure. No problem. Well, Jason, at the federal level you can record any phone call as long as one of the parties knows it is happening. So, if you are having a conversation with your friend and I want to record it without either of you knowing it, that is out-and-out illegal everywhere. Some states also have laws about recording phone calls. Most of the states have effectively the same kind of

DOI: 10.4324/9781003542612-27

one-party consent but ten states have what are called two-party consent laws and another 4 states have 'mixed consent' which basically mean 'it's complicated.'

"In two-party consent states both parties to the conversation need to know that the call is being recorded. Now it is difficult to know exactly where the other party is located so even if you are not in the state that requires it you cannot always be sure that the other guy is not in one of those states. That's why, when you are on with customer service, you often get a blanket announcement that the call is being recorded for 'training purposes.'

"But CallJar is different. Our position is that we are not actually recording a phone conversation. We are only recording half of the conversation, the half of the conversation that the app user downloaded on his or her phone. Since we are not recording anything the other party says, we do not think two-party consent laws apply at all. We just sidestep the entire issue."

"Do the two-party consent laws specifically say that they do not apply if you are not recording the unknowing party?"

"Well, no. I mean, it is not like they had anything like CallJar in mind when the laws were drafted."

"So how do you know the regulators in one of those states won't come after you?"

"Well, we spoke to our lawyer about it and he said that one of his colleagues who specializes in telecom looked over the laws and he thinks we have a good case."

"A good case still can mean millions of dollars in legal fees if the regulator disagrees with you. Even if you win, that could be expensive. Would your law firm write a letter officially stating that position that you can show to investors to make them a little less nervous about the possibility?"

"Actually, I asked for exactly that. He said that they would have to do a deeper dive but that they were willing to do that and could issue a formal statement of their opinion – no guarantees, of course – for $50,000.

"Bear in mind that the app user can simply tell the other party that he is recording the phone call if he is really worried about it. We will put the stuff about single- and dual-party consent in the FAQ's and draft the Terms of Use to make it clear that we are not guaranteeing that. Worst case scenario, we could build an option into the setup that automatically plays a notification at the start of every call. We do not think that is necessary and we would prefer not to go down that path if we don't have to."

"Good job, Marcus. Now let's step out of character for a moment. You and I have already talked about this a little bit so nothing you said above was a complete surprise. $50,000 might even be on the less expensive side for something like this. Don't get me wrong – there is no way you are spending $50,000 in legal fees at this stage of the game unless you absolutely have to.

"So let's talk about how to convey what you just said visually and concisely."

Jason starts sketching on the whiteboard something that, if you look at it just right, could be a map of the United States. He has shaded in California and Washington and Florida pretty accurately. There's a large blob in the Northeast where Massachusetts and New Hampshire are (that probably also includes chunks of Vermont and Maine) and another large blob more or less where Pennsylvania, Delaware, and Maryland are. He has some interesting ideas as to where Illinois, Nevada, and Montana might be located. But considering we spoke about this weeks ago, his memory for which states require two-party consent is pretty damn good.

"Whatever, you get the idea. You start with a map like this on the left side of the page, two shades, with a key explaining which states are single- versus two-party consent states. You'll explain in the voice over what that means but I think it'll be pretty self-explanatory even without the commentary."

Jason adds a couple of bullets to the right side of the map. It takes me a moment to realize that the scribble he puts next to each board is not even intended to be words.

"Then, on the right side of the map you add a couple of bullets. The first will be something along the lines of 'Since CallJar only records the app users' half of the conversation, we believe it sidesteps these laws entirely' and the second bullet will be something about the other points that you raised about the terms of use and easy alternatives.

"You put a note at the bottom of the slide to see the appendix for more detail and in the appendix you can lay out some of the arguments a little better. If not having that legal opinion letter becomes the one thing standing between you and checks, we can talk about getting that letter.

"But I do not think it will be an issue. I think you get into the market and this thing either fails quickly, in which case nobody cares, or starts to pick up steam pretty quickly. In that case, by the time regulators get their collective ass in gear enough to make any noise, you are big enough to just hand it off to your lawyers to handle. I have seen that movie play itself out a couple of times and, by and large, I think other early-stage investors will be willing to take a flier on it as well. But we will see what the market says."

Key Takeaways

- A Regulatory slide is necessary if a startup operates in a heavily regulated industry or has technology or a business model that may be impacted by regulations.
- This slide should explain the potential regulatory risks and lay out the steps the startup is taking to address them.
- If the majority of potential investors have questions related to regulations, address the issue proactively by putting the Regulatory slide in the main body of the pitch deck (as opposed to in the appendix).

Chapter 26

Getting Up to Speed on Accelerators

Subject: Talkcelerator interested in CallJar
From: Marcus Williams
To: Jason Murath

Jason,

Cheryl called me a moment ago. She told Tim about CallJar and he is interested. Should I apply to Talkcelerator?

Sincerely,
Marcus

"Damn. Are you okay?"

I tell all my sparring partners to go a little rough on me. Don't psychoanalyze me. I learn faster when mistakes hurt. That is why I picked up snowboarding so much faster than skiing. When you catch an edge on a snowboard, that freaking hurts.

"All good. My mind was not in the game. Let's-"

But the instructor cut me off. "Water break! Two minutes!"

I have got to stop thinking about my last meeting with Jason while I am trying to block punches. I keep missing the blocks ... and the punches that get through derail my train of thought.

DOI: 10.4324/9781003542612-28

As I sip my water, I consider our conversation. Apparently, the accelerator's offer was more or less "market": 6% of CallJar for $150,000 plus mentoring, customer and investor introductions, and a grab bag of freebies and discounts on things like Amazon web hosting credits and the like. I could sort of put a value on the credits and discounts and even adding that to the cash, the implied valuation was really low, significantly below even the small angel investments Jason made. It all comes down to the coaching and the connections. But how do I value that? How do I know if what I am getting is worth the equity I am giving up?

"Line up! I want everyone to practice a block-punch-kick combo. Imagine that someone just came up to you and sucker punched you. Your goal is to react quickly, avoid getting knocked out, and create some space. The attacker could come at you with a jab or a roundhouse or an uppercut and use either hand. So, mix up your blocks and practice your punches and kicks from either side."

I like these kinds of drills. Visualize a combination and then execute. Work on making the moves precise and fluid. Gradually speed it up. It's all about creating muscle memory so that, if the time never comes, my reflexes take over. It also requires less close attention to outside factors so I can ponder Jason's advice without getting hit in the face.

Out of the corner of my eye I see the instructor going from student to student, correcting one student's stance, repositioning another student's arm to make the block more effective, tapping another on the shoulder to congratulate him or her for a sequence well executed.

Maybe I am thinking about this the wrong way. In a way, an accelerator is not all that much different than this dojo. We all started the beginner class around the same time. We are learning the same skills at roughly the same pace. The instructor comes around and gives us specific feedback and advice that we need to improve. There is no way I could pick up martial arts by reading some blogs and watching some YouTube videos.

There is no way I could have gotten CallJar to where it is now without the one-on-one coaching I am getting from Jason. And not only is he not charging me anything, he wrote me a check! But a lot of startups are not that lucky; they do not have someone like Jason in their corner. So, I guess an accelerator might make a lot of sense.

Before I signed up for the course, I briefly considered private lessons. In addition to being a lot more expensive, it also seemed a bit lonely. Something about martial arts felt like it should be a group learning experience. Going through the startup journey shoulder to shoulder with a bunch of other talented founders could have value too.

Heck, if one Jason is good to have in my corner, having a whole team of Jasons might be even better. After all, some people take both private lessons and group lessons and they typically progress faster. Maybe I should do both. Maybe I should be optimizing for speed and success rather than valuation? After all, Jason knows a lot of people but he doesn't know everybody.

On the other hand, is more really that much better? At some point, I am sure there are diminishing marginal returns on the number of Jasons; after a while, each new Jason brings fewer and fewer new potential introductions to the table.

"Follow through on your punches. It does you no good to react fast if there's no power in your punch or in your kick. You are not going to create any distance with a light poke."

"Hmmph." (which the instructor correctly understands to mean, "Got it, I will work harder")

Of course, the quality of the instructor makes a big difference. I did a lot of research on several martial art forms before picking Krav Maga (and yes, before you ask, I am the only Black man in the room). Then I looked at a couple of different classes to get a sense of who the instructor was, their qualifications, their teaching style, etc. before enrolling here.

While Jason says that Talkcelerator is one of the better accelerators out there, he is just one data point. Their focus on speech-based startups is definitely a plus. But if I decide I want to go the accelerator route, I need to talk to a lot of the startups who went through the program. I would especially want to see how the startups who had their choice of programs think the different programs stack up.

Before choosing Krav, I spoke to some people who had taken classes in multiple martial art forms. I hear it is pretty rare for a startup to go through multiple accelerators but they would have a very interesting perspective.

I would also want to talk to as many angel investors as I could to get their impression of the quality of the startups that come out of the program. How often do they invest in those startups? How do investors rank Talkcelerator against its peers?

Hmm … What would the karate equivalent of angel investors be? Security firms who hire the graduates? Nah. Give it up Marcus. No analogy is perfect.

Wait. Maybe there is an analogy. Krav doesn't make a big deal about earning belts – heck, we do not even wear karate gis – but many of the other styles I researched were very focused on preparing the students for the big test days when they could level up and earn a new belt.

In a way, I guess that is like an accelerator's demo day. Except that instead of getting a colored belt from the instructor, you get cash from investors. If I am trying to get a sense for how valuable an accelerator's investor introductions are, maybe I need to start by asking them for hard numbers. How many of their startups raise a round within six months of completing the program? That should be a fairly easy stat for an accelerator to measure.

Perhaps I should have asked each of the instructors what percentage of their students made it to their first belt within six months of taking lessons? Not a perfect analogy; after all, the dojos take all students, first come first serve, at least until they hit capacity. Accelerators, though, make a big deal about their rigorous selection process so the percent raising rounds is even more on point for them.

Looking around at the other students in the Krav Maga class, I do not think any of them are focused on belts. Most just want to learn critical self-defense skills. If your skills are good, belts happen. Or not. Honestly, my skills are good; I could not care less if I earn a belt. It's like Jason always says, "You do not build a company to get funded; you get funded if you have built a great company. And if you can build a great company without taking any funding, that is even better."

Then there are guys like David. He is here for fitness. He lives in a doorman building in a good neighborhood. As far as he's concerned, Krav is just good cardio. Plus, it fits his schedule. He jokes that if pole dancing were not on Friday nights, he would be doing that instead.

Cheryl mentioned a startup like this in the current Talkcelerator batch. The founder's family was pretty wealthy. He was not worried about raising money. He could get as much as he wanted just by pulling out his checkbook. For him, it was all about sales. He just did not have the connections to potential customers and he had never sold into that industry. I wonder how many deals he closed as a result of the introductions they made for him?

Average sales generated per startup … Maybe I could ask the different accelerators for that statistic? Hmm. Direct to consumer startups do not really work that way so the different mix of types of startups in the accelerator cohort may make it difficult to compare apples to apples. Also, the long lead time to close an enterprise sale and the multiple touch points might make it hard for an accelerator to track this stat even for only their B2B startups. I think I will ask the question anyway. How they answer it might tell me almost as much as the stats themselves.

When the instructor makes a point that he thinks all his students should hear, his voice carries across the room.

"Sarah, all your combinations end with a right foot kick. Nine out of ten people are righties. Your opponent is used to fighting righties. Mix it up a bit. Use your left foot more. Fight different."

That reminds me. I need to look into the Diverse Founder Initiative. DFI doesn't take any equity so that is a plus. But I took a look at their portfolio page and a lot of their startups were more small business than tech startup and I didn't see anything speech focused so I am not sure if the fit is right. But free is free. Except that it is not really free, is it? There is always the time commitment.

I guess I need to dig into their team some more to see if they have built and sold any companies at all like mine. After all, if there is one thing I have learned so far, it is that there is no shortage of people willing to give startups advice even if they have zero actual qualifications … and bad advice is the most expensive kind.

Key Takeaways

- It can be difficult to assess whether the benefits of a given accelerator program are worth the startup's equity and time that the accelerator demands.
- Some accelerators focus on specific industries or technologies. Others are generalists.
- The cash investment an accelerator makes is typically at a very low valuation.
- Accelerators typically also offer mentorship, customer introductions, and assistance fundraising. The value of each of these benefits varies with each startup's specific circumstances.
- Startups without active mentors and advisors benefit more from an accelerator.
- Startups who will be actively fundraising soon also benefit more from an accelerator, especially if this is their first time doing so.
- Startups with less sales experience or who have access to fewer large customers or marketing channel partners may also benefit more.
- It can be difficult for an accelerator program to accurately quantify the business development and fundraising benefits they provide … but founders should not be shy about asking anyway.
- A lot of people who confidently offer advice to startups have little to no actual relevant experience so research the backgrounds and reputation of the accelerator staff carefully.

Chapter 27

20/20 Vision

"So, Marcus, I am sitting in the chair in the optometrist's office waiting for these eyedrops to kick in and make everything blurry and it occurs to me you never spoke about your Vision slide."

I do my best to imitate Jason's voice. "Hi, Marcus. How are you doing? Are you busy? There is something I want to ask you."

"Yeah, that. Whatever. Now tell me what your Vision for CallJar is."

"After we start getting some traction with contractors and realtors, I figured we would look at expanding into other professions. Not sure which ones but I was meaning to look at doctors and …"

"No, no. I mean yes, you should do that. But no, that is not what I mean by vision. Vision is not just more of the same. Something different, categorically bigger. It is your big hairy audacious goal. It is the 'but wait there's more!' "

"What do you mean?"

"Remember the part in those late-night infomercials after they tell you that the set of six awesome steak knives are going to cost $19.99 and then they say" (pause for deep breath and transition to carnival barker voice) "BUT WAIT THERE'S MORE!! How would you like a bread knife so sharp, it can cut through a can? Now how much would you pay!? Wait, do not answer yet! We'll also throw in a set of three paring knives and the only vegetable peeler you'll ever need. And if you order now, you'll also get this lovely knife block to store it all in! All for the low, low price of $19.99" (and dropping to a whisper) "plus shipping and handling."

"I am amused and confused and ever so slightly afraid of you all at the same time."

"Didn't you ever see those commercials? They come on at midnight or 1:00 a.m., over and over and over again."

DOI: 10.4324/9781003542612-29

"We cut the cord five years ago and only use streaming services. I can't remember the last time I saw a commercial."

"Jesus, that is the most polite "okay boomer" I've heard in a while.

"Okay, wait. Think of Amazon. When they were first founded, all they sold were books. So, imagine you are Jeff Bezos pitching selling books over this new interweb thing to a VC fund. He has just convinced them that there is a huge market selling books online and everyone is going to get rich. Then he gets to his Vision slide and says, "But wait, there's more." Then he goes on to tell them about how he is not going to stop at books. He is going to sell everything from clothing to televisions to sport equipment to groceries to medicine and so on and so on. And then, just when the VC wraps its mind around the fact that the market is even huger than the one they were already excited about, he says again, 'But wait there's more.' Then he goes on to tell them that, once he has built this super-efficient logistics operation to support shipping all these products all over the world, he is going to open up that logistics system to other businesses so that anyone who wants to sell product anywhere in the world can do it without having to deal with putting their products in boxes, putting stamps on it, taking it to the post office, etc., etc. Amazon will take care of all of that behind the scenes, for a fee. Now, even the super huge market of selling everything to everybody starts seeming pale in comparison. That is what I mean by vision.

"So, after pretty much everybody in the world has CallJar on their phone, what do you do next?"

"Well, then we go back to the original idea and start selling to businesses. We build out more detailed admin controls around what should or should not automatically be shared. We create plug-ins for Salesforce, Hubspot, Pipedrive and other Customer Relationship Management software. Maybe we even build our own CRM-lite."

"That is pretty good. You see, that gives the VC a choice. Some VCs will be more excited about the B2B angle. That vision statement tells them that you get them, that the whole B2C play is only a means to an end for what they think is the actual big play. Other VCs might look at it and think that there is no way the B2B market will remain untapped for the three to five years you need to make major inroads on the consumer side. They will just write off the B2B angle, treat it like a lottery ticket – potentially huge but unlikely to pay off. Fortunately, if you have sold them on the Market Size slide, you can win them over on the potential of the B2C market alone."

Now it is my turn to go all infomercial on Jason. "But wait, there's more!"

"I was actually thinking about that the other day. I was stuck in customer service hell. The AVR – sorry, automated voice response – system was absolutely horrible and could not get anything I said right. No matter how many times I hit zero or said 'Operator,' it refused to put me through to living, breathing, arguably human being. I don't think I have much of an accent so I can only imagine how bad it is for people who do.

"Once we have people who have been using CallJar for even just a few months, as they correct the transcripts of their calls before sending them, they are basically training the algorithm to understand their accent and speech habits better. That means that we will have the equivalent of a voice profile for every one of our users. We also have that user's telephone number. That is a really interesting dataset. I wonder if we could license out that customization to other companies? That customer service center may have no information on a caller other than the telephone number that they are calling from but if that number is in our database, they could use our profile to instantly increase the accuracy of their AVR dramatically. I am pretty sure we could do without revealing any PII. Sorry, that is Personally Identifiable Information …"

"I know what PII is. Not my first rodeo."

"Sorry, I was not sure. My point is, once we are at scale, we could license out the voice profiles to any other companies' customer service departments. Even if we charge a small fraction of a penny per minute of audio, that could add up very quickly.

"Is that what you mean?"

"That is exactly what I meant."

Key Takeaways

- A Vision slide can help get investors even more excited about a startup's potential but it is not always necessary.
- This slide is more than just the long-term product roadmap.
- The vision is a big, hairy audacious goal above and beyond conquering the market already described in the pitch deck.
- The Vision slide essentially gives investors a choice: they can find the additional, often even larger, opportunity presented in the Vision slide to be credible making the startup even more attractive *or* they can discount it entirely but still invest in the startup based on its primary product and market.

Chapter 28

Getting (Mile)stoned

"It feels a bit weird coming in here the same day the company filed for bankruptcy. I mean, nothing looks different. The coffee tastes the same …"

It has been a while since Jason and I have actually sat at the same table together. Now that we have been working together for several months, we have been able to push forward a lot with phone, text, and email but there is still no substitute for reconnecting face-to-face every so often. Plus, I really do like the coffee here.

Jason looks up from his mug. "I have been saying for years that coworking startups were doomed to bankruptcy or a serious down-round for years now. It is times like this that I wish I actually blogged so I could point to a post and say, 'I told you so.' If only there were some way to short a startup stock, I would have made a killing."

"What made it so obvious to you?"

"They are a tech-enabled real estate company but they were getting valued and funded as if they were a tech startup. That almost always ends badly. The underlying economics of a tech-enabled real estate company is real estate; it scales like real estate. The margins may be a bit better than their pure real estate peers because of the tech but they are still real estate-like margins. And the metrics they live or die on are real estate metrics. What's worse, their technology gave them an edge over the competition but only until the competition got its own technology. There was nothing in their innovation that was defensible in the long term. If there is no way to prevent competition from developing the same technology, that means that all the benefits from the new technology will ultimately flow to the customers, not to the companies who use it.

"For coworking spaces, it was even worse. WeWork's big accomplishment was that it made coworking cool and at the same time made it possible to fit 20% or 30% more people into the same space. The first part meant that demand skyrocketed so things seemed rosy at first. But the second part meant that,

 DOI: 10.4324/9781003542612-30

ultimately, they just created 30% excess capacity. So once the other players copied their model and the initial surge of increased demand for co-working space played out, what was left was an industry with serious oversupply. It was entirely predictable from the get-go."

"If it was so predictable, why didn't investors see it coming?"

"Not everyone is as lucky as you to have a freaking genius as their angel and mentor."

"No. I guess they got the modest ones."

I timed that one perfectly. Jason had just started to take a sip when he cracked up. I think a little coffee came out of his nose.

"Kidding aside, a lot of people did not see it because WeWork had really good initial traction and a great salesman for their CEO. He was able to convince a lot of people that now everything was different. So, WeWork closed up-round after up-round after up-round … until the music stopped."

"Actually, Jason, that is exactly what I wanted to talk about today."

"What? You own shares in coworking spaces and you want me to tell you how to write those off on your taxes?"

"That is only funny because you know I do not."

"It would still be funny to me."

"You know, Jason, you are kind of an asshole."

"That is far from the first time I have been called that. In fact, I think that is the third time today. But the first two times were my wife so I don't know if that counts."

"Think we can get back to work anytime soon?" Jason shrugs so I continue, "I have been struggling with my Traction slide. I don't know what to put there."

"That is not entirely surprising considering you basically do not have any. Remember what I told the Talkcelerator group investors want?"

He holds up one finger, "Recurring revenue. You don't have any."

Second finger, "Any other kind of revenue. None of that either."

Third finger, "Unpaid pilots or users. None of those either."

Fourth finger, "Awards? Agreements with meaningful partners. Nope. All you have is an almost complete MVP and a bunch of customer interviews. Not nothing, but also not super sexy."

"So, what do we do for our Traction slide, Jason?"

"In this case, just skip it. Getting to a working prototype and some test users is okay early traction for a startup at your stage but not all that impressive standing alone. I would roll it into your Milestones slide."

"I do not think I have ever heard of a Milestone slide."

"That is not totally shocking. To the extent that anything in this industry can ever be called 'standard', this is not one of the standard slides. I usually see this information spread across a couple of slides and in my not-so-humble opinion, it is more efficient to have it all in one place."

Jason is drawing on the whiteboard again but this time it actually looks somewhat intelligible.

"This horizontal line is a timeline. It usually starts when you founded your company. This dotted vertical line is now. Everything to the left of the dotted line are things that you have accomplished. Everything to the right of the dotted line are things you are planning to do or expect to achieve.

"I also like to split the milestones up by type. Below the horizontal timeline, I like to show the things you control that are the inputs to your startup's success: when you founded the company, when you released your MVP, when you added or plan to add new features – especially the ones that unlock new revenue streams! – when you plan to expand into new geographies, etc. I would include fundraising activity here, too.

"On top of the timeline are things that you achieve or earn. Basically, the outputs: first customer, 20th customer, when you hit $100,000 in recurring revenue, then $1M, and so on. You could also include key marketing or other agreements, awards received, and other meaningful accomplishments.

"I usually recommend you extend the timeline out for the next 18 months. Most startups raise in 18-month chunks so when you talk about this slide you will usually end by saying that you plan to get to that revenue target within 18 months which leads nicely into your Ask slide.

"Damn, gotta take this call. I promise, it will be quick."

It was not. But while he was on the call, he did pull up this example, which, other than missing the vertical 'now' line, pretty much matches his description:

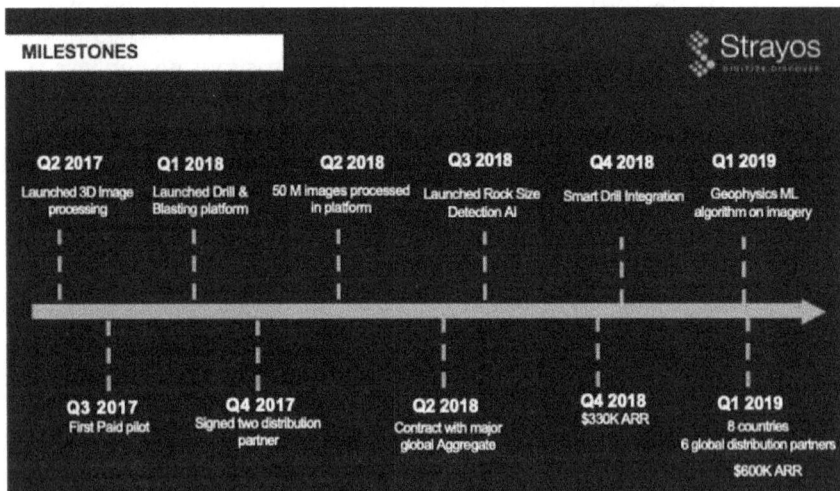

Figure 28.1 Milestones slide example

Source: Strayos Investor Deck, www.strayos.com

Key Takeaways

- A Milestones slide shows the progress that the startup has made since inception and its plans for the immediate future.
- The timeline extends out 18–24 months from the current date as that is typically when a startup will be raising its next round.
- It can be helpful to separate out inputs (e.g., funds raised, features built/to be built) from outputs (e.g., revenue targets/achieved, numbers of customers). One way to do this is to put inputs below the timeline and outputs above it.
- An entrepreneur can use this slide to impress the investor with how far his or her startup has come in a short time and with minimal resources.
- This slide transitions easily to the Ask slide so these slides are often paired.

Chapter 29

The Art of the Ask

Jason is still on his call and, as luck would have it, my phone starts to ring. It's Kofi. I wave to Jason, he shrugs and smiles weakly, and I move over to the far side of the room.

"Dad, I am stressing about my project."

Stressing is his new word. He's been using it almost daily for the past three weeks, like it was a new toy although God knows where he heard it. I mean, really – what's a ten-year-old have to stress about?

I answer in my least patronizing tone of voice, "What's stressing you out, buddy?"

"It's my history project. We are out of popsicle sticks so I can't make the Viking long houses ..." (Kofi skipped the dinosaur phase and is obsessed with Vikings so naturally his history project is on the Viking settlement in North America) "... and the project is due tomorrow."

"Hey, hey, don't sweat it buddy. I will go to CVS on the way home and get some popsicle sticks."

"But grandma is coming tonight and we are going out for dinner. I won't have time to work on it tonight and the project is due tomorrow!"

Before I can point out that the project was assigned over a week ago, the words start to tumble out.

"And then my cousins are coming to visit so I can't work on it over the weekend and I don't want to use Lego men for Vikings, I want real Vikings and the website won't deliver until Monday and ..."

"Buddy, buddy, buddy, wait. Slow down. Take a breath. I promise you it will be okay. Let me understand. If I get the sticks and order the Viking miniatures from the website tonight, can you work on it Monday after school?"

Sniffle. "Yeah"

DOI: 10.4324/9781003542612-31

"So, if I ask your teacher for an extension until Tuesday, can you get her a kick-butt diorama by then?"

"Yeah"

"Okay then. Don't stress. I will email the teacher right away."

"Thanks, Dad. I love you."

"Love you too, buddy." Click.

"And that is a good Ask slide."

I was so focused on Kofi that I hadn't noticed Jason finishing his call. So, I responded with one of my typically witty comebacks.

"Huh?"

"When a lot of startups get to the Ask slide, they tell you in detail how they want to use the money – who they are going to hire, how much they will spend on marketing, etc. – but they do not tell me what they actually accomplish with the money. When you ask Kofi's teacher for a few more days, you aren't going to promise her popsicle sticks and Viking miniatures. You are going to promise her a kick-butt diorama by Tuesday."

"I might not actually say 'kick-butt.'"

"Details, Marcus. Big picture. Focus.

"When a startup asks me for money, I want to know

1. How much do they need?
2. What meaningful milestone that gets them to? and
3. When will they get there?

Basically, I tell all the startups I work with that the headline for their Ask slide should be:

"Raising X dollars to get to Y milestone by Z month-year.

"Simple, clear, and to the point. They can put use of funds in the body of the slide because that tells me a bit more about whether or not the plan they have to get to that goal seems reasonable to me or not, But honestly that is secondary."

"Is it really?"

"Absolutely. After all, does your kid's teacher really care that you are going to order figurines from an online geek store? That granny is coming for the weekend? Not really. She might ask to make sure that there was a legitimate reason to believe that the project she gets on Tuesday will be meaningfully better than what she would get tomorrow if she stuck to the original deadline. But at the end of the day, she probably only really cares that your son learns the material and enjoys doing it. If giving him an extra day or two will make that happen, she should be thrilled."

"What do you mean by a 'meaningful milestone?'"

"Well, ever hear the expression that no one wants to put half the tank of gas into a rocket ship?" (Apparently, we are well beyond the point where Jason even waits for me to respond.) "With very, very, very few exceptions, the startups I invest in are going to have to raise more money to continue to grow. If they want to be able to do that, they need to be able to get to a point where they are attractive to the next stage of investors. Let's say you are a pre-revenue startup ..."

"I think I can empathize."

"Less lip, more listen.

"Okay, so let's say I give you some money to finish building your product. You do that but still have no revenue. Maybe that is enough of a milestone to raise your next round but what if new investors do not consider that enough traction to want to invest? Then, I really only have two choices. Put more money in or let your company fail. I do not want to be in that situation. In that case, your milestone should also include getting to a certain level of revenue since that would make your startup attractive to future investors.

"When you get a little further along, your milestones could include expanding into new cities or countries. An especially meaningful milestone is cash flow breakeven. At that point, if you decide to raise more money, you are doing it because you *want* more money to accelerate growth, not because you *need* it. That's a huge difference."

"I guess that makes sense. How do I know what milestone I should be shooting for?"

"The technically correct answer is to ask a later stage investor. You should be talking to some of those investors anyway in a 'hey, I know that I am early for you right now so I am not pitching you for investment but I would like to tell you what I am doing and get a sense of whether it would interest you down the road' sort of way. While you are talking to them, you ask them what they would be looking for in order to invest in the next round and that informs what your goals should be. I even recommend that you put that target in your thank you email to them. Then, when you do hit them up for money in a year or two, you reply to that same thread. It makes it a little awkward for them to hem and haw when you have hit the explicit target they gave you.

"But – wait for it – I digress. Practically speaking, most experienced angels have a pretty good sense of what you need to accomplish to be fundable down the road and can give you some guidance there as well."

Subject: Ask slide
From: Marcus Williams
To: Jason Murath

What do you think of this as the Ask side?

Ask: Raising $500K to get to $500K ARR by the end of 2025

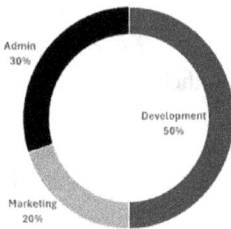

Use of funds
- ❖ Salaries
- ❖ Office
- ❖ Servers

Figure 29.1 CallJar Ask slide

Sincerely,
Marcus

Subject: Re: Ask slide
From: Jason Murath
To: Marcus Williams

Perfect. Add it to the deck. Send me your Team slide as well and will go over it at our meeting.

Yours,
Jason

Key Takeaways

- The Ask slide is more than just how much money a startup is looking to raise and what they intend to spend it on.
- Investors want to know what meaningful, fundable milestones you will achieve with their money, not just what you intend to spend it on.
- The Ask should include how money is being raised, what milestone or milestones the startup intends to hit, and how long it will take them to get there.
- A milestone can be releasing the product/specific new features, a level of revenue, getting to cash flow breakeven, expanding into new markets, etc.
- Entrepreneurs can talk to later stage investors to confirm that the startup is aiming for a milestone that is sufficient to enable them to raise their next round of financing.
- The specific use of funds is only relevant in how it supports the founders' claim that they can get to that milestone with the time and money they are asking for.

Chapter 30

Team (Why, not Who)

Subject: Team slide

From: Jason Murath

To: Marcus Williams

Okay, this one's relatively quick so why do not we bang this out over email and focus on your Financials at our next meeting

The biggest mistake startups make on their Team slide is they think the slide is about who when really it is about why. No disrespect, but I do not give a flying fig about who you are. I want to know why you are the team that is going to crush all the other wannabes.

If a founder has prior exits, that is the gold standard. Put it right there in the headline.

Prior startups that did not get to a meaningful exit get you a silver medal. At least I know this is not your first rodeo. Plus, I can hope that you have made the really stupid mistakes on someone else's dime.

Deep experience in an industry or technical category is worth the bronze.

I think Cheryl has a startup skeleton or two in her closet so your Team slide headline would be something like this:

"Founding team with deep technical, customer acquisition, and X prior startups."

It ain't poetry but it does the trick.

DOI: 10.4324/9781003542612-32

On the page itself, get decent headshots for the two of you with similar, neutral backgrounds. You do not need to have professional photos taken but it should not look like a bad dating profile photo with your ex-girlfriend cropped off the side of the photo and her hand still visibly draped over your other shoulder.

Name and title below each photo. Don't make me guess what each of you do.

You can have a line or two under that explaining why you are awesome. Sometimes, it is more space efficient and aesthetically pleasing to simply put the logos of your university and past employers below your photos. Assuming, of course, you did not go to the local community college and work at the local dry cleaner. Cheryl probably didn't mention it but she majored in marketing and business at Northwestern. That is the kind of thing that answers the question 'Why these guys?' when you see it below a startup's CMO.

Here is an example of a really good Team slide:

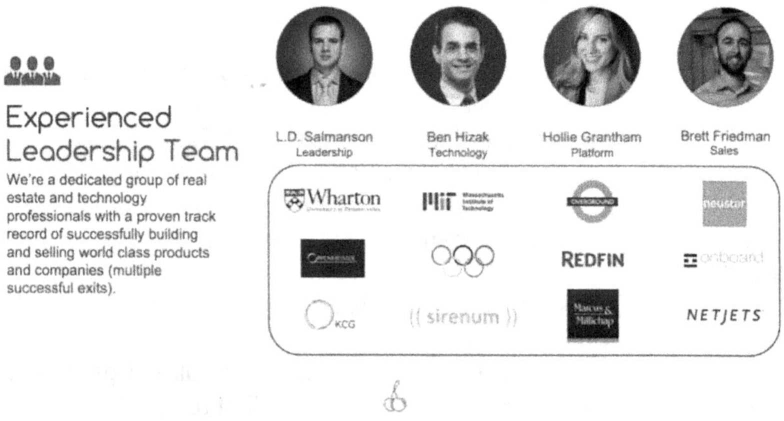

Figure 30.1 Team slide example

Source: Cherre Investor Deck, https://cherre.com

(I would have shouted "multiple successful exits" in the headline but this team was oddly modest. I had to twist the founder's arm to get him to agree to highlighting the phrase in red.)

Last thought: You can put me on the Team slide as well. Just make sure I am clearly separated from the team – over to the side, possibly with a dotted line between us – and clearly marked as a mentor or advisor. Better yet, "Mentor and Investor." If you had a larger team and/or more advisors and investors worth highlighting, I would suggest putting us all on a second slide but this is fine for now.

Yours,
Jason

Key Takeaways

- The Team slide is about more than who does what.
- This slide should answer the question, why is this the right team to make this startup a success?
- Highlighting prior exits (viz., sales of prior startups the team members had founded) is a great way to give investors confidence in the team
- Prior startup experience, even if the entrepreneurs did not achieve an exit or were not the founders also shows that the team will not make rookie errors.
- Listing relevant prior employers is also a good way to show founder quality and prior industry experience.
- Using logos from prior employers and universities instead of words is a good way to keep the Team slide visually interesting and uncluttered.

Chapter 31

Show Me the Money Financials

"So I am a little bit stuck on what I should put on the Financial projections slide."

"Why is that? You have already built your model, identified the critical variables, done your best to de-risk your assumptions. The Financials just fall out of that."

"But those are all still mostly guesses. How am I supposed to say with confidence what I think revenue is going to be in five years?"

"You can't. But don't sweat it. Truth is, the only thing I know for certain when I see a Financials slide is that the numbers are wrong. But that is not what I am looking for on this slide."

"Really? If you aren't trying to figure out how the startup is going to grow, what are you looking for?"

"For me, the financial projections are really just a kind of sanity check. If everything in the deck looks good, I am ultimately going to need to see your full model, play around with the variables, prove to myself that you – and I! – really understand the risks and the steps you are taking to mitigate them. But there is no way I am going to get that from the deck itself. Plus, that is a lot of work. I am only going to do that later in the process when I am mostly convinced that I want to make the investment.

"What I am looking for here is to see whether this is the kind of business that venture funding makes sense for. For example, if a typical startup tells me that in five years they are going to be at $2 million in revenue, they just are not growing fast enough for this to be a venture backable business. Either the founders do not understand how aggressive they need to be and will be out competed by other teams or it is really a small market regardless of what the Market slide said. Or

DOI: 10.4324/9781003542612-33

customer acquisition is going to be so slow and painful that it will take forever for them to grow into a meaningful sized business and that will kill my ROI.

"On the other hand, if they are showing $20 million in revenue in year two, they are probably clueless or smoking ganja or both."

"No one calls a ganja anymore, Jason. You're just embarrassing yourself."

"Really? I can still call it weed, right?"

"Sure, Jason. Knock yourself out."

"Good to know. But back to our regularly scheduled program.

"I am an angel investor and I am used to inexperienced founders. When I see a startup I like with financial projections that are too modest or too wildly optimistic, I have a conversation with the founders to try to understand what assumptions they made and why their projections are what they are. But if the numbers do not change – and I mean, change with a good reason, not just because they are telling me what I want to hear – that is all I need to know to pass on the deal."

"Okay, that makes this slide a little less intimidating. So, what do I do? Just put a table with my high-level projections on the slide?"

"You could do that. It's a little boring but I wouldn't ding you too hard for that. Hang on, I think I got a deck earlier today with a table for their financials ... Ah, here it is:

Financial Forecast

	2019	2020	2021	2022
		Pandemic Adjusted Forecast		
Gross Revenue	$.19M	$.56M	$2.1M	$5.0M
ARR	$.12M	$.36M	$1.5M	$3.8M
Operating Income	($1.3M)	($.95M)	($1.4M)	($.36M)
Paid Users	275	800	3,000	7,500
Freemium Users	---	200	1,500	15,000

Figure 31.1 Financials slide example

Source: Stringbean Investor Deck, www.stringbean.tech

"A little boring but it does the trick. If you wanted to make it a bit more interesting, you could show revenue graphically as a bar or line graph. If you are likely to get to profitability fairly quickly, you could also show profit on the same axis. I have got an example of those floating around here somewhere ...

FINANCIAL SUMMARY

● ● ●

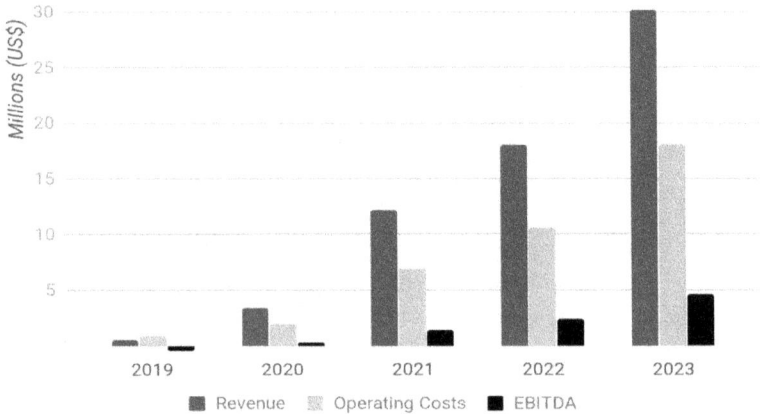

Figure 31.2 Financials slide example

Source: Kognition Investor Deck, www.kognition.ai

"If there are major drivers of revenue that you want to highlight such as number of customers, you could even add a two- or three-line table below the chart with those drivers. Just be prepared. Investors like to do simple math. If you show revenue and number of customers, I will do the math to calculate revenue per customer and if there is a big jump in that metric, I am going to ask you what's causing it. Now this can be a good thing. As you roll out new features that increase the number of services you can sell to a particular customer, your average revenue per customer should go up. So, if this coincides with a major feature release planned on your timeline, the story sticks together nicely. You might even want to proactively highlight this jump in your voiceover to this slide. But if you start fumbling and stuttering and cannot explain why the numbers move the way they do, that is a big red flag for an investor.

"Remember: your deck is not a test to see if you got the right answer. Your deck is part of a conversation that you want to have with a potential investor. Your Financial slide is no different."

Key Takeaways

- Early-stage investors do not expect a startup's financials to be 100% accurate. There are simply too many unknowns at this stage.
- An angel or VC investor looks to the Financials slide to confirm that the projections are reasonable.
- Implausibly rapid growth is a red flag and may indicate that the entrepreneurs do not understand what it takes to scale a business.
- Slowly growing revenue may indicate that the startup is not the kind of rapidly growing business that is venture-backable.
- To determine whether the startup's assumptions are defensible and projections are detailed and sound, the investor will need to see the spreadsheet with the full financial model … but that is time consuming and most investors will not commit to that until they are further in the process.

Part III

Finding and Meeting Investors

OK, our pitch deck is ready! Now how do you find investors to show it to? This section takes you through the process of identifying relevant investors, getting warm introductions to them, holding investor meetings, and running an effective fundraising process overall.

DOI: 10.4324/9781003542612-34

Chapter 32

Prospecting for Investors

"So, Marcus, now that the designer is prettying up the deck, what are your plans for fundraising?"

"Well, I was going to ask you if you knew any other angel investors I should speak to."

"About 95% of the founders who I ask that question say just about the same thing.

"The good news is that I know a few and will absolutely make those introductions. The bad news is, that is a piss-poor way to go about finding potential investors."

"Uh, thanks? Why is that so bad? How else would you do it?"

"The human mind doesn't work that way. It's not like it runs a SQL query, lining up the characteristics of your startup against the desired investment criteria of every angel investor I know. If you ask somebody that kind of broad question, a handful of names will jump to mind and then they will kind of run dry.

"On the other hand, the human mind is great at Yes or No questions. If you ask me whether someone specific is a good match for your startup, it is very easy for me to answer that. Your first question can always be 'Who do you know ...?' to see who jumps to that investor's mind right away but if you really want to maximize the number of warm introductions you get, you want to pull your list of prospects out of your back pocket to see who they know and think would be worth contacting."

"I guess that makes sense but how do I come up with that prospect list?"

"The process is actually fairly straightforward but it is iterative and a bit time-consuming. Here's how it goes in a nutshell."

Jason is writing on the whiteboard as he speaks. I have long since given up on actually trying to read anything he scribbles so I take notes in tandem:

DOI: 10.4324/9781003542612-35

1. Come up with a few startups that are in the same general space as your startup
2. Find out who the early investors were in that startup
3. Research those early investors to confirm that they make sense for you
4. See what other startups those investors have backed that are potentially relevant to you
5. Go back to step #2

"By the time you have looped through that a few times, you should have a list of relevant startups on the one side and a list of prospective investors on the other. You want to have at least 50 – and better yet 100 – prospects before you start reaching out to anyone. It may take you a few hours of mind-numbingly boring work, but you will get there."

"That seems simple enough. What exactly do you mean by startups in the same general space as CallJar?"

"A startup is relevant to you in this case if it is in a similar industry or function or technology. Basically, what you are looking for is a pattern. Investors who like certain types of startups are more likely to be interested in CallJar than others. Someone who only invests in cybersecurity or healthtech, probably is not worth wasting your time on. Here is the acid test. When you ask somebody for a warm intro to that investor, you are going to want to be able to say, 'Angel McVestor invested in startup A, B and C so I think he could be interested in CallJar.' For example, if an investor invested in Uber and Lyft, there is a good chance he might be interested in hearing about a scooter share like Lime. But if your startup is a direct-to-consumer high end linen company, that sentence makes no sense."

"Angel McVestor?"

"I give this spiel at least a dozen times per year and I get laughs every time."

"Pity laughs."

"You want to go into comedy or do you want to pitch a startup?"

"Sorry, please continue Obi Wan."

"So, Padawan, what makes a startup similar to CallJar?"

"Well … I guess if it involves speech recognition, that would count."

"Absolutely. What else?"

"Um … actually, I do not know."

"Think broad. What kind of customer are you selling to?"

"We are starting with realtors and contractors and more generally with any on-the-go professional who wants to be more productive."

"So, what if I am an angel investor who has invested in other productivity tools aimed at professionals and small or midsize businesses? That is a bit of a specialized market. It takes a different kind of sales process than you need if you are selling software to large businesses at $20,000 plus a pop. An investor who has backed companies like that before would not only be potentially more open to investing in yours but could also bring a fair bit of relevant advice to the table."

"I see. That makes sense. What if I also approached angels who have invested in proptech or construction tech? I realize that those are only my initial markets but they might be able to help me get some good early traction."

"Absolutely. Especially if your initial markets are a little niche. Those kinds of investors often love startups that begin in their backyard but have the potential to spread across many other verticals."

"Okay, I get that part. But how do I find out who invested in those startups?"

"Sometimes you can just Google the name of the startup and invest plus an asterisk. The 'invest*' will capture investors, invests, investment, and any other variations on the word that might be in an article about the startup's funding. Occasionally the angel investor will have his own website with his investment thesis and portfolio companies laid out for you. More often than not you are going to want to look at one of the online databases. Crunchbase is a pretty good one and there is a free version of it if you do not want to spend the extra couple of bucks for the full features. You could also look at Pitchbook, Mattermark, or a couple of other databases. They are all kind of the same. That said, they tend to be better at capturing institutional investors and can be a little hit or miss on the angel side."

"I see. I assume that, if I can look up a startup and find out who invested in it, I can also look at the investor and see what else he or she invested in in the same place?"

"Exactly. Before you ask, if an investor has invested in your direct competitor, obviously you do not reach out to them. Just be very tightly focused on what you consider a direct competitor. Some founders have such a broad interpretation of that term that it pretty much excludes anyone who might be remotely relevant to them. If you are on the fence, when you get connected to the investors you can describe your startup in broad terms and ask them point-blank whether they think they have a portfolio conflict. Most investors are very careful to avoid even the appearance of a conflict. If we get a bad reputation for something like this, you can pretty much guarantee that we will never see any of the best startups ever again."

"Wait. I think you skipped a step. How do I go from having a list of prospects to actually getting a meeting with them?"

"You get down on your knees and praise God for inventing LinkedIn."

"I am pretty sure that was Reid Hoffman."

"The Lord works in mysterious ways. And you are missing the point. You want to use LinkedIn here the same way you use it to get a job."

"I do not know how to break this to you Jason, but I was a developer for most of my career. I have never had to look for a job in my life. Recruiters always reached out to me."

"Oy Jesus. Okay Marcus, listen up. When savvy but ordinary mortals want a job, they don't just apply for it online. After they submit an application, they look for people at the same company, preferably in the same department, ideally the person that they would report to. Then they find people they know who are connected to the people at the company they want to work for and ask the people they know to put in a good word for them.

"Before LinkedIn, it was incredibly hard to figure out who knew whom. Now, you just plug your target's name into the search bar and LinkedIn will tell you how many degrees of connection away you are from the target. If you are a second-degree connection, that means that there is at least one person who is linked to you both and can, at least theoretically, make a warm introduction.

"As a practical matter, some people will connect with anyone on LinkedIn. If they do not actually know your target well enough that the target values their recommendation or if they don't really know you well enough to vouch for you, they are useless to you as an introducer. But if one of your mutual LinkedIn connections legit knows each of you and believes in what you do enough to vouch for you, that is the best way to get in front of a prospective investor."

"That makes sense. So, once I have a prospective investor, I jump into LinkedIn, find a mutual introduction, and ask for a warm intro."

"You can do it that way. But I generally recommend finding all the investors first, taking a break, finding all the potential connections, taking a break, and then asking for all the introductions in one shot. Personally, I just find it easier to do this in batches. First, I do all of the same task all the way through. Then the next task and so on. I find it less efficient to jump from CrunchBase to LinkedIn to email and back again.

"Plus, it helps to get an overall picture of who can make warm introductions for you before requesting them. You will generally find that there are some people who are hyper-connected and, if you are not careful, you will end up asking them for a dozen introductions. Some of your contacts won't mind that. Current investors like me, your best friends, your mom – we will make as many introductions as you ask us for. On the other hand, most people are happy to make a few introductions and might get a little annoyed after the third or fourth request. If you get a good overall view of who can connect you to whom first, before you start asking for introductions, you can spread the love around a bit better. Tap the people who can only make one intro for you first so that you do not ask your super connectors for intros you can get elsewhere."

I nod. Put that way, it does sound more efficient, not to mention more courteous, to do it in batches.

"Makes sense to me. I will set aside twenty minutes or so every morning to start crunching through this all. That way it won't be as, how did you put it, mind numbingly boring?"

"No, no, no, no, no. You want to do this as a series of sprints rather than a marathon."

Wow. That is just about the most passionate I have seen Jason in a long time. My shock must be showing on my face because he immediately continues.

"Would you rather have one job offer in hand or five?"

"Is that a trick question? Of course, the more the merrier. When I was at my last job, I got an offer to move to a different company. The pay was better and I think I would have liked the work as much or better than the company I was at. But I was not pressed to move and I thought I could get a better deal so I countered with a higher number. I never heard back from them. A few months later I got another offer which I ultimately took. The salary was close but not exactly as high. But by that point, things were getting a little shaky at the job I was at so I took it. I do wonder every so often at what would have happened if I had not tried to negotiate and had just taken the other offer."

"What would you have done if you were unemployed at the time you got that first offer?"

"I probably would have jumped at it."

"And what would you have done if you had had both job offers in hand at the same time?"

"Good question ... I think I would have gone back to the second offer and highballed them. If they agreed to my number, then I would have gone back to the first offer and asked them to match or beat it. But if the second company did not come back with a better offer, I probably would have taken the first offer as is."

"So, you see how different the dynamic is between having both offers at the same time versus having to consider them separately?

"Let's assume that roughly the same number of investors will give you a term sheet regardless of how you approach this. If you spread the process out over a couple of weeks, by the time you get warm intros, set up pitch meetings, respond to follow up information requests, have additional meetings, and all that jazz, your term sheets will start dribbling in weeks apart. Most of the time, you have a week or two to agree to a term sheet that you have been offered so you will only have one term sheet in hand when you have to make that decision.

"But if you just suck it up and run the process as a series of three, two-to-three-hour sprints, all your intro request emails will be going out at the same time. This gives you a fighting chance of getting enough conversations to the term sheet stage at the same time that you might be able to pit one investor against the other."

"Damn. I think you are right about that."

"Of course I am right about that. This is not my first rodeo, you know.

"One last piece of advice on prospecting for investors before I have to jump on my 10 a.m. Zoom: have a system for staying on top of your intro requests. You don't know if your intro request email got sent to spam or just got lost in your friends' overflowing inboxes. Or perhaps they got your email and have been too busy to actually reach out to the target on your behalf. Maybe they even forwarded your email but have not heard back. It is even possible that the investor wrote back to them but that email is lost in their inbox. Raising money for your startup is not their top priority; you need to stay on top of the process. Wait a week and if you have not heard back, email them again. If they missed your first email, hopefully they will see this one and send it out. If they did send out the intro request, this will nudge them to search their inbox for responses and to follow up on the intro request if necessary.

"By the way, it is also possible that they do not actually know the prospective investor you want to reach well enough to make an intro. Remember: not everyone is as discriminating about who they connect with on LinkedIn. It is even possible that they do know the investor but they just do not believe in your startup enough to want to put their reputation on the line requesting the intro. In a perfect world, they would just come out and tell you that. In reality, they may be embarrassed to admit it and decide to ghost you instead, hoping that you will forget about it and spare them the unpleasantness. But you want this process to move along quickly and likely have someone else who you can ask for that introduction so a quick 'No' beats not knowing any day. By following up in a week, they realize that you are not going to let them off the hook that easily.

"If they still have not responded a week after your first follow-up email, you can send another one. But if they still have not responded a week after your second follow-up, move on to someone else for that warm introduction.

"Damn. Now I am late for my Zoom …"

Key Takeaways

■ To successfully raise a round of financing, a startup should begin with a list of 50–100 relevant investors.

■ Relevant investors are ones who invest at the current stage of the startup into similar (but not competitive) startups. This could include startups in the same industry, who sell to the same customers, with the same business models, etc.

■ The acid test for determining whether another startup is similar enough is to use it in this sentence and see if it makes sense: "I see that [investor] has invested in [startup A], [startup B], and [startup C] so I think [he/she/they] will be interested in your startup ..."

■ Finding investors is much more than simply asking, "Do you know any investors I should speak to?" It is a process.

■ Databases like Crunchbase, Pitchbook, Mattermark, etc. can help entrepreneurs identify investors in similar startups.

■ Investors are swamped with messages from startups. Cold outreach is rarely effective.

■ Founders can use LinkedIn to find mutual acquaintances who can make warm introductions to the investors they have identified.

■ Many mutual acquaintances may not actually know the people they are linked to on LinkedIn so the founder should be prepared to ask other mutual acquaintances for those introductions

■ Many mutual acquaintances may (unfortunately) simply not respond so founders must be systematic about following up and, if a mutual acquaintance remains unresponsive, reach out to another mutual acquaintance instead.

■ In order to maximize negotiating leverage, the startup wants to get multiple offers at the same time. To increase the odds of that happening, contacting investors should be a sprint, not a marathon.

Chapter 33

"I'd Like You to Meet ..." (Warm Intro Requests)

Subject: CallJar investor prospects

From: Marcus Williams

To: Jason Murath

Jason,

Just came off of four hours of looking for relevant potential investors and my eyes are starting to glaze over. But at least that is done. Sharing a Google Sheets file with you so you can review it.

Since you told me that you are good for an unlimited number of warm introduction requests, please mark up that file to let me know which investors you can reach out to so I know not to reach out to other people for those introductions.

Thanks in advance for those emails.

Sincerely,
Marcus

DOI: 10.4324/9781003542612-36

Subject: Re: Your call with Marcus Williams 2023-12-04 03:41 p.m. (GMT+5)

From: Jason Murath

To: Marcus Williams

Wow, the alpha version of the app worked pretty damn well. The transcript below has almost no typos (e.g., "interests" instead of "intros", "fun name" instead "fund name") and it picked up the pauses in the conversation to punctuate it really well. As far as I can tell, it picked up every longer break when you were speaking and turned that into a new paragraph. Very impressive.

It could use a few more commas and it seems a little odd to have a numbered list with the numbers spelled out (one instead of 1). Do you think you could train the speech recognition engine to recognize when somebody is making a list?

The most annoying part is that it kept writing call jar (and once, call charm) instead of CallJar but who's quibbling?

Since we do not have-auto sharing setup, I am forwarding the transcript of my half of the conversation to you so you have it in writing.

Yours,
Jason

----------- FORWARDED MESSAGE -----------

Subject: Your call with Marcus Williams 2023-12-04 03:27 p.m. (GMT+5)

From: noreply@CallJar.com

To: Jason Murath

[Transcript begins]

That is not how it works buddy. But I realize that I was a little bit rushed at the end last week so I forgive you.

Yeah, yeah, yeah, listen up. First the good news. That is a good list to start with. I recognize a good 20 names on the list and I am happy to reach out to them. I marked the names of the people I can introduce you to on the shared doc so you can focus on getting warm interests for the other investors.

You're welcome. But here's the bad news. If you ask someone to do that much work for you they will do it later, also known as never. If you want someone to do you a favor you have to make it the bare minimum amount of work possible. Basically, I should be able to just hit forward and add a sentence along the lines of I invested in these guys and you should too. If you make it that easy, I will bang the emails off right away. If only to get them out of my inbox.

Exactly. So, send me a separate email for every intro you want. It's a little more work for you but you are asking me for a favor so you should be willing to go the extra distance to make things easy for me. Subject line should be something like call jar would like to meet investor name with his fun name in parenthesis if the investor is a VC rather than an angel so it is immediately obvious from just the subject to me, to the target, and to you when you get an email back for me who is being introduced to whom. Also, you want to make sure the subject line is different enough that Gmail doesn't merge different introduction requests into a single thread. It's very easy to miss a reply that way.

I know. I hate blank subject lines the worst too. The body of the email should be basically three sentences.

One. As you know, call jar does XYZ. Don't make me think about how I should describe your startup. Too much effort. Besides, you can do it better than me. So why make the first thing the investor you want to meet read about your startup be less than ideal?

Yes, of course I know that I basically wrote the elevator pitch with you but some of the guys you are going to ask for a warm intro will be hearing about this for the first time or aren't investors so do not necessarily think about how to describe things in ways that would appeal to an investor. Take the opportunity to put the best words in their mouth.

Good to know that. Let's continue.

Two. I see that you are connected to so and so. He or she invested in A B and C so I thought that they might be interested in call jar as well. Got it? This way neither I nor the prospective investor need to think about whether you are a good potential fit. You have just done the thinking for us.

Sure. Of course you could be wrong. Investment theses change or there might be some other reason the investor was interested in those startups that does not really carry over to call charm. But at least your reasoning will be plausible and if the connector or the investor disagree you still come off as someone thoughtful who did their homework. I can't tell you how many startups just blindly spray and pray.

Oh right. Almost forgot.

Third sentence. Do you know so and so well enough to make an introduction? This part is critical. If the person you're asking has any reservations about making the introduction you want them to tell you no rather than just ghost you. This gives him or her an easy out.

Your deck? Sure. Attach your deck if you would like. Some people feel strongly about not attaching the deck because they think that will somehow cost them a meeting they could other-wise get based on just the email alone. My thinking is that in that case you will lose the investor at the first meeting anyway so why bother taking up their time? The only time you would legitimately lose a meeting that could actually go somewhere is if your deck is so bad that it turns them off. In that case shame on you. You should put in the effort to make a really good deck.

I can't remember. Do you have a video showing the product in action?

No? Okay then this is academic but if you decide to make one you can attach a link to it in the body of the email. Just keep it to 90 seconds or less. Some investors actually like video more than text but many of them hate to have to sit through long and rambling videos.

Love you too babe.

[Transcript ends]

Key Takeaways

■ To maximize the chance of getting a warm introduction, the entrepreneur needs to do everything in his or her power to minimize the effort required from the mutual acquaintance.

■ An intro request email should be concise and to the point.

■ It should include a brief description of what the startup does both to avoid making work for the mutual acquaintance and to ensure that the description is as effective as possible.

■ The email should also reference other investments the target investor has made to make it immediately clear that the opportunity is relevant to the investor.

■ All intro requests should give the mutual acquaintance an easy out in case he or she is reluctant to make the introduction, enabling the entrepreneur to quickly move on to another mutual acquaintance.

Chapter 34

Mastering the Investor Meeting

Subject: Your call with Marcus Williams 2023-12-13 10:07 am (GMT+5)

From: noreply@CallJar.com

To: Jason Murath

Thank you for our call a moment ago. This call today was important to me and I use a service called CallJar to transcribe my half of the conversation. Only my half of the conversation is recorded; for your privacy, nothing you said was recorded.

[Note from Marcus]
I have made a couple updates to the app. Standard intro text gets added at the beginning of every transcript that is sent and now the user can add a personal note (like this) one at the top of the transcript before it sends.

I have also added a layer of intelligence that automatically boldfaces key information like dates and times, telephone numbers, addresses, and the like.

[Transcript begins]
Jason, great news.
What? No. The Cubs aren't even in the running.
Ah. Yeah. Not so funny.

DOI: 10.4324/9781003542612-37

I have got an investor who wants to meet. David Owens at New Seeds responded to a warm intro request I sent. He wants to meet next week.

That is exactly what I was going to ask for. **9:00 a.m. Friday** at your office is perfect.

Yeah, you got me. That was me repeating back to what you said to make sure that call jar caught it. See you then.

[Transcript ends]

The New Seeds office looks nice … but not too nice. It says, "We are doing well enough to have a nice office but we don't waste our investors' money on anything as silly as a really nice office." In a way, I guess that makes sense. If they are going to expect the startups they invest in to make every penny count, they might as well also show that they don't spend money frivolously either.

"Marcus Williams, here to see Mr Owens."

The receptionist looks up and says, "Certainly, David is expecting you. He is just wrapping up a call. Please make yourself comfortable in the conference room behind me and help yourself to coffee or some water."

While I am waiting, I might as well figure out how to cast my screen onto the monitor. There is a website … and a code … there! Got the presentation up on my laptop … and there it is on screen. All set. Now we wait …

"Sorry to keep you waiting. Marco?"

"Just Marcus, and not a problem at all. There is always plenty of email to catch up on."

Okay, time to start taking some of Jason's advice. Step number one, confirm that you are talking to the right person. He looks enough like his LinkedIn photo and the picture on the website that I am going to skip confirming it explicitly.

I was worried there a moment when the receptionist said David was stuck on a call. According to Jason, it would not be the first time a partner took a meeting, only to pawn it off on an associate when the startup showed up. That would not have been the end of the world; I might have had to work a little harder to spell out the talking points for an associate to use at the fund's weekly meeting so he could make the case to the partners to spend more time on CallJar. Easy enough to do but it is nice to know that I am speaking to someone senior who won't need the extra hand holding. I still need to get a feel for David's level of technical expertise but let's not skip the time check.

"I heard that your prior call went long. I hope everything is okay?"

"Yeah, yeah, nothing too crazy. Just a little bit of founder drama. But we've talked everyone off the ledge and it is going to be fine. Thanks for asking."

I can't tell how much of that is him joking and how much of that is business as usual so I think I am just going to play it straight.

"Are we still good until 2?"

"Actually, I have got another call at 2 p.m. and it would really help if I had ten minutes to prep for that."

Jason and I have been practicing the pitch for days now. If he lets me get through without interruption – and according to Jason investors almost never do – it takes me about seven minutes to get through the deck. That plus another 15 minutes or so for questions means that 20 to 25 minutes is really all that I need. We were starting ten minutes late so if we had booked a half hour, time would be getting a bit tight. But we had booked an hour so even wrapping up ten minutes early, I have got plenty of time. But now I know roughly how much time to budget for creating a good rapport.

"Brian mentioned you guys used to work together at Lucent but I didn't get too many of the details …"

David is smiling so that must have been a good way to start.

"Brian was my first boss out of college. I had no idea what I wanted to do but my father knew Brian's father and he was six or seven years ahead of me so we knew each other slightly growing up. I was the only non-engineer on the team so it was definitely a bit rough at first. They told me to ask whatever questions I needed to ask, that there were no stupid questions … and then I'd ask a question and they would say, 'except that one' and make me fetch coffee for the team. But I learned a lot and, by the time I went to business school, I knew I wanted to work somewhere in technology. I kind of fell into VC, but that is a different story. How about you? How did you end up building a startup?"

David and I do not have anyone else in common other than Brian (at least as far as LinkedIn knows) and I didn't see anything on the fund website or his other social media profiles that would suggest any common hobbies. But he is comfortable with engineers so I'll work with that. I launch into my background and the story behind CallJar, playing up the move from being an engineer to managing them. Jason had me practice this part over and over again until I could do it in my sleep. Then he had me do it over and over again until it didn't sound like I had rehearsed it. Meanwhile I am thinking ahead.

It sounds like he has a decent amount of technical chops after all. He is not coming from a software background so I probably won't have to go into the details about how we hacked into the accessibility options to make the app work. On the other hand, he probably does not know enough to know that figuring that out was actually really hard so I should probably stress it a bit more than I otherwise would. He has the telcom background so he may geek out a little bit on the legalities of one versus two party consent but I am very comfortable there so that should work well.

"… so bottom line, I just couldn't find anything that did the trick and decided to build it myself. Would you like me to take you through the deck?"

Not the most eloquent transition but Jason warned me that some investors prefer to just chat it out, rather than go through the deck. I am not concerned about presenting without the deck – I have practiced it enough time both ways that I am perfectly comfortable pitching blindfolded if necessary – but if we go that route I want to have a little bit of extra time in case we go off on tangents because if that happens, time might get a little tight.

"Sure. You can cast it on the screen … oh, I see you have already got that hooked up. Nice job. Let's jump right in."

So far, so good. The pitch feels good. Problem slide goes pretty much exactly as planned. Solution slide also goes well.

"So, hang on. How do you get around dual party notification laws? If the caller or the other party is in a two-party state, do you have to get their prior consent before recording?"

Just as I suspected, he asked that early so I will just jump to that slide in the deck and have that conversation right now.

That seemed to satisfy him. Let's pick the story back up where we left off …

He seems engaged and he is asking good questions but it is almost a little bit anticlimactic. Jason said some investors would pepper me with questions and I needed to be able to present the information in whatever order they wanted. But other than the question about regulations, David seems happy to let me go through the deck in order.

That sounded like his last question. Time for the moment of truth.

"So, is this the kind of startup you might be interested in investing in?"

Jason warned me that every so often, I would get an outright no. That the investor would say something like, 'we only invest in direct-to-consumer fashion brands.' Or gaming. Or crypto. I did my homework on New Seeds pretty thoroughly. Not only did CallJar fit the description of what they invested on their website, there were at least five startups on their portfolio page targeting similar types of users or with similar models. So, I do not expect an outright fail but I would be lying if I said I was not nervous.

Slowly, thoughtful, David says, "Possibly …"

I let out a breath that I didn't know I was holding and wait for him to continue.

"We really like vertical SaaS plays, especially ones with clear visibility into their first niche or two, and I am still processing your ultimate vision. If it plays out like that, the revenue from licensing voice profiles could make the software revenue look like table scraps. But it is also possible that voice recognition gets so good that it does not even need profiles. Fortunately, the market size on the software side alone is big enough and the investment it will probably take to get there is reasonable enough that the opportunity can stand on the software proposition alone.

"My concern is that you might be too early for us."

Is this the famous 'VC soft no' that Jason warned me about? Let's see if we can figure out if he really means that we are too early or he is just looking for a polite way to pass.

"Respectfully, David, I looked at your site and you do invest in pre-revenue startups. Can you walk me through why this would still be too early?"

"You are absolutely right that we do make pre-revenue investments. It is just that the bar is higher in those cases. For us to make a pre-revenue investment, we are looking for a truly exceptional team. I am not casting any shade on you and Cheryl but some of the pre-seed investments we have made are in teams that have had two or more large prior exits. You guys are a strong team, the kind of team that we would have no problem backing if you already had some revenue. But without revenue, it is a closer call.

"Of course, sometimes it is not the team that puts them over the top but the technology. But as much as I love what you are doing with speech to text, the underlying speech recognition engines are not your technology …"

"Well, the LLM is all ours."

"Absolutely, if you did not own the language model, there would be nothing here that was ultimately defensible and we would not be having this conversation at all. But there is a qualitative difference between owning proprietary data and owning the technology that generates all the proprietary data."

"I guess I understand when you put it that way. There is not much we can do about the team right now and the tech is what the tech is. So, I guess that leaves traction. How much traction would make this an easy decision for you?"

My gut tells me David is being genuine, that he really wants to invest but that we are too early. My hands are on the table so I figuratively cross my fingers.

"That is a tough question to answer …"

I just got that sinking feeling in the pit of my stomach. According to Jason, not being willing to put down a target number is one of the signs that I am getting the dreaded 'soft no.'

"… but I'd say if you had 1,000 paying users anytime within the next year, that would be pretty compelling. In fact, even if you had only 100 paying users but got them within a few months, that might even push us over the edge."

A wave of relief washes over me. I knew he was for real. It is still not an investment, but at least he is still in play.

"I see and completely understand. A little bit disappointed, but I appreciate the guidance. I hope it is okay for me to add you to our update list?"

"Absolutely. Please do."

I can't wait to tell Jason about this meeting

* * *

"Well aren't you excited, Marcus?"

Jason had listened quietly, with a small smile on his face, for the full five minutes it took for me to tell him about the meeting.

"Of course. Shouldn't I be?"

"Of course you should be. Your first investor pitch is a big milestone. Like your first kiss on the cheek in 6th grade. Objectively, it is just a little kiss on the cheek. But it was a huge deal at a time and you still remember it vividly 50 years later.

"And I agree with your assessment. I think David is sincere about wanting to invest but won't do it until you have a little more traction."

"So, what do I do now?"

"You add him to your monthly investor update email and leave him alone until you have 100 users."

"That sounds so ... anticlimactic."

"What else would you expect? He told you what he is looking for. Until you have that, or until something else meaningful changes, anything else would just be wasting his time."

"What counts as meaningful?"

"Ideally, something that triggers FOMO. If another investor was coming in. But not just your Uncle Jim. Ideally, it is a super angel or VC fund that is going to lead your round. If that happens, New Seed will miss this round and have to hope they can get in on your Series A round. There is nothing like Fear of Missing Out to get a VC to rethink whether you are actually too early or not. Even if they are not your lead, a commitment from an investor with street cred in your space whose opinion carries weight might get David to take a second look.

"Short of that, a really big partnership that could lead to a lot of revenue in the short term might also be meaningful traction. For example, if a large realtor association decided to endorse CallJar and promote it to all its members, that could get a VC fund who thinks you are just a little bit too early to reconsider."

"Oh, I see."

"Hey, why so glum? This is actually good news. You are going to kiss a lot of frogs before you find your prince. If we are reading David's response correctly, now you have a little more optionality than you had just a few days ago. Let's say that you can't raise the full $500,000 you want right now but you are able to raise, say, $100,000. That won't get you to the revenue target that you want to hit. But if it gets you to 100 users in just a few months – that is $1,000 monthly recurring revenue, right? – or if it gets you to 1,000 users in about a year – $10,000 a month, $120,000 annual – you can go back to David and see if he wants to invest at that time."

"I guess that is more of a glass-half-full way to look at things."

"That is the spirit. More importantly, did he have any leads for you?"

"What do you mean, leads?"

"Didn't you ask David ... oh!"

(I have never seen anyone actually hit their forehead with the palm of their hand. I didn't know anyone did that in real life.)

"I completely forgot that we got cut off last week. There are a whole bunch of other questions you need to ask before you leave a meeting that we didn't get to."

"Now you tell me?"

"Well, I was expecting to talk about it today but the meeting came in faster than expected. Don't sweat it. We can ask most of the questions in your thank you follow up email.

"Normally, after figuring out whether or not there is genuine interest there, you would want to ask the investor what their average check size is for an investment at your stage. They will probably come back to you with a range which should tell you where they can fit into the round. In order to lead your round, their check generally has to be for at least half of the total amount you want to raise. After all, the lead investor is setting terms of the round – valuation, option pools, preferences – do not worry. I will explain all of that later. The point is that it is hard to tell other investors that they need to accept these terms if the lead is not the largest investor in the round.

"Now I have seen some rounds led by an investor who put in a third of the total but, more often than not, they were co-leading it with another fund so it is basically the same thing.

"Plus, if the lead or co-leads are not a good chunk of the round, that does not get you close enough to the finish line that the other, smaller investors feel the pressure to get off the fence or lose the opportunity.

"On the flip side, if their minimum check is bigger than the amount that you want to raise, you have to have a discussion with them as to whether they are willing to write you a smaller check or whether you need to consider raising more money. If the difference is relatively small, usually either option is fine. But if the gap is really large, it might not be possible to come to a compromise. Typically, when that happens, it is because you are talking to a later stage investor than you ought to be targeting.

"The investor may also tell you that they have minimum ownership targets, say 10% or 15% or even as much as 20% of the company. With that information and the check size they want to write, you can often back into the typical valuations that they invest at. Assume that the rest of the money in the round, if any, comes in from other investors at the same valuation. You can estimate how much of your company you are giving up in this round. If that comes out to too much dilution, you may not want to take money from this investor … assuming, that is, you have any choice in the matter. If that is the only investor to give you a term sheet, obviously it is take it or leave it."

"I think I followed that. Since I forgot to ask that in the meeting, is that the kind of thing I can ask in my follow-up email?"

"I don't see why not. After confirming the user targets he gave you, you can continue with something like, 'assuming we reach those targets, what size investment do you think you might make?'"

"Sure, but why do I need to reiterate the targets he gave me? He already knows that information."

"Maybe no reason. I can't prove it but I feel it is harder for investors to move the goalpost later if you memorialize it in the follow up email. Let's say the market is a little softer when you hit the mark they gave you – or maybe the investor is just in a less generous mood – and the investor is tempted to ask for more traction before investing. If you have replied to the follow up email and lead with, 'When we spoke in February, you said to reach back out to you when we had 1,000 paying users (see below) ...', it is a bit harder for an investor to say, 'Actually, I changed my mind. Come back when you have 2,000.' They might anyway. We can be shameless schmucks that way. But on the margin, I think it helps, even if I can't prove it."

"I guess that makes sense and it can't hurt. After I reiterate the targets he cited and ask what his typical check size is, what else should I have asked that I can put in the follow up email?"

"You definitely want to ask for introductions to other investors in this case. Nothing complicated. A simple, 'Also, while I appreciate that we are a bit too early for you, any introductions you can make to investors who do invest at a slightly earlier stage and who would be interested in CallJar would be warmly appreciated' should do the trick."

"Just in this case? Why not always?"

"Let's play this out. Say I passed because I did not believe in the venture, whether I said that explicitly or not. It is in my strike zone thematically and stage-wise. You ask me for intros. How does that work? 'Hey Bob, I got a startup you might want to look at. What? No, I am not investing in it. But you might love it.' 'Gee, thanks Jason. Why am I so lucky?' See? Awkward."

"So the referral only works if CallJar is not in the investor's strike zone. 'Well, Bob, I considered it but you know I only invest post-revenue. But I am interested and tracking their progress.' That is a good referral."

"I guess that makes sense too. Plus, if they do introduce me to some earlier stage investors, that is a good sign, right? I mean, they would not put their reputation on the line and recommend that another investor look at us if they were not genuinely interested, would they? If I were really getting a soft no, I would guess that they would not want to make any introductions for me."

"Spot on. They would probably tell you that they will think about it, but then not offer up any names. But if they make a warm introduction to another investor, they are putting their street cred on the line and that is definitely a good sign."

"Sweet. I will get started on that email right away."

Key Takeaways

- Entrepreneurs need to prepare for and actively manage meetings with investors.
- Always starts by confirming the meeting length.
- Confirm / get a feel for the investor's level of familiarity with the startup's industry and (if relevant) level of technical expertise
- Allocate some time early in the meeting for establishing a good rapport ... but take care not to spend too much time chatting at the expense of discussing the startup.
- Some investors will listen to the founder walk through the pitch deck, others will more proactively ask questions. An entrepreneur should be comfortable jumping around their deck ... and even presented without the deck entirely.
- Investors may decline to invest stating that the startup is too early for them. While this can be the truth, it can also be a way for them to pass without actually saying no.
- To distinguish between genuinely too early and the "VC soft no", the entrepreneur should follow up by asking what traction would be sufficient. A definitive answer may mean that the startup is genuinely too early.
- Fear of Missing Out can motivate interested investors to move faster and potentially invest earlier. Investor FOMO may be triggered when another investor commits to invest, the startup wins important new clients or more generally is rapidly hitting revenue targets. Signing a big partnership can also trigger FOMO.
- Startups should add interested investors to a monthly newsletter so they can see the progress the startup is making.
- An investor who passes because the startup is objectively not in their strike zone (e.g., wrong industry or stage) can be a source for referrals to other, more suitable, investors so the entrepreneur should ask.
- An investor who passes despite the startup being otherwise suitable is not a good source of referrals.

Chapter 35

Portco Jujitsu

I am not sure why I am here but Jason's advice was, "At this stage of your startup, when in doubt, take the meeting." So here I am.

'Here' is the Knowify office. From their website, it looks like they make software for small contractors and subcontractors to manage their business better. From the screenshots, the software looked pretty slick. Thinking back on the renovations we did when we moved into our new apartment, I really wish the contractor we worked with had used Knowify. He sent us contracts with handwritten amendments on them, texted us or called us with important updates and changed orders that were never actually documented anywhere. I would not be surprised if he showed up at his accountant at the end of the year with a shopping bag full of receipts.

The reception area is nice. Not nearly as nice as the VC office but still very respectable. There is no one at the reception desk. For some reason, I get the impression that it has been a long time since anyone has sat there regularly. But the newspaper on the coffee table is up to date. I can see a little down the hall, through the glass wall, into one of the conference rooms. Nice table, large screen monitor on the wall, microphone speaker combo on the center of the table … pretty standard. The two guys in there are using the whiteboard on the other wall. Whatever they are discussing, it seems pretty intense.

"Welcome to Knowify, I am Marc," I hear from just over my shoulder. I jump a little bit. Not that I feel guilty about snooping or anything. I mean, the chair I am in is practically pointed straight at the conference room …

Marc is dressed in typical 'startup casual': decent jeans and a well-worn fleece with the company logo on it. His English is clear and correct but with a definite accent that I can't seem to place but which feels vaguely European.

"Nice to meet you, Marc."

DOI: 10.4324/9781003542612-38

"Same here. Ah, I see the conference room is taken. Let's go down to my office. We can swing by the break room to pick up some coffee if you would like."

Seems pleasant enough. The coffee is good, although the room does not seem as well stocked as I thought it would be.

As we head down the stairs, The decor gets … less. My poker face must not be what I thought it was because Marc notices.

"The dungeon is not as nice as the castle, eh?" Smiling, Marc continues. "We are subletting. The company upstairs raised a lot of money and took a five-year lease for two floors in anticipation of rapid growth. Things started to get bumpy for them and they put hiring on hold. But they were stuck with all this extra space that they could not get out of. So, we sublet some of their space. Naturally, they did not get around to furnishing this floor so we did it ourselves. We did not raise nearly as much money as they did – plus, I am cheap to begin with – so unlike upstairs, our rooms look more ah … 'rustic' than rich."

"At least the coffee is good."

"The coffee is in the sublease agreement. A man has to have priorities."

I like Marc already but I still have no clue why he asked me here. My poker face must be off today because Marc asks, "Have you figured out why I asked you here yet?"

Well that was uncanny.

Chuckling, Marc continues, "We are a New Seeds portfolio company. I had an update Zoom with David and he mentioned you."

"Really?"

"Yeah. All he said was, 'They are targeting subcontractors. Maybe you should talk to them.' I was not sure if you planted that seed – sorry, bad pun – in David's mind or if he came up with it on his own."

"First I am hearing about it."

"That's a shame. Asking a VC for an intro to one of his portfolio companies is a smart move. VCs are lazy. Or as they would say, 'swamped.' So David has no bandwidth to dig any deeper. But since he mentioned it to me, I have to talk to you and report back."

"Do you really have to?"

"Officially? No. Unofficially, if it takes 30 minutes to make a key investor happy …"

"I see."

"So now you get another shot on goal. If I tell him that I am impressed, he may dig in. If I think what you are doing is promising enough to test out a pilot, when the pilot is done, you get another shot on goal. Not that I am anything special. I am doing well enough that he trusts my opinion a bit and he owns enough of Knowify that he can ask for it for free.

"In fact, when I talk to an investor, I always check out their portfolio. If there is a match, I 'offer to help.' Even if the startup is defunct, the fund will often make the intro just to get another data point on me."

"That is brilliant."

"Well, I can't take credit. One of my early advisors and angel investors gave me the idea."

"Really? He is into construction tech and he has good ideas like that. Maybe I should speak to him. Who was the investor?"

"Jason Murath. Have you heard of him?"

Key Takeaways

- Meeting with other, ideally more mature, startups in your space is a good way to pick up useful information and advice and can lead to introductions (to investors, to customers, etc.) and partnerships.
- Investors sometimes ask their portfolio companies to meet with prospective investments to get another, informed opinion about that startup.
- Startups can take advantage of this dynamic by proactively asking investors for intros to their relevant portfolio companies.

Chapter 36

Dry Funds

Subject: Your call with Jason Murath 2023-12-21 04:07 p.m. (GMT+5)

From: noreply@CallJar.com

To: Marcus Williams

Thank you for our call a moment ago. This call today was important to me and I use a service called CallJar to transcribe my half of the conversation. Only my half of the conversation is recorded; for your privacy, nothing you said was recorded.

[Transcript begins]

Hi, Jason. I just got out of the meeting with HNM Capital.

I thought it went well right up until I asked your question. How did you know to tell me to ask when they had raised their last fund?

He said they did their final close about two and a half years ago. I followed up to ask if they had any dry powder available for new investments and he said that they were currently just making follow-on investments until they got to the first close on their next fund.

Well, if you knew they had no money, why did you let me take the meeting?

I guess that is fair. He did say that they have been raising their next fund for a while so I guess it was possible that they had managed to raise more money since the last time you spoke to them.

Yeah, it didn't hurt to practice either. Of course, had I known that they had no money, it would have been a heck of a lot less stressful. Why do they take these meetings if they can't invest?

That is kind of a dick move, taking meetings, wasting startups' time, all simply to make it look like they are still active.

Well, if they really do think they are getting close to a first close on their next fund and if so many of the startups they meet are just a little early, then I suppose it does make sense for them to keep taking meetings so that they are ready to write checks the moment they have money in the bank. But the more I learn about VC, the less charitable I feel.

So, what am I supposed to do? If they do not have money, I don't really feel like I need to spend a lot of time following up with them.

Sure, what's one more email address to add to the monthly investor updating mail I send out anyway?

[Transcript ends]

Key Takeaways

- Not all 'investors' actually have money to invest.
- VC funds typically raise funds in three-year cycles.
- It is entirely appropriate for entrepreneurs to ask a fund when they last raised capital and if they are still making new investments.
- If it has been over two years since the VC closed its most recent fund, they may not have much money left (viz., "dry powder") to make investments in new startups.
- Sometimes a fund that is out of money for initial investments but whose partners think that they will be raising a new fund soon will take meetings anyway so their pipeline of potential investments stays full.
- Dry funds may be a good source for finding other potential investors so it often pays to take the meeting anyway.

Chapter 37

Pay to Play Doesn't Pay

"How's your love life?"

"Been better, been worse."

Ritual observed, we clink beer mugs and each take a drink. Jackson was back in town to visit family over Christmas … so naturally we snuck away from both our families to catch up.

"Seriously Jax, any progress on that front? Last time we spoke, you said you were quitting the apps."

Jax looks a little tired. "Yeah, Marcus. The apps are pretty much all about hookups these days."

I shoulder Jax a bit to preempt a pity party. "I know. I have been living vicariously through you."

Apparently, I am only partly successful. "No, Marcus. I mean *all* about hookups. Even when I say in my profile that I am looking for something more serious, I end up going on a few dates, getting physical, and then it just fades out. Sometimes it is even a first date hookup and then I get ghosted. I know this will shock you a little bit but I am actually kind of beyond that right now."

"What's the verbal equivalent of the head exploding emoji?"

"Cute … not. But I do have an update for you."

"Are you going to make me drag it out of you?"

"I signed up for one of those executive matchmakers."

I channel my best Dr. Phil. "So how's that working for you?"

"Waste of $5,000. It started out well. I sat down with a real, live human being and talked to her about what I was looking for and what was important to me. It really felt like she was getting to know me and what I needed in much more depth than any of the apps. She immediately set me up on a couple of dates.

"On the plus side, the women I met were at least serious about potentially finding a real relationship. But that is about where the good news ended. Many

DOI: 10.4324/9781003542612-40

of them were a lot older than they claim to be – I do not mean a few years, I mean 'was that your niece in the photo?' older."

"Ouch."

"Yeah. Some of the others were awkward to the point of being on the spectrum. Don't get me wrong. Everyone deserves someone to love and I would not totally rule out someone" pausing briefly for the right words "neuro-atypical if we clicked. But man were those dates painful. I completely understand why they needed a matchmaker's help.

"The only normal, attractive woman I met told me that she was quitting the service because she met someone through a friend and it was looking like it might get serious."

"I am sorry it didn't work out. Do you think you just chose the wrong matchmaker?"

"That was my first thought but I have been thinking about it for a while now and I think the basic concept is flawed. If you, or better yet, Julia, introduce me to someone, then both the woman and I know that someone we both trust is vouching for the setup. Julia would not offer to make the setup unless she really thought there was a fit. A paid matchmaker will basically take anyone whose check clears. Even though they claim to be 'discriminating,' at the end of the day, their incentive is to get more clients. Maybe they weed out the truly unmatchable but it is not the same filter as someone putting her reputation on the line."

Something clicked. "I know exactly what you mean."

"Marcus, is there something going on between you and Julia that I should know about?"

"No, no. We are all fine. I am thinking about something that happened with the startup.

"I was approached by a group called Broad Network Ventures. They have the word 'ventures' in their company name so I assumed that they are investors. But they are not. They make introductions to investors on behalf of startups.

"They were asking for $5,000 a month retainer for them to open up their network and to let me pitch at their monthly events. They also wanted a 5% success fee if any of their introductions led to funding. They said they might take some or all of the success fee as equity rather than cash but I did not pursue it because something about it felt a little off."

"Because they are willing to pimp out any crappy startup whose check clears? You wondered how much their introductions are actually worth?"

"Exactly!

"Jason – the investor who has been coaching me – keeps telling me to get warm introductions, that cold emails are useless. I thought that was going to be a bit of a struggle but it turns out that startup investors are incredibly networked. They are generally pretty active on social media and have loads of connections on LinkedIn. It has actually been easier than I expected to find mutual connections to hit up for introductions. I don't know if this will still be true at later stages with corporate or family office investors – those guys keep really low profiles! – but at the early stage, it really is not so hard.

"In fact, now that I've tried it, stepping into an investor's shoes for a second, if someone came to me through a paid service rather than finding a warm intro, I guess I would wonder just how weak that founder's network was."

"Absolutely, Marcus, absolutely. It is basically the same thing that I tell the guys on my business development team. The kinds of mid- to senior-level decision makers we target live their lives with LinkedIn open in the background. Even though a well-timed cold call can sometimes work wonders, being able to name drop a few mutual connections at the start of a call can go a long way."

"Hmm ... I do have a handful of investors that I still have not been introduced to. Sometimes my connector tells me they have sent an introduction request along but have not heard back, sometimes I just have not heard back from the connectors I reached out to. Either way, I guess sending a cold email that name drops them right in the beginning is better than doing nothing."

"Makes sense ... But enough about you. We always talk about your startup. This time we are talking about me. And I just had an idea."

"Really? How's that feel? Does it hurt much?"

"In about five seconds I am going to do something to you with my beer mug and I'll be waiting outside the proctologist's office just waiting to ask you, 'does it hurt much?' "

"Okay, okay, Jax! I'll be good. I'll just shut up and drink my beer for a few minutes."

"I always knew you were a smart guy, Marcus. Now where was I ... Ah.

"You know that I am a pretty outgoing, social guy – I am probably not going to get along with a wallflower. The women I am likely to be attracted to probably are pretty active on Instagram. I am thinking that I should go through a few of my close friends' accounts and see if any of their friends look interesting."

"Uh, that might be a little ... stalker-ish. But if you talk to Julia first and explain what you have in mind, she might agree to go through her friend list with you. That might surface a potential match or two that she would not have otherwise thought of without the prompt."

"I can drink to that."

Key Takeaways

- There are brokers who offer to help startups raise money.
- Typically, the brokers charge the startups a small percent (~5%) of the amount raised. They may also charge a monthly retainer.
- Unlike warm introductions from mutual acquaintances who are implicitly endorsing the startup with their reputation, startup brokers are incentivized to take on any clients who are able to pay so there is no positive signal to their introductions.
- Also, the better entrepreneurs are able to network to investors themselves so it tends to be lower quality startups who use startup brokers at the early stages.
- Consequently, most investors view these startup brokers negatively.

Chapter 38

The Perils of Corporate Partnerships

Jason looks up from his phone. "Well, my 4:30 just canceled. It is a standing Zoom and he says he forgot to tell me that he was on vacation Christmas week. Got anything else you want to talk about today, Marcus?"

"Actually, yes. I got an email from someone at MojoSales. They are a relatively new CRM system going up against Salesforce. He said he had heard about CallJar and wanted to set up a call to 'explore potential partnership opportunities.' How do I play this?"

"The short answer is, take the call but do not get your hopes up just yet. Large companies and even midsize companies are still a heck of a lot larger than you are. They typically have people working on partnerships or corporate development. It is their job to go out and talk to as many other startups out there that might, possibly, maybe be useful to their company. They start a lot of conversations and only end up pursuing very few actual partnerships. The partnerships guy will start asking for a lot of information, may even ask if you have certain capabilities that they might want. The startup then gets really excited that they are talking to such a large company. They focus on the upside, on how the right deal with this corporate can basically put them on the map. They are not wrong, just overly optimistic. The problem is that the startup ends up putting a lot of time into the conversation, they might even adjust their development schedule to build features that they think will appeal to this potential corporate partner. But the corporate has no skin in that game. To them it is just talk, just exploring possibilities. If it sucks up one person's time for a few months, that is no big deal in the cosmic scheme of things ... to them, that is. For the startup on the other hand, who

DOI: 10.4324/9781003542612-41

doesn't have that much extra bandwidth to play with, every hour spent trying to close the big deal is an hour taken away from their original plan."

"So I should basically just ignore them? What if there really is the potential to make a game changing deal?"

"I am not saying ignore them. Just be really disciplined about how much time you are willing to put into these discussions. You have decided, for all the reasons we discussed months ago, to begin with a B2C strategy and to only pursue the B2B strategy after you have a decent chunk of traction. A deal with MojoSales could mean turning your strategy upside down. I would be very careful about putting too much time against this unless you have a fairly high confidence that a deal is going to go forward.

"Go ahead and talk. Understand what they are looking for. Get a sense of how important they think the functionality you bring to the table is to them. If they want you to spend any time customizing the product for them or building integrations that you would not otherwise need for any other customer, talk to me before committing to anything.

"What I will probably tell you to do is to price out that extra work as if it were a consulting assignment. Tell them you are a lean startup and all your dev resources are already committed to projects. You can tell him that you would love to proceed but you won't be able to put anyone on it for another six months … unless they want to sign an agreement where they pay you so you can hire the additional programmers that it would take to customize the product sooner rather than later. If they actually agree to pay for it, then there is a fighting chance that they are serious. But if they start to hem and haw and ask you to do a little bit of it for free just to be able to 'shop it around internally', I would recommend that you tell them that you just don't have the capacity right now and that you would be happy to revisit it in three to six months."

"Okay, I think I see the plan. One other wrinkle, though. They say they sometimes invest in startups who are strategic to them. Does that change anything?"

"Ah, corporate venture capital. CVCs are a slippery pig …"

"One of these days, I have to find out where you get these phrases."

"From friends who grew up in the south, of course. After all, the best expressions come from there. Or the military. Or both, come to think of it."

"So, tell me, o wise one, why is corporate venture a 'slippery pig?'"

"Because done correctly, it can be huge. But nine times out of ten, it is not done correctly and ends up being a huge wombat."

I know he is dying for me to ask. I am going to wait him out this time. Oh, what the heck. He seems so eager …

"Okay, I'll bite. What is a wombat?"

"A wombat is an Australian marsupial. Kind of cute actually. But here it stands for Waste Of Money, Brains And Time.

"Here is what makes corporate venture capital great: if they like what you do, they can get you pilots within the parent organization that can generate revenue.

Also, the fact that they have invested can be a strong signal to other investors and other potential customers that you are worth a look.

"The problem with CVCs are that it doesn't always work out that way. Often, they are in their own little corner of the organization, sometimes even geographically removed from the rest of the organization, and do not have the strong ties with the operating units that it takes to truly get pilots to happen. Also, they generally move pretty slowly. The ones that have good, high-level support also tend to have pretty heavy oversight. Imagine trying to get time on the calendar of a CFO of a Fortune 100 company to get permission to make a $1 million investment. He or she says they are committed to innovation but just has so many other deals on his or her plate and most of those deals have two or three more zeros attached to them. So, the corporate venture fund has to wait weeks for that meeting before they can pull the trigger. What's more, because of the corporate BS and because of how the funds are often structured, the investors at a CVC generally do not get the same kind of payoff as a partner at a regular venture fund. So, the economics for them are a lot worse, which means that the people running the corporate venture fund tend not to be the A players. Not always, of course. I know some really good corporate venture funds run by superstars but they are the exception rather than the rule."

"So, what does that mean here? I should ignore corporate venture funds altogether?"

"No, not at all. All other things equal, the fact that MojoSales does make investments in startups is a plus. First, find out if the person you are speaking to is involved in the venture fund or only on the business side. As part of your conversation with him, ask him how the venture fund works with the business units. Maybe even ask for a couple of successful examples where they both piloted and made investments so you truly understand the level of coordination between the units and how things play out in an ideal scenario. Sometimes, the funds won't invest until there is a business unit sponsor that is engaging with the startup. Other times, the fund will invest first and then look for business units who can benefit from the startup. You want to understand that dynamic.

"Either way, it is worth trying to get an introduction to someone at the corporate venture fund to get a sense of what prior investments they have made and how those played out. Did they invest before the business unit piloted the startups software or vice versa? How are things going with those startups? Will they introduce you to those startups so you can discuss the experience from their perspective? You get the idea.

"If you can get the CVC to invest upfront, in advance of any engagement with the business, that is probably the least disruptive for you at this point. Then you can leave it in their court to sell you to the business units before you make any meaningful investment in customizing your product to meet their needs."

"Sounds like a plan."

Key Takeaways

- Some large companies have employees whose jobs it is to look for new startups that might be useful to the larger company.
- Sometimes the large companies also invest in startups, either directly or through a corporate venture fund that the company has set up.
- These potential partnerships can be a big opportunity for a startup ... but can also be a dangerous distraction.
- Large companies can afford to talk to many startups even if very few of those conversations result in a partnership.
- Startups have limited time and resources. Whatever they do comes at the expense of the startup's original plan. So, it is critically important for the startup not to misread the level of interest and allocate too much time to pursue a partnership that may not come to fruition.
- There are ways a startup can safely engage with a much larger company and not devote too many resources to the discussion until it is confident that the partnership is likely to happen.

Chapter 39

Monthly Update Emails for Fun and FOMO

Subject: Example>> xxx Investor update Apr 2023

From: Jason Murath

To: Marcus Williams

Marcus,

Thanks for sending me your latest investor update email. I would like to say it is a good first attempt. Only it kind of sucked. Really badly, actually.

Sorry. But it is true. Fortunately, you sent it on the afternoon of December 29 and there isn't an investor on the planet who is paying any attention right now. Don't sweat it, though. We will make January's update email great.

The thing to keep in mind when you are writing an investor update email – writing pretty much any kind of email you are sending, actually – is this: What do I need to tell the recipient of this email in order to get them to do what I would like them to do?

Since you are fundraising right now, your primary goal is to get one of these investors to decide that you are the kind of startup they want to invest in right now. They will almost always want to see signs of progress. Sales are ideal but a major new partnership signed might move the needle for them. You might also put in a new key hire if that person is especially strategic. As you

DOI: 10.4324/9781003542612-42

are starting to get some commitments, showing that the round is starting to fill up could also create some FOMO.

I have forwarded an email below from one of my other founders who writes a really good investor update email.

(I have taken out the name, the numbers, and cut short other specific details in each paragraph for confidentiality.)

I especially like how the key points are all bulleted up front so an investor who is short on time can just read the top few bullets. I also like how each bullet gets its own, clearly marked, paragraph later so if I only really care about one or two of the points, I can jump right down to those details.

Notice also how they include an Ask. Even prospective investors want to help. They often like to pay it forward so that when and if you do get to the point where they want to invest, you will remember what they have done for you and will take their money instead of another investor's. When you are actively fundraising, introductions to other investors is going to be your main ask. Introductions to customers, or in your case, to organizations or other channel partners who can get you in front of large numbers of busy, on-the-go professionals is always a good ask. You may also need to make key hires and you can ask your investors if they know anyone who fits the description. The same goes for introductions to subject matter experts who you might want to meet.

Without further ado, see below.

Yours,
Jason
---------- FORWARDED MESSAGE ---------

Subject: xxx Investor update Apr 2023

Dear Investors,

Here's the latest monthly update. Please feel free to reach out to me directly if you have any questions, suggestions, introductions, etc.

Xxx by the numbers:

- Traction: $$$ ARR run rate (up from $$$ at the end of 2022)
- Traction: Key new customers: XXX …
- Series A: $$$ committed ($$$ target raise)
- Product: QuickBooks integration launched
- Small setback: XXX let go
- Ask: investors, investors, investors

Details and commentary:

Traction

Q1 2023 was good to XXX. Our sales team closed a number of large new customers including XXX, XXX, and XXX resulting in us ending the quarter with a $$$ ARR run rate. This compares to $$$ coming out of Q4 2022 and $$$ ARR at the end Q1 last year. We have also closed a number of smaller customers and continue to experience no meaningful churn.

Fundraising

While the current fundraising environment is not as frothy as it was last year, we continue to get meetings with prospective investors. Of the $$$ we are targeting for our Series A we have $$$ in hard commitments from existing investors. Additionally, XXX has soft committed to investing $$$ once we get a lead investor to set the valuation in this round.

Product

We have finally completed the QuickBooks integration that we have talked about in prior update emails. This will make it considerably easier for us to onboard XXXXXX

The next modules we hope to roll out are XXXXXX

Challenges

Unfortunately, we had to let XXX go earlier this month. As we discussed, we hired XXX in August as SVP of sales in order to put more structure around our sales processes to prepare us to scale the sales team rapidly once we have raised our next round. Unfortunately XXXXXX

Asks

While we always welcome introductions to potential customers and are actively recruiting a new SVP of sales, what we need most now are introductions to institutional investors who can lead our Series A. In addition to funds who focus on our industry, we think industry agnostic VC funds who focus on vertical SaaS solutions and/or marketplaces could also be good leads or co-leads for this round. Even if you do not have a direct connection to the fund, please let us know if you have anybody in mind so we can look to see if we have other potential warm introductions to that investor.

Key Takeaways

- Startups should send out monthly investor update emails while they are actively fundraising.
- These emails should highlight the startup's progress ... and hopefully entice an investor to invest.
- Even potential investors like to be helpful ("pay it forward") so an update email can also include a request (e.g., to potential investors, customers, subject matter experts, new hires, etc.).

Part IV

Sealing the Deal

Congratulations! You have a funding offer from an investor. Don't drop the ball just yards away from the endzone. Here's how to make sure you are getting the best deal possible for your startup.

DOI: 10.4324/9781003542612-43

Chapter 40

Notes, Safes, Priced Rounds

"… and then he said he does not do notes or safes. I told him that was okay. Was it okay, Jason?"

"Don't sweat it. You stumbled onto the right answer, Marcus, even if by the look on your face you have no idea what any of those things are."

"Well, I have heard of them …"

"Nah, it is my fault. I am like the parent of a 16-year-old who should have had the birds and bees chat years ago."

"I don't think anyone calls it the birds and bees chat anymore."

"Details. Moving on … Either way, I should have walked you through Notes, SAFEs and priced rounds before you went out to your first investor meeting. My bad. Sit back, get comfortable, and get educated.

"Your basic, vanilla fundraise is called a 'priced round'. What that means is that an investor is giving you money in exchange for a fixed number of shares. The investor will tell you what he thinks your company is worth right now. That's the 'pre-money valuation.' Assuming you accept that valuation, you use that number to calculate the price per share and then you use the share price to figure out how many new shares your startup needs to give the investor for his, say, $2 million investment. That investment plus the pre-money is what your company is worth after the round closes. Since we investors are super creative, we call that your 'post-money valuation.' There can be 101 wrinkles and complications but that is it in a nutshell. Makes sense?"

"So far."

Jason leans over and without quite getting up scrawls something that, with a little imagination, might read as "Convertible Notes" on the marker board.

DOI: 10.4324/9781003542612-44

"Okay, here is where it gets complicated. How did they teach you to value a business in school?"

"Uh, discounted cash flow?"

"Which is …?"

"You take the company's expected revenue over time, subtract the costs, look at the bottom line over the next 20 or 30 years and then use a slightly complicated formula with the interest rate to correct for the fact that money you get in ten years is worth less to you than money in hand right now."

"Bingo. Don't get cocky. That was just the setup. How do you value a company using discounted cash flow if the company has no revenue? Or maybe it has a little revenue but you expect revenue to grow by leaps and bounds over the next couple of years. How do you come up with a 30-year forecast based on that?"

"Good question. Whenever we did it in school, I think we just assumed that revenue grew 5 or 10% a year. But that is not really realistic for a startup. How do VCs do it?"

"If the startup is reasonably far along, they might try to do a discounted cash flow analysis. Or they might just forecast out revenue until they think the growth will start leveling off. Then they look at what publicly traded companies in the same space are valued at. Then they calculate what multiple of revenue that valuation is and apply that same multiple to the startup's future revenue to figure out what expected exit value is.

"Unfortunately, the earlier the startup is, the more guesswork is evolved. At some point, it is all pretty much just make believe. Fortunately, at the early stage, valuation does not really matter all that much. If you got into Google's seed round, it did not matter if the valuation you invested at was $5 million or $10 million. Either way you made buckets of cash.

"The dirty little secret is that experienced investors have a rough idea what a seed or Series A startup is valued at in general. They might bump it up a bit for a specific startup if something about the startup is especially awesome or if they are in a bidding war for that startup with another fund. Market conditions also factor in. In a tough fundraising market, investors may low-ball startups. In a hot market, they pay more. In a very frothy market, some of the more experienced investors will pass altogether rather than overpay. That takes a lot of discipline and most of us are FOMO-driven lemmings so …" Jason shrugs and then continues, "But it is not really a precise calculation at all for the most part.

"That said, there is an alternative to guessing and that's why God created …" Jason taps on the words Convertible Notes "… these."

(I am going to let that one pass.)

"Convertible Notes are basically a way to kick the can down the road a little bit. It is a way to admit that we do not really know what the startup is worth right now and we are going to wait until the startup raises another round and, presumably, is further along and has generated more revenue. Then we use that new round's valuation to retroactively come up with the valuation for the earlier round. Here is how it works in practice:

"Let's say that an investor gives the startup money in its Seed round. This money is technically a loan. That is the 'Note' part of Convertible Note. Like all loans, it has a duration – usually 18 months to two years – and earns some small amount of interest. If nothing else happens, when the Note comes due, the startup has to pay the investor back with interest.

"That almost never happens. The goal is for the startup to make progress and raise a Series A round in the not-too-distant future. Presumably, the Series A is a priced round and that gives the startup a valuation. When that happens, the money that the investors loaned the startup turns into shares. That is the 'Convertible' part of Convertible Note."

"So, the Seed investors end up retroactively buying shares at the same share price as the Series A investors?"

"In theory. That would mean that the Convertible Note was uncapped and had no discount. A really hot startup might get that or really stupid – sorry 'unsophisticated' – investors might agree to that. But most Convertible Notes have a discount and a cap."

"That is starting to sound familiar."

"It should sound familiar. When I invested in CallJar it was with a Convertible Note with a 20% discount and a $4 million cap."

"I know it is a little late to be asking this, but is that good?"

"For me it is. You got royally screwed." Jason bursts out laughing, "If only you could see the look on your face right now …

"No, you actually got a pretty good deal. Discounts are typically 20–25% and a cap on a pre-launch startup could be as low as $2 million or less. But if this works, the upside is so big that it was not worth nickel and diming you. I didn't want you to look back when you were older and wiser and feel like I had taken advantage of you."

"Well, that is a relief. Maybe you can walk me through exactly what a 20% discount and a $4 million cap mean?"

"I thought you would never ask. Let's start with the discount.

"Ever worked on a project for weeks, run the ball down most of the field, then have someone new added to the team who helps you get the last ten yards to the endzone … and then gets equal credit for the goal?"

"God, I hate that."

"So do angels. If I believed in you enough to give you money before you even have a working product and then someone new invests a year or two years later when you have customers and revenue, why should they get to invest at the valuation?"

"They shouldn't. You took more risk, your money was tied up longer."

"Exactly! But at the same time, I do not know how to, or at least I may not want to, put a valuation on your company. So how do I peg my valuation to the future investment without screwing myself? I bake in a discount.

"If my Convertible Note has a 25% discount and the next investor comes in and invests in your company at a $10 million pre-money, my Note will convert at a $7.5 million valuation. We take the amount I lent you under the Note plus interest and divide it by the price per share based on that $7.5 million valuation and that's how many shares I get. Easy peasy, right?"

"Sounds pretty straightforward."

"Most of the time it is. Next scenario: what happens if the startup I invested in really blows the door off the hinges? What if they are able to take the small check I gave them and start generating a lot of revenue. Then, when they want to raise their next round, they get a $100 million pre-money. Is it fair that I only got a 25% return on that initial investment? I picked a huge winner. Shouldn't I get a much bigger payout?"

"Well, when you put it that way, I guess not. You should get something more if you are the first money into a huge success."

"Exactly! And that is where the cap comes in. Many Convertible Notes will also have a cap on the valuation for just that situation. So, in addition to the 25% discount on the Convertible Note I just mentioned, I might also have a $20 million cap. In the example I gave before where the next investor comes in at a $10 million pre-money, the cap is irrelevant. But in the second example where the company hits it out of the park, the cap comes into play and, instead of my investment retroactively coming in at a $75 million valuation, it comes in at the $20 million valuation set by the cap. Instead of a measly 25% return on a stellar pick, I get a 5X return.

"To be honest, it is a little schizophrenic. 'I do not know how to set a valuation so I am going to use a Convertible Note … but I do not think you are worth that much so I also want a cap.' It is a bit of trying to have it both ways but it generally works. My philosophy is, the cap bridges the gap between what the founder thinks the company is worth and the investor's skepticism. If the company does do as well as the founder expects, the founder gets the valuation he or she wanted because of the cap. If the startup does well but not quite that well, the investor gets the lower valuation that he or she suspected was more accurate."

"That is it?"

"There are sometimes more nuances but usually, yes. Convertible Notes are pretty vanilla."

"So, what's a SAFE?"

"Same, same but different."

"I am pretty sure that spells out SSBD, not SAFE."

"A SAFE is a Simple Agreement for Future Equity. It basically acts the same as a Convertible Note, pegging the valuation of an early round to the valuation in the next round, complete with discounts and caps, just like Convertible Notes. In my not so humble opinion …"

"Jason, I don't think you have had a humble opinion in over a decade."

"Details. Now hush up, I am on a roll. Where was I …?

"Oh, yeah. SAFEs. So the one theoretical downside of a Convertible Note is that it is actually debt. If the startup can't pay off the loan when the Note matures, in very theoretical theory, the investor could force the company into bankruptcy."

"But only in theory?"

"If the startup has not raised a new round, one of two things is happening. The first is that it is taking off like a rocket ship and does not need to raise money. In that case, it can pay off the loan with interest and does not have to give up any equity. As an investor, I am not thrilled with that outcome but it is a risk I can take … especially since it virtually never happens. This is one reason some investors won't ever do Convertible Notes.

"The second and overwhelmingly more likely scenario is that the startup is failing. In that case, I have zero interest in forcing the startup into bankruptcy. If the founders are willing to keep trying to turn it around, why would I stop them? I know the founders are afraid that an investor would take advantage of momentary weakness to force them out and take over the company but honestly, I have got dozens of active investments at any one point in time and I have a life beyond angel investing. If I wanted to run a startup, I would found one myself. I have absolutely zero interest in taking over a startup that is failing to get traction. I have much better uses for my time."

"So, all the horror stories about investors forcing founders out of their company are urban legends?"

"Hell no! That definitely happens. I have had to do it a few times myself. Those are completely different situations. That happens when you have a startup with good early traction and a reasonable chance of success that has outgrown the founder's skill set. If the founder cannot grow with the company, he or she is just holding it back. If that goes on too long, the competition catches up and the startup fails. Replacing a founder is an absolute last resort and most investors err on the side of giving the founder time to grow into the new role. Looking back on every time I have had to replace a founder, I wish I had moved faster every single time. The number of times we switched jockeys too late and the horse lost the race far, far outnumbers the times founders were able to up their game.

"But that is a totally different situation from when a Convertible Note reaches its term and the startup cannot pay off the loan. That is usually a failing startup, one where the basic concept did not prove out. If they do not even have product market fit, it is pretty rare that any other founder would be able to do anything with the startup anyway."

"So, if investors do not really use a Convertible Note to take over a company that is running short on money, why do we need a SAFE?"

"To be honest, I am not really sure but maybe it does not matter if the fear is justified or not. All that matters is that founders are afraid of the scenario. So, when Y Combinator created SAFEs in 2013 ..."

"What? God did not create SAFEs too?"

"Silence blasphemer! God would never involve himself in something so trivial! But I digress ...

"So when Y Combinator created SAFEs, they became a popular option for founders because they are not loans and they do not have a fixed maturity date and they don't accrue interest. It is not even theoretically possible for an investor to take over the startup in this situation. And if the top accelerator in the world starts doing it, the other accelerators and angel investors have to seriously consider offering it as well. Since SAFEs and Notes basically act the same, an investor does not really care that much which of the two instruments he or she uses.

"Basically, you can treat them as roughly the same and focus on the discount, cap, and other terms rather than which instrument you use."

Key Takeaways

- Early-stage investments are typically structured as Convertible Notes, SAFEs, or priced rounds.
- Priced rounds are conceptually simplest. The investor and the founders agree on a valuation for the startup and use that to calculate a price per share. The startup then issues shares to the investor at that price.
- Coming up with a precise valuation for very early-stage startups is difficult so investors often use Convertible Notes and SAFEs to invest while deferring coming up with the startup's valuation until later.
- Convertible Notes are essentially debt that becomes equity when the startup raises its next round of financing.
- The valuation used to convert a Convertible Notes to equity is typically the valuation of the next round, less a discount, subject to a maximum valuation called a "cap."
- Because Convertible Notes are debt, if the startup is unable to pay it back the investors could force the startup into bankruptcy. For practical reasons, it is generally not in their interests to do so.
- SAFEs function much like Convertible Notes but are a contractual agreement to receive equity at a later date.
- Since SAFEs are not debt, there is no way investors can use them to force a startup into bankruptcy.

Chapter 41

Terms of Endearment

Subject: Call between Jason Murath & Marcus Williams 2024-01-23 5:17 p.m. (GMT+5)

From: noreply@CallJar.com

To: Marcus Williams; Jason Murath

Calls between two CallJar subscribers who opt to automatically share conversations are transcribed and merged. We have done our best to format the conversation accurately but errors occur, especially when parties to a conversation talk at the same time.

[Transcript begins]

MW: Jason, great news! I just got a term sheet.
JM: Congratulations. That must feel pretty good. Send me the term sheet when you have a chance and I will give it a once-over.
MW: Yes, I will forward it on to you as soon as we're off this call.
JM: (inaudible) You know you do not have to do that repeating what I say thing now that we're both using the app. You'll have my half of the conversation as well. How long do you have to respond?
MW: Hold on, I will check.
MW: It says I have one week to sign or that the offer expires.
JM: Ask them for three weeks. Tell them that you are very excited and would like to move forward with that but that

	your lawyer is on a family vacation for the next week and a half.
MW:	Why?
JM:	Remember how we talked about how fundraising is a sprint, not a marathon? Why did I say you need to sprint?
MW:	Because we want to get multiple term sheets at the same time so we have a little leverage.
JM:	Exactly. And how many term sheets do you have right now?
RW,	Uh, one.
JM:	And how many more do you think you can get in just one week?
MW:	Okay, I see where this is going. The odds of another term coming in over the next week is much lower than the ones of getting one over the next three weeks.
JM:	Exactly! Plus, we are not going to just wait passively and see what happens. You have a term sheet in hand. Now is the time to use that to create FOMO. How many investors have you spoken with at least once who are still quote thinking about it unquote?
MW:	Six, although I am pretty sure that one of them is out of dry powder and just meeting with startups to look like they are still in the market while trying to raise their next fund.
JM:	Gotcha. So here is the plan. You are going to call, not email, each of those five funds. Heck, call the sixth fund too. Won't take you much time and you never know. Tell them that you are excited to share with them that you have a term sheet in hand. The terms are good but you really enjoyed your conversation with insert fund name here and that, all other things equal, you would prefer to have their money because insert plausible reason based on something that that fund arguably does better. For example, if the fund you are emailing has been around awhile, you tell them that you prefer a lead investor with more experience. If the fund is focused on or has a lot of prior investments in startups doing something with speech recognition, tell them that you want someone with deep domain knowledge. Then end with unfortunately the term sheet expires soon so you are calling to see if they are still interested. That is short enough that you can leave it as a voicemail and send a follow up email if you don't catch them live.
MW:	Okay, I can do that ASAP. Do I tell them what the terms are?

JM: If this were a job offer, would you tell the other companies you were interviewing with what your offer was and who it was from?

MW: I see your point. No, I wouldn't tell them the offer because I want the other guys to make their own offers and don't want them to just match or slightly beat the one I have in hand. If they come in low and I prefer them if only they match the other company, I might reveal that offer at the final stages of the negotiation but definitely not right away. Do I tell them who the fund is? It is a pretty reputable one for what that is worth.

JM: Would you tell the other companies who the offer was from?

MW: Hmm. That is a tougher one. I might be a little worried that word would get back to my current employer and they would try to sabotage the offer but I do not think that applies here.

JM: Probably not. But the VC world is actually pretty small, especially for the funds that specialize in the same sectors. There is a very good chance that the other six investors you have in the pipeline know someone at the fund who just gave you a term sheet. They might pick up the phone and try to get a sense of what the offer is from the other VC. Often, the lead investor does not take the entire round so they might invite the second VC to offer to take the rest of the round on the same terms rather than bid up the terms the way you want things to play out. So if they ask who the term sheet is from or what the terms are, just say that you are bound by confidentiality.

MW: Okay, will do.

[Transcript ends]

Key Takeaways

- Once a startup receives a term sheet, it should use that term sheet to prod other interested investors to come to a decision.
- Most investors will issue a term sheet with a tight timeframe for the startup to respond or lose the offer.
- There are ways a startup can attempt to extend the deadline.

Chapter 42

Beyond Valuation

"Thanks, Jason, for making time on such short notice but I have these three, very different term sheets to look over and I figured it would be easier just to print out the term sheets and look at them side-by-side."

"Paper? Okay boomer."

Did I just get okay boomered by a guy who grew up on black and white TV?

"Relax, Marcus. I'm kidding. Sometimes the simpler tool is the better tool for the job. First of all, congrats. Most startups fail to get even a single term sheet and you have three to play with. Let's see what we have here …

"Interesting. You got one of each: a Convertible Note, SAFE, and a priced round. Let's look at the Note first.

"Atlatl Ventures is offering to lead this round by investing $300,000 of the $500,000. That is fair.

"A $5 million cap feels right in this market given that you have your beta ready but are pre-revenue. Maybe even a bit generous.

"10% interest is high but interest rates in general are three to four points higher ever since COVID so that is not too crazy. Plus, for a startup that will take off or bust, it really does not matter all that much in the cosmic scheme of things.

"Eighteen month maturity is spot on the market … no prepayment too …"

"Why no prepayment? I can pay my mortgage and car loans off early."

"Because the bank wants you to pay off the loan eventually; investors want the Note to convert to equity. The whole idea is that you will raise more money before the Note matures and that will trigger a conversion."

"Ah."

"Moving right along … $1 million for a qualified financing is normal. A qualified financing is the minimum amount of money you need to raise in the next round to trigger the Note to convert to equity. The idea is that if you take out a $25,000 loan, that does not affect the Note. It has to be a 'real' financing."

 DOI: 10.4324/9781003542612-46

"I see."

"20% discount on the conversion is completely fair. Oh, this is interesting. If there is a change of control – typically you selling the company – they get a choice. They can either be paid the greater of the Note plus interest OR 2X the face value of the Note OR they can have the Note convert into equity at the cap and then get paid out that way. That is a little non-standard but they just want to protect themselves. If you flounder and there is a fire sale, they get their 2X. Say it takes three years before that happens, that is a 26% IRR. Pretty good downside protection … unless the startup sells for less than that amount or even shuts down entirely, both entirely plausible outcomes. On the other hand, if you take off like a rocket ship, they get the upside. You can live with this. If the startup is not doing well, you are not walking away with much any way you slice it.

"They can also trigger conversion to equity at the cap if you have not yet raised a qualified financing and cannot pay them back with interest. Less common but far from unusual. Most of the time, if you cannot pay the investors back, they prefer to remain a Noteholder because debt gets paid off first in case of a bankruptcy but some investors like to have the option to convert.

"All in all, pretty reasonable Note. Let's take a look at the SAFE …

"Gearing Capital is willing to lead with $250,000 of the $500,000. Also fair.

"The SAFE also has a $5 million cap but that cap is a post-money cap so that is really the equivalent of a $4,500,000 pre-money cap. Eh, slightly worse but not really a big deal.

"Same 20% discount rate so that is a wash. Since it is a SAFE, there is no interest so that is slightly better than the Convertible Note. Very slightly better. The interest is basically rounding error. Nor is there a fixed maturity. It just keeps going as we discussed before so no need for any 'what if you can't pay it back' arrangements.

"Same $1 million qualified financing trigger for conversion so no surprises there and it just converts to equity if there's a change of control. No 2X return if the purchase price is low but if that is the outcome, you are probably going to walk away with a zero anyway.

"Yeah, this one is pretty clean too. The cap is ever so slightly less rich but if you feel strongly about not having to worry about potentially being forced into bankruptcy, you could go with the SAFE instead of the Note. Fielder's choice.

"Now let's take a look at the priced round.

"Rah Partners willing to take the whole $500,000 and a $7 million pre-money valuation is a nice improvement. Not only is it higher than either of the other caps, you get it no matter what, even if your next round is a down-round. Nice.

"Wait. Things are getting a bit funky here. They want 2X liquidation preference. Hmm …"

"Is that bad?"

"It's not ideal. Usually in a plain vanilla price round you get 1X liquidation preference. What that means is, if there is an exit, the investors get their investment back before the rest of the proceeds are split among the investors. If it is not a very good sale, that preference can be larger than they would get simply for the percentage of the company that they own. And if they are getting their money first, that means the founders get their money after the investors. When the purchase price is low, the founders get less or even no money because the investors need to be paid first. Obviously, the higher the liquidation preference, that bigger risk that is. If you have a nice, big exit, it is all academic. But it can bite you if the exit is smaller.

"It's unusual to see this in a Seed or Series A round. It gets a little bit more common later on when you are getting more private equity style investors who want to protect themselves against different outcomes. But early stage tends to be either a big win or a total loss so this kind of thing is unusual.

"But let's move on. Let's see ... Uh uh. Full ratchet anti-dilution protection. Now that is just evil."

"Jason, I am nodding along as if I have any idea what you mean."

"Okay, buckle up. This one's a little complicated. If all goes well, each time you go to raise another round, the valuation goes up. If the first round is at $1 per share, then the second round is at $3 a share. When that happens, everything is peachy keen. But what happens if you hit a rough patch the next investor is willing to invest, but only at $0.80 per share? No, don't answer that. That was a rhetorical question. When that happens, it is called a 'down-round' because, duh, the valuation went down. But the big problem is that anyone who was invested previously, including the founders who have common shares – you can think of them as the original investors who bought their shares with sweat – get squeezed. Whenever a new investor invests, the company issues new shares so the existing investors are diluted. Now that is okay in an up-round because even though you have a smaller percentage of the company, the value of the shares you have went up. So net net you are happy. But in a down-round, you get all the dilution of issuing new shares for the new investors and on top of it the value of the shares you already have go down."

"I see. That does sound pretty unpleasant."

"Yeah, things can get nasty when down-rounds happen. So that is why investors will sometimes ask for protection against a down-round. The way full ratchet anti-dilution protection works is that an investor will say, 'If you miss your mark and there is a down-round, I need you to make me whole by giving me more shares.' That way, even though the value of the shares that the investor owns has just gone down, you are giving them enough new shares that the total value of their investment stays the same. So, the startup has to issue new shares for the new investor and then issue even more new shares to make the prior investor whole. That means even more dilution for the founder. Again, if things go well and you just raise up-rounds, this is all academic. But if you stumble at all and have a down-round, you could end up with a very small percentage of the company when the dust settles.

"There is a lot more here about governance provisions, option pools, yada, yada, yada but I am not going to go into any of that because the deal is already bad enough as it is. Even if everything else is kosher, I would not go with this one, not when you have other options."

"So, I should just turn this one down and go with one of the other two?"

"Yes, but not yet. We are going to see if we can use their offer to make one of the other guys work a little harder.

"Normally, I would have done it the other way around as well. The valuation on the priced round term sheet is much better and when you have other term sheets it is sometimes easier to go back to the higher bidder and say that you want to go with them but the other offers have 'cleaner terms.' Often the higher bidder will drop the annoying terms. If it were just one or two things, that would be the way to go but these guys feel predatory to me. It feels like they are trying to see how much they can take advantage of your ignorance. Most early-stage investors are not trying to take advantage of the founders they invest in you. They do not mind leaving a little money on the table to keep the founders happy because that will help them get other startups to take their money. Or at least the reverse is true; once you have a reputation for screwing founders, the best startups do not even want to talk with you. So even if you push back and get a clean offer from these guys, I get the vibe that they are always going to be trying to take advantage of you one way or another. You are going to be tied to these investors for five to ten plus years. It's your company so you can do what you want but I would not get into bed with these guys."

"But you told me not to turn them down right away?"

"Because you can still use their offer. The same way you used the first term sheet you got to get two more funds to get off the fence, you are going to use this to see if you can get a better deal from either of the other two guys.

"You are going to call the two funds the same way you called them last time and tell them something along the lines of, 'Hey, I am really excited to get the offer from you and I really want to move forward with you. But I have received two other term sheets with terms that are better than the ones you offered me. I would really like to move forward with you guys because …' and fill in the blank with whatever reason you gave them in the first place about how they are more awesome than the other funds you are talking to. Best thing you could do is to talk to them live and see if they are willing to improve their offer. Use your judgment about if and when you want to actually reveal that the price round was valued at $7 million. Personally, I would hold on to that card just a little bit to see how high their counter offer will be without giving them a target to shoot for. My guess is they won't go above $7 million on the first counter offer – if they ever do – but you never know. If they come back at $6 million, you can always show your cards at that point and see if they will match it and make this an 'easy decision' for you. Just be careful to leave the door open for you to come back and take their offer even though it is lower than the third one. Most VCs have healthy enough egos that if you tell them that you are taking their offer even though it is not the best offer financially but because you value the other things they can bring to the table, they will probably believe you.

"Make both of these calls right away. Remember, you are trying to get both pots of water to come to a boil at the same time."

"I am already getting my phone out."

Key Takeaways

- There is more to a term sheet than valuation.
- Some investors may offer a startup a good valuation but include other terms that make their offers less attractive than other, lower-valuation offers.
- Some terms are essentially attempts to take advantage of unsophisticated and unsuspecting founders.
- An experienced adviser (or lawyer who specializes in startup funding) can tell a startup what is typical ("market") vs. non-standard but acceptable vs. predatory.
- With multiple term sheets in hand, a startup can (gently!) play the offers off each other to get the best deal.

Chapter 43

Sealing the Deal

Subject: Got a better offer

From: Marcus Williams

To: Jason Murath

Just got off the phone with Atlatl (the Convertible Note fund) and they upped the cap to $6 million. They would not go any higher nor drop the 2x return floor, even after I told them that the other fund was offering a $7 million pre-money. I think they caught on that I didn't really want to take that offer. Maybe if I played it a little better they might have gone higher. Maybe not. I guess we will never know.

As I mentioned yesterday, Gearing (the SAFE guys) upped their cap to $6 million too and changed it to a pre-money cap so that puts both offers basically on par. Having the extra protection of a SAFE instead of a Convertible Note (for what it might be worth) and not having the 2x return floor are nice but not such a big deal IMHO. If I thought that one of the funds could add more value or had a better "name brand," I would just go with the better fund. But I think both funds are good and can help in different but equally valuable ways so I am going to sign Gearing's term sheet.

(Yes, I ran the SAFE by the lawyer you recommended just to be – no pun – safe and he said that it was "plain jane" and that if

DOI: 10.4324/9781003542612-47

I wanted to sign it, I "had his blessing." Is no one you work with entirely normal?)

Sincerely,
Marcus

Subject: RE: Got a better offer

From: Jason Murath

To: Marcus Williams

Mazal tov. You officially have a lead investor.

Right after you sign with Gearing, call Atlatl (see? I remember who's who), tell them "it was a tough decision yada yada yada" and ask them if they are interested in taking the rest of the round. The terms are close enough and, since Gearing is leading with $250,000, that leaves $250,000 for Atlatl, not that much less than the $300,000 they wanted to lead with. Cross your fingers because if they say yes, your work is done.

If they pass, we will email all the other investors you spoke with, give them the good news, and see who bites. Hopefully, we can get one or two of them to fill out the rest of the round but if we need to grind the rest out with small checks from five or ten angels or small funds who could not lead the round, so be it.

Yours,
Jason

Key Takeaways

■ The lead investor may not finance the entire round.
■ Once a term sheet is signed, the startup has a set period of time to raise the rest of the money.
■ While the lead startup will likely help, this is the startup's responsibility.
■ Other investors who offered term sheets are likely prospects, followed by other investors who showed interest but did not offer to lead the round.
■ All other things equal, it is nice to fill the round with a few, large checks but it may be necessary to raise the rest from several, smaller investors.
■ Many angels and small funds cannot write checks large enough to lead a round but make good prospects for the remainder of the round.

Chapter 44

Money in the Bank

Subject: Money money money

From: Marcus Williams

To: Jason Murath

Good news: I just checked the bank account and the last of the money cleared!

The round is officially closed.

Thanks again for all your help ... and for all the help yet to come.

Sincerely,
Marcus

Subject: RE: Money money money

From: Jason Murath

To: Marcus Williams

Congrats, kid. Couldn't have happened to a nicer guy.

Now get the f*** back to work.

Yours,
Jason

 DOI: 10.4324/9781003542612-48

For Product Safety Concerns and Information please contact our EU
representative GPSR@taylorandfrancis.com
Taylor & Francis Verlag GmbH, Kaufingerstraße 24, 80331 München, Germany

www.ingramcontent.com/pod-product-compliance
Lightning Source LLC
Chambersburg PA
CBHW052111230326
41599CB00055B/5546

9 781032 883540